Sunset

BEST HOME PLANS

Traditional Home Plans

Outside, this classic Victorian is reminiscent of yesteryear; inside, it's a comfortable family home with all the amenities of today. See plan HFL-1050-MD on page 96.

Sunset Books Inc. ■ Menlo Park, California

SUNSET BOOKS INC.
Director, Sales & Marketing:
   Richard A. Smeby
Editorial Director:
   Bob Doyle
Production Director:
   Lory Day
Group Marketing Manager:
   Becky Ellis
Art Director:
   Vasken Guiragossian
Assistant Editors:
   Kevin Freeland, Lisa Anderson
Contributing Editor:
   Don Vandervort

A Dream Come True

Planning and building a house is one of life's most creative and rewarding challenges. Whether you're seriously considering building a new home or you're just dreaming about it, this *Traditional Home Plans* book offers a wealth of inspiration and information to help you get started.

On the following pages, you'll learn how to plan and manage a home-building project—and how to ensure its success. Then you'll discover more than 200 proven home plans, designed for families just like yours by architects and professional designers. Peruse the pages and study the floor plans; you're sure to find a home that's just right for you. When you're ready to order blueprints, you can simply call or mail in your order, and you'll receive the plans within days.

Enjoy the adventure!

Photographers: Mark Englund/
HomeStyles: 4, 5; Philip Harvey:
10 top; Stephen Marley:
11 top left and right; Russ Widstrand:
10 bottom; Tom Wyatt: 11 bottom.

Cover: Pictured is plan DD-2928-A on page 185. Cover design by Vasken Guiragossian. Photography by Mark Englund/HomeStyles.

Third printing September 1997

Copyright © 1992, Sunset Books Inc., Menlo Park, CA 94025. First edition. All rights reserved, including the right of reproduction in whole or in part in any form. Library of Congress Catalog Card Number: 92-81030. ISBN 0-376-01194-3. Printed in the United States.

♻ Printed on recycled paper

For more information on Sunset's *Best Home Plans: Traditional Home Plans* or any other Sunset book, call (800) 526-5111.

Single-level ranch offers a happy marriage of economical construction and stunning design. See plan E-2700 on page 213.

Contents

Traditional Appeal

What kind of a house feels like "home" to you? If it's the simplicity of a Cape Cod saltbox, the stateliness of a Colonial, or the nostalgia of a Victorian, this book is for you. Although all of the styles presented here are firmly rooted in the past, the houses themselves offer all the features you expect to find in homes today—convenient floor plans, ample storage, up-to-date kitchens, and much, much more.

Traditional homes feel comfortable: their appearance is familiar, they rarely look out of place in any neighborhood, and they represent styles that have withstood the test of time. Even if you're just dreaming about building your own home, you're sure to enjoy browsing through the hundreds of plans in this book.

The two keys to success in building are capable project management and good design. The next few pages will walk you through some of the most important aspects of project management: you'll find an overview of the building process, directions for selecting the right plan and getting the most from it, and methods for successfully working with a builder and other professionals.

The balance of the book presents professionally designed stock plans for traditional houses in a wide range of styles and configurations. Once you find a plan that will work for you—perhaps with a few modifications made later to personalize it for your family—you can order construction blueprints for a fraction of the cost of a custom design, a savings of many thousands of dollars (see pages 12–15 for information on how to order).

Durable stone blends with wood siding on this wide, country-style home. Dormer windows flood the two-story living and dining areas with light. See plan DD-3467 on page 203.

Symmetrical design of this stately four-bedroom traditional is accented by a gable centered over the entrance. See plan D-2928-A on page 185.

Victorian beauty, enhanced by gingerbread detailing, masks a thoroughly modern interior complete with an island kitchen. See plan V-2440 on page 210.

Classic French-style farmhouse features a two-story great room and a private master suite on the main level. Upstairs, bedrooms are located at each of the four corners. See plan VL-2716 on page 212.

The Art of Building

As you embark on your home-building project, think of it as a trip—clearly not a vacation but rather an interesting, adventurous, at times difficult expedition. Meticulous planning will make your journey not only far more enjoyable but also much more successful. By careful planning, you can avoid—or at least minimize—some of the pitfalls along the way.

Start with realistic expectations of the road ahead. To do this, you'll want to gain an understanding of the basic house-building process, settle on a design that will work for you and your family, and make sure your project is actually doable. By taking those initial steps, you can gain a clear idea of how much time, money, and energy you'll need to invest to make your dream come true.

The Building Process

Your role in planning and managing a house-building project can be divided into two parts: prebuilding preparation and construction management.

■ **Prebuilding preparation.** This is where you should focus most of your attention. In the hands of a qualified contractor whose expertise you can rely on, the actual building process should go fairly smoothly. But during most of the prebuilding stage, you're generally on your own. Your job will be to launch the project and develop a talented team that can help you bring your new home to fruition.

When you work with stock plans, the prebuilding process usually goes as follows:

First, you research the general area where you want to live, selecting one or more possible home sites (unless you already own a suitable lot). Then you choose a basic house design, with the idea that it may require some modification. Finally, you analyze the site, the design, and your budget to determine if the project is actually attainable.

If you decide that it is, you purchase the land and order blueprints. If you want to modify them, you consult an architect, designer, or contractor. Once the plans are finalized, you request bids from contractors and arrange any necessary construction financing.

After selecting a builder and signing a contract, you (or your contractor) then file the plans with the building department. When the plans are approved, often several weeks—or even months—later, you're ready to begin construction.

■ **Construction management.** Unless you intend to act as your own contractor, your role during the building process is mostly one of quality control and time management. Even so, it's important to know the sequence of events and something about construction methods so you can discuss progress with your builder and prepare for any important decisions you may need to make along the way.

Decision-making is critical. Once construction begins, the builder must usually plunge ahead, keeping his carpenters and subcontractors progressing steadily. If you haven't made a key decision—which model bathtub or sink to install, for example—it can bring construction to a frustrating and expensive halt.

Usually, you'll make such decisions before the onset of building, but, inevitably, some issue or another will arise during construction. Being knowledgeable about the building process will help you anticipate and circumvent potential logjams.

Selecting a House Plan

Searching for the right plan can be a fun, interactive family experience—one of the most exciting parts of a house-building project. Gather the family around as you peruse the home plans in this book. Study the size, location, and configuration of each room; traffic patterns both inside the house and to the outdoors; exterior style; and how you'll use the available space. Discuss the pros and cons of the various plans.

Browse through pictures of homes in magazines to stimulate ideas. Clip the photos you like so you can think about your favorite options. When you visit the homes of friends, note special features that appeal to you. Also, look carefully at the homes in your neighborhood, noting their style and how they fit the site.

Mark those plans that most closely suit your ideals. Then, to narrow down your choices, critique each plan, using the following information as a guide.

■ **Overall size and budget.** How large a house do you want? Will the house you're considering fit your family's requirements? Look at the overall square footage and room sizes. If you have a hard time visualizing room sizes, measure some of the rooms in your present home and compare.

It's often better for the house to be a little too big than a little too small, but remember that every extra square foot will cost more money to build and maintain.

■ **Number and type of rooms.** Beyond thinking about the number of bedrooms and baths you want, consider your family's life-style and how you use space. Do you want both a family room and a living room? Do you need a formal dining space? Will you require some extra rooms, or "swing spaces," that can serve multiple purposes, such as a home office–guest room combination?

■ **Room placement and traffic patterns.** What are your preferences for locations of formal living areas, master bedroom, and children's rooms? Do you prefer a kitchen that's open to family areas or one that's private and out of the way? How much do you use exterior spaces and how should they relate to the interior?

Once you make those determinations, look carefully at the floor plan of the house you're considering to see if it meets your needs and if the traffic flow will be convenient for your family.

■ **Architectural style.** Have you always wanted to live in a Victorian farmhouse? Now is your chance to create a house that matches your idea of "home" (taking into account, of course, styles in your neighborhood). But don't let your preference for one particular architectural style dictate your home's floor plan. If the floor plan doesn't work for your family, keep looking.

■ **Site considerations.** Most people choose a site before selecting a plan—or at least they've zeroed in on the basic type of land where they'll situate their house. It sounds elementary, but choose a house that will fit the site.

When figuring the "footprint" of a house, you must know about any restrictions that will affect your home's height or proximity to the property lines. Call the local building department (look under city or county listings in the phone book) and get a very clear description of any restrictions, such as setbacks, height limits, and lot coverage, that will affect what you can build on the site (see "Working with City Hall," at right).

When you visit potential sites, note trees, rock outcroppings, slopes, views, winds, sun, neighboring homes, and other factors. All will impact on how your house works on a particular site.

Once you've narrowed down the choice of sites, consult an architect or building designer (see page 8) to help you evaluate how some potential houses will work on the sites you have in mind.

Is Your Project Doable?

Before you purchase land, make sure your project is doable. Although it's too early at this stage to pinpoint costs, making a few phone calls will help you determine whether your project is realistic. You'll be able to learn if you can afford to build the house, how long it will take, and what obstacles may stand in your way.

To get a ballpark estimate of cost, multiply a house's total

Working with City Hall

For any building project, even a minor one, it's essential to be familiar with building codes and other restrictions that can affect your project.

■ **Building codes,** generally implemented by the city or county building department, set the standards for safe, lasting construction. Codes specify minimum construction techniques and materials for foundations, framing, electrical wiring, plumbing, insulation, and all other aspects of a building. Although codes are adopted and enforced locally, most regional codes conform to the standards set by the national Uniform Building Code, Standard Building Code, or Basic Building Code. In some cases, local codes set more restrictive standards than national ones.

■ **Building permits** are required for home-building projects nearly everywhere. If you work with a contractor, the builder's firm should handle all necessary permits.

More than one permit may be needed; for example, one will cover the foundation, another the electrical wiring, and still another the heating equipment installation. Each will probably involve a fee and require inspections by building officials before work can proceed. (Inspections benefit *you,* as they ensure that the job is being done satisfactorily.) Permit fees are generally a percentage (1 to 1.5 percent) of the project's estimated value, often calculated on square footage.

It's important to file for the necessary permits. Failure to do so can result in fines or legal action against you. You can even be forced to undo the work performed. At the very least, your negligence may come back to haunt you later when you're ready to sell your house.

■ **Zoning ordinances,** particular to your community, restrict setbacks (how near to property lines you may build), your house's allowable height, lot coverage factors (how much of your property you can cover with structures), and other factors that impact design and building. If your plans don't conform to zoning ordinances, you can try to obtain a variance, an exception to the rules. But this legal work can be expensive and time-consuming. Even if you prove that your project won't negatively affect your neighbors, the building department can still refuse to grant the variance.

■ **Deeds and covenants** attach to the lot. Deeds set out property lines and easements; covenants may establish architectural standards in a neighborhood. Since both can seriously impact your project, make sure you have complete information on any deeds or covenants before you turn over a spadeful of soil.

---

square footage (of livable space) by the local average cost per square foot for new construction. (To obtain local averages, call a contractor, an architect, a realtor, or the local chapter of the National Association of Home Builders.) Some contractors may even be willing to give you a preliminary bid. Once you know approximate costs, speak to your lender to explore financing.

It's a good idea to discuss your project with several contractors (see page 8). They may be aware of problems in your area that could limit your options—bedrock that makes digging basements difficult, for example. These conversations are actually the first step in developing a list of contractors from which you'll choose the one who will build your home.

Recruiting Your Home Team

A home-building project will inter-ject you and your family into the building business, an area that may be unfamiliar territory. Among the people you'll be working with are architects, designers, landscapers, contractors, and subcontractors.

Design Help

A qualified architect or designer can help you modify and personal-ize your home plan, taking into account your family's needs and budget and the house's style. In fact, you may want to consider consulting such a person while you're selecting a plan to help you articulate your needs.

Design professionals are capable of handling any or all aspects of the design process. For example, they can review your house plans, suggest options, and then provide rough sketches of the options on tracing paper. Many architects will even secure needed permits and negotiate with contractors or sub-contractors, as well as oversee the quality of the work.

Of course, you don't necessarily need an architect or designer to implement minor changes in a plan; although most contractors aren't trained in design, some can help you with modifications.

An open-ended, hourly-fee arrangement that you work out with your architect or designer allows for flexibility, but it often turns out to be more costly than working on a flat-fee basis. On a flat fee, you agree to pay a specific amount of money for a certain amount of work.

To find architects and designers, contact such trade associations as the American Institute of Architects (AIA), American Institute of Build-ing Designers (AIBD), American Society of Landscape Architects (ASLA), and American Society of Interior Designers (ASID). Although many professionals choose not to belong to trade associations, those who do have met the standards of their respective associations. For phone numbers of local branches, check the Yellow Pages.

■ **Architects** are licensed by the state and have degrees. They're trained in all facets of building design and construction. Although some can handle interior design and structural engineering, others hire specialists for those tasks.

■ **Building designers** are generally unlicensed but may be accredited by the American Institute of Building Designers. Their back-grounds are varied: some may be unlicensed architects in apprentice-ship; others are interior designers or contractors with design skills.

■ **Draftspersons** offer an economi-cal route to making simple changes on your drawings. Like building designers, these people may be unlicensed architect apprentices, engineers, or members of related trades. Most are accomplished at drawing up plans.

■ **Interior designers,** as their job title suggests, design interiors. They work with you to choose room fin-ishes, furnishings, appliances, and decorative elements. Part of their expertise is in arranging furnishings to create a workable space plan. Some interior designers are em-ployed by architectural firms; others work independently. Financial arrangements vary, depending on the designer's preference.

Related professionals are kitchen and bathroom designers, who con-centrate on fixtures, cabinetry, appliances, materials, and space planning for the kitchen and bath.

■ **Landscape architects, design-ers, and contractors** design out-door areas. Landscape architects are state-licensed to practice landscape design. A landscape designer usual-ly has a landscape architect's educa-tion and training but does not have a state license. Licensed landscape contractors specialize in garden construction, though some also have design skills and experience.

■ **Soils specialists and structural engineers** may be needed for proj-ects where unstable soils or uncom-mon wind loads or seismic forces must be taken into account. Any

structural changes to a house re-quire the expertise of a structural engineer to verify that the house won't fall down.

Services of these specialists can be expensive, but they're impera-tive in certain conditions to ensure a safe, sturdy structure. Your build-ing department will probably let you know if their services are re-quired.

General Contractors

To build your house, hire a licensed general contractor. Most states re-quire a contractor to be licensed and insured for worker's compensa-tion in order to contract a building project and hire other subcontrac-tors. State licensing ensures that contractors have met minimum training standards and have a spec-ified level of experience. Licensing does not guarantee, however, that they're good at what they do.

When contractors hire subcon-tractors, they're responsible for overseeing the quality of work and materials of the subcontractors and for paying them.

■ **Finding a contractor.** How do you find a good contractor? Start by getting referrals from people you know who have built or remodeled their home. Nothing beats a personal recommendation. The best contractors are usually busily moving from one satisfied client to another prospect, adver-tised only by word of mouth.

You can also ask local real estate brokers and lenders or even your building inspector for names of qualified builders. Experienced lumber dealers are another good source of names.

In the Yellow Pages, look under "Contractors–Building, General"; or call the local chapter of the National Association of Home Builders.

■ **Choosing a contractor.** Once you have a list of names of pro-spective builders, call several of them. On the telephone, ask first whether they handle your type of job and can work within your schedule. If they can, arrange a meeting with each one and ask them to be prepared with references of former clients and photos of previous jobs. Better still, meet them at one of their current work sites so you can get a glimpse of the quality of their work and how organized and thorough they are.

Take your plan to the meeting and discuss it enough to request a rough estimate (some builders will comply, while others will be reluctant to offer a ballpark estimate, preferring to give you a hard bid based on complete drawings). Don't hesitate to probe for advice or suggestions that might make building your house less expensive.

Be especially aware of each contractor's personality and how well you communicate. Good chemistry between you and your builder is a key ingredient for success.

Narrow down the candidates to three or four. Ask each for a firm bid, based on the exact same set of plans and specifications. For the bids to be accurate, your plans need to be complete and the specifications as precise as possible, call-

ing out particular appliances, fixtures, floorings, roofing material, and so forth. (Some of these are specified in a stock-plan set; others are not.)

Call the contractors' references and ask about the quality of their work, their relationship with their clients, their promptness, and their readiness to follow up on problems. Visit former clients to check the contractor's work firsthand.

Be sure your final candidates are licensed, bonded, and insured for worker's compensation, public liability, and property damage. Also, try to determine how financially solvent they are (you can call their bank and credit references). Avoid contractors who are operating hand-to-mouth.

Don't automatically hire the contractor with the lowest bid if you don't think you'll get along well or if you have any doubts about the quality of the person's work. Instead, look for both the most reasonable bid and the contractor with the best credentials, references, terms, and compatibility with your family.

A word about bonds: You can request a performance bond that guarantees that your job will be finished by your contractor. If the job isn't completed, the bonding company will cover the cost of hiring another contractor to finish it. Bonds cost from 2 to 6 percent of the value of the project.

Your Building Contract

A building contract (see below) binds and protects both you and your contractor. It isn't just a legal document. It's also a list of the expectations of both parties. The best way to minimize the possibility of misunderstandings and costly changes later on is to write down every possible detail. Whether the contract is a standard form or one composed by you, have an attorney look it over before both you and the contractor sign it.

The contract should clearly specify all the work that needs to be done, including particular materials and work descriptions, the time schedule, and method of payment. It should be keyed to the working drawings.

A Sample Building Contract

Project and participants. Give a general description of the project, its address, and the names and addresses of both you and the builder.

Construction materials. Identify all construction materials by brand name, quality markings (species, grades, etc.), and model numbers where applicable. Avoid the clause "or equal," which allows the builder to substitute other materials for your choices. For materials you can't specify now, set down a budget figure.

Time schedule. Include both start and completion dates and specify that work will be "continuous." Although a contractor cannot be responsible for delays caused by strikes and material shortages, your builder should assume responsibility for completing the project within in a reasonable period of time.

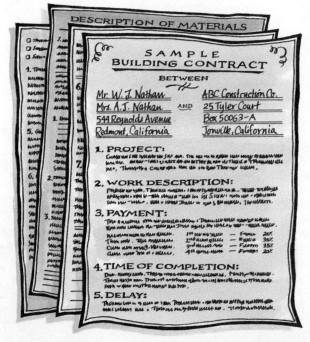

Work to be performed. State all work you expect the contractor to perform, from initial grading to finished painting.

Method and schedule of payment. Specify how and when payments are to be made. Typical agreements specify installment payments as particular phases of work are completed. Final payment is withheld until the job receives its final inspection and is cleared of all liens.

Waiver of liens. Protect yourself with a waiver of liens signed by the general contractor, the subcontractors, and all major suppliers. That way, subcontractors who are not paid for materials or services cannot place a lien on your property.

Personalizing Stock Plans

The beauty of buying stock plans for your new home is that they offer tested, well-conceived design at an affordable price. And stock plans dramatically reduce the time it takes to design a house, since the plans are ready when you are.

Because they were not created specifically for your family, stock plans may not reflect your personal taste. But it's not difficult to make revisions in stock plans that will turn your home into an expression of your family's personality. You'll surely want to add personal touches and choose your own finishes.

Ideally, the modifications you implement will be fairly minor. The more extensive the changes, the more expensive the plans. Major changes take valuable design time, and those that affect a house's structure may require a structural engineer's approval.

If you anticipate wholesale changes, such as moving a number of bearing walls or changing the roofline significantly, you may be better off selecting another plan. On the other hand, reconfiguring or changing the sizes of some rooms can probably be handled fairly easily.

Some structural changes may even be necessary to comply with local codes. Your area may have specific requirements for snow loads, energy codes, seismic or wind resistance, and so forth. Those types of modifications are likely to require the services of an architect or structural engineer.

Plan Modifications

Before you pencil in any changes, live with your plans for a while. Study them carefully—at your building site, if possible. Try to picture the finished house: how rooms will interrelate, where the sun will enter and at what angle, what the view will be from each window. Think about traffic patterns, access to rooms, room sizes, window and door locations, natural light, and kitchen and bathroom layouts.

Typical changes might involve adding windows or skylights to bring in natural light or capture a view. Or you may want to widen a hallway or doorway for roomier access, extend a room, eliminate doors, or change window and door sizes. Perhaps you'd like to shorten a room, stealing the gained space for a large closet. Look closely at the kitchen; it's not difficult to reconfigure the layout if it makes the space more convenient for you.

Above all, take your time—this is your home and it should reflect your taste and needs. Make your changes now, during the planning stage. Once construction begins, it will take crowbars, hammers, saws, new materials, and, most significantly, time to alter the plans. Because changes are not part of your building contract, you can count on them being expensive extras once construction begins.

Specifying Finishes

One way to personalize a house without changing its structure is to substitute your favorite finishes for those specified on the plan.

Would you prefer a stuccoed exterior rather than the wood siding shown on the plan? In most cases, this is a relatively easy change. Do you like the look of a wood shingle roof rather than the composition shingles shown on the plan? This, too, is easy. Perhaps you would like to change the windows from sliders to casements, or upgrade to high-efficiency glazing. No problem. Many of those kinds of changes can be worked out with your contractor.

Inside, you may want hardwood where vinyl flooring is shown. In fact, you can—and should—choose types, colors, and styles of floorings, wall coverings, tile, plumbing fixtures, door hardware, cabinetry, appliances, lighting fixtures, and other interior details, for it's these materials that will personalize your home. For help in making selections, consult an architect or interior designer (see page 8).

Each material you select should be spelled out clearly and precisely in your building contract.

Finishing touches can transform a house built from stock plans into an expression of your family's taste and style. Clockwise, from far left: Colorful tilework and custom cabinetry enliven a bathroom (Design: Osburn Design); highly organized closet system maximizes storage space (Architect: David Jeremiah Hurley); low-level deck expands living space to outdoor areas (Landscape architects: The Runa Group, Inc.); built-ins convert the corner of a guest room into a home office (Design: Lynn Williams of The French Connection); French country cabinetry lends style and old-world charm to a kitchen (Design: Garry Bishop/Showcase Kitchens).

What the Plans Include

Complete construction blueprints are available for every house shown in this book. Clear and concise, these detailed blueprints are designed by licensed architects or members of the American Institute of Building Designers (AIBD). Each plan is designed to meet standards set down by nationally recognized building codes (the Uniform Building Code, Standard Building Code, or Basic Building Code) at the time and for the area where they were drawn.

Remember, however, that every state, county, and municipality has its own codes, zoning requirements, ordinances, and building regulations. Modifications may be necessary to comply with such local requirements as snow loads, energy codes, seismic zones, and flood areas.

Although blueprint sets vary depending on the size and complexity of the house and on the individual designer's style, each set may include the elements described below and shown at right.

■ **Exterior elevations** show the front, rear, and sides of the house, including exterior materials, details, and measurements.

■ **Foundation plans** include drawings for a full, partial, or daylight basement, crawlspace, pole, pier, or slab foundation. All necessary notations and dimensions are included. (Foundation options will vary for each plan. If the plan you choose doesn't have the type of foundation you desire, a generic conversion diagram is available.)

■ **Detailed floor plans** show the placement of interior walls and the dimensions of rooms, doors, windows, stairways, and similar elements for each level of the house.

■ **Cross sections** show details of the house as though it were cut in slices from the roof to the foundation. The cross sections give the home's construction, insulation, flooring, and roofing details.

■ **Interior elevations** show the specific details of cabinets (kitchen, bathroom, and utility room), fireplaces, built-in units, and other special interior features.

■ **Roof details** give the layout of rafters, dormers, gables, and other roof elements, including clerestory windows and skylights. These details may be shown on the elevation sheet or on a separate diagram.

■ **Schematic electrical layouts** show the suggested locations for switches, fixtures, and outlets. These details may be shown on the floor plan or on a separate diagram.

■ **General specifications** provide instructions and information regarding excavation and grading, masonry and concrete work, carpentry and woodwork, thermal and moisture protection, drywall, tile, flooring, glazing, and caulking and sealants.

Other Helpful Building Aids

In addition to the construction information on every set of plans, you can buy the following guides.

■ **Reproducible blueprints** are helpful if you'll be making changes to the stock plan you've chosen. These blueprints are original line drawings produced on erasable, reproducible paper for the purpose of modification. When alterations are complete, working copies can be made.

■ **Itemized materials list** details the quantity, type, and size of materials needed to build your home. (This list is extremely helpful in obtaining an accurate construction bid. It's not intended for use to order materials.)

■ **Mirror-reverse plans** are useful if you want to build your home in the reverse of the plan that's shown. Because the lettering and dimensions read backwards, be sure to buy at least one regular-reading set of blueprints.

■ **Description of materials** gives the type and quality of materials suggested for the home. This form may be required for obtaining FHA or VA financing.

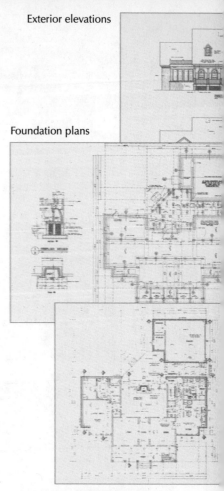

Exterior elevations

Foundation plans

Detailed floor plans

■ **How-to diagrams** for plumbing, wiring, solar heating, framing and foundation conversions show how to plumb, wire, install a solar heating system, convert plans with 2 by 4 exterior walls to 2 by 6 construction (or vice versa), and adapt a plan for a basement, crawlspace, or slab foundation. These diagrams are not specific to any one plan.

NOTE: Due to regional variations, local availability of materials, local codes, methods of installation, and individual preferences, detailed heating, plumbing, and electrical specifications are not included on plans. The duct work, venting, and other details will vary, depending on the heating and cooling system you use and the type of energy that operates it. These details and specifications are easily obtained from your builder or local supplier.

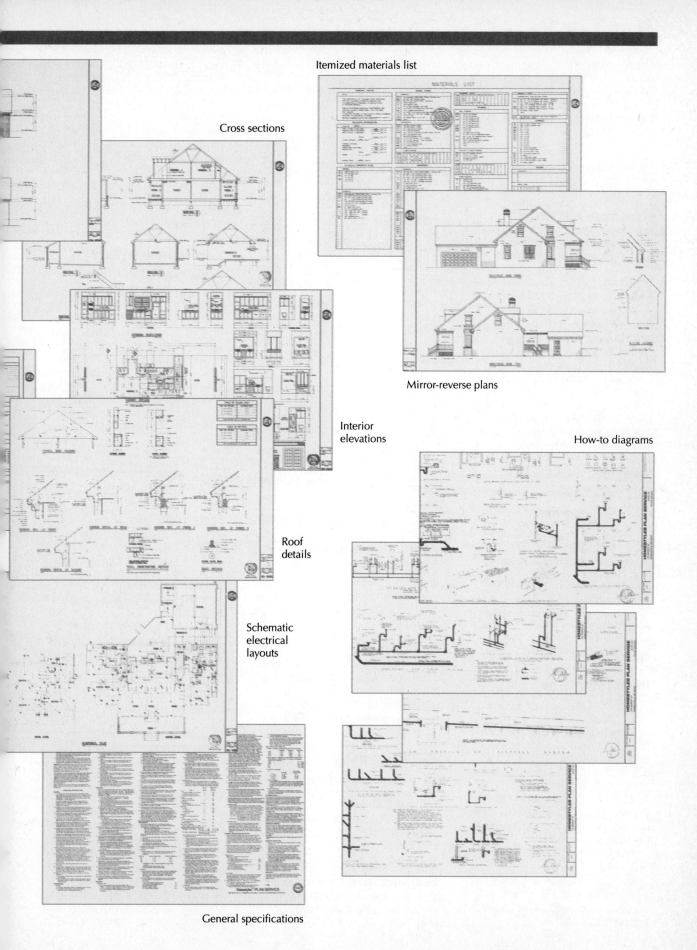

Itemized materials list

Cross sections

Mirror-reverse plans

Interior
elevations

How-to diagrams

Roof
details

Schematic
electrical
layouts

General specifications

Before You Order

Once you've chosen the one or two house plans that work best for you, you're ready to order blueprints. Before filling in the form on the facing page, note the information that follows.

How Many Blueprints Will You Need?

A single set of blueprints will allow you to study a home design in detail. You'll need more for obtaining bids and permits, as well as some to use as reference at the building site. If you'll be modifying your home plan, order a reproducible set (see page 12).

Figure you'll need at least one set each for yourself, your builder, the building department, and your lender. In addition, some subcontractors—foundation, plumber, electrician, and HVAC—may also need at least partial sets. If they do, ask them to return the sets when they're finished. The chart below can help you calculate how many sets you're likely to need.

Blueprint Checklist

____ Owner's set(s)

____ Builder usually requires at least three sets: one for legal documentation, one for inspections, and a minimum of one set for subcontractors.

____ Building department requires at least one set. Check with your local department before ordering.

____ Lending institution usually needs one set for a conventional mortgage, three sets for FHA or VA loans.

____ TOTAL SETS NEEDED

Blueprint Prices

The cost of having an architect design a new custom home typically runs from 5 to 15 percent of the building cost, or from $5,000 to $15,000 for a $100,000 home. A single set of blueprints for the plans in this book ranges from $245 to $685, depending on the house's size. Working with these drawings, you can save enough on design fees to add a deck, a swimming pool or a luxurious kitchen.

Pricing is based on "total finished living space." Garages, porches, decks and unfinished basements are not included.

Building Costs

Building costs vary widely, depending on a number of factors, includ-

Price Code (Size)	1 Set	4 Sets	7 Sets	Reproducible Set
AAA (under 500 sq. ft.)	$245	$295	$330	$430
AA (500-999 sq. ft.)	$285	$335	$370	$470
A (1,000-1,499 sq. ft.)	$365	$415	$450	$550
B (1,500-1,999 sq. ft.)	$405	$455	$490	$590
C (2,000-2,499 sq. ft.)	$445	$495	$530	$630
D (2,500-2,999 sq. ft.)	$485	$535	$570	$670
E (3,000-3,499 sq. ft.)	$525	$575	$610	$710
F (3,500-3,999 sq. ft.)	$565	$615	$650	$750
G (4,000-4,499 sq. ft.)	$605	$655	$690	$790
H (4,500-4,999 sq. ft.)	$645	$695	$730	$830
I (5,000 & above)	$685	$735	$770	$870

ing local material and labor costs and the finishing materials you select. For help estimating costs, see "Is Your Project Doable?" on page 7.

Foundation Options & Exterior Construction

Depending on your site and climate, your home will be built with a slab, pier, pole, crawlspace or basement foundation. Exterior walls will be framed with either 2 by 4s or 2 by 6s, determined by structural and insulation standards in your area. Most contractors can easily adapt a home to meet the foundation and/or wall requirements for your area. Or ask for a conversion how-to diagram (see page 12).

Service & Blueprint Delivery

Service representatives are available to answer questions and assist you in placing your order. Every effort is made to process and ship orders within 48 hours.

Returns & Exchanges

Each set of blueprints is specially printed and shipped to you in response to your specific order; consequently, requests for refunds cannot be honored. However, if the prints you order cannot be used, you may exchange them for another plan from any Sunset home plan book. For an exchange, you must return all sets of plans within 30 days. A nonrefundable service charge will be assessed for all exchanges; for more information, call the toll-free number on the facing page. Note: Reproducible sets cannot be exchanged.

Compliance with Local Codes & Regulations

Because of climatic, geographic and political variations, building codes and regulations vary from one area to another. These plans are authorized for your use expressly conditioned on your obligation and agreement to comply strictly with all local building codes, ordinances, regulations and requirements, including permits and inspections at time of construction.

Architectural & Engineering Seals

With increased concern about energy costs and safety, many cities and states now require that an architect or engineer review and "seal" a blueprint prior to construction. To find out whether this is a requirement in your area, contact your local building department.

License Agreement, Copy Restrictions & Copyright

When you purchase your blueprints, you are granted the right to use those documents to construct a single unit. All the plans in this publication are protected under the Federal Copyright Act, Title XVII of the United States Code and Chapter 37 of the Code of Federal Regulations. Each designer retains title and ownership of the original documents. The blueprints licensed to you cannot be used by or resold to any other person, copied or reproduced by any means. The copying restrictions do not apply to reproducible blueprints. When you buy a reproducible set, you may modify and reproduce it for your own use.

Blueprint Order Form

Complete this order form in just three easy steps. Then mail in your order or, for faster service, call toll-free.

1. Blueprints & Accessories

BLUEPRINT CHART

Price Code	1 Set	4 Sets	7 Sets	Reproducible Set*
AAA	$245	$295	$330	$430
AA	$285	$335	$370	$470
A	$365	$415	$450	$550
B	$405	$455	$490	$590
C	$445	$495	$530	$630
D	$485	$535	$570	$670
E	$525	$575	$610	$710
F	$565	$615	$650	$750
G	$605	$655	$690	$790
H	$645	$695	$730	$830
I	$685	$735	$770	$870

A reproducible set is produced on erasable paper for the purpose of modification. It is only available for plans with prefixes A, AG, AGH, AH, AHP, APS, AX, B, BOD, BRF, C, CC, CDG, CPS, DCL, DD, DW, E, EOF, FB, G, GA, GL, GSA, H, HDS, HFL, HOM, IDG, J, JWA, K, KD, KLF, L, LRD, LS, M, NBV, NW, OH, PH, PI, RD, S, SDG, SG, SUL, SUN, THD, TS, U, UD, UDA, UDG, V, WH.
Prices subject to change

Mirror-Reverse Sets: $50 surcharge. From the total number of sets you ordered above, choose the number you want to be reversed. *Note: All writing on mirror-reverse plans is backwards. Order at least one regular-reading set.*

Itemized Materials List: One set $50; each additional set $15. Details the quantity, type, and size of materials needed to build your home.

Description of Materials: Sold in a set of two for $50 (for use in obtaining FHA or VA financing).

Typical How-To Diagrams: One set $20; two sets $30; three sets $40; four sets $45. General guides on plumbing, wiring, and solar heating, plus information on how to convert from one foundation or exterior framing to another. *Note: These diagrams are not specific to any one plan.*

2. Sales Tax & Shipping

Determine your subtotal and add appropriate local state sales tax, plus shipping and handling (see chart below).

SHIPPING & HANDLING

	1–3 Sets	4–6 Sets	7 or More Sets	Reproducible Set
U.S. Regular (5–6 business days)	$17.50	$20.00	$22.50	$17.50
U.S. Express (2–3 business days)	$29.50	$32.50	$35.00	$29.50
Canada Regular (2–3 weeks)	$20.00	$22.50	$25.00	$20.00
Canada Express (5–6 business days)	$35.00	$40.00	$45.00	$35.00
Overseas/Airmail (7–10 businessdays)	$57.50	$67.50	$77.50	$57.50

3. Customer Information

Choose the method of payment you prefer. Include check, money order, or credit card information, complete name and address portion, and mail, fax, or call using the information at the right.

SS01

COMPLETE THIS FORM

Plan Number _____ **Price Code** _____

Foundation_____
(Review your plan carefully for foundation options—basement, pole, pier, crawlspace, or slab. Many plans offer several options; others offer only one.)

Number of Sets: $_____
- ☐ One Set   (See chart at left)
- ☐ Four Sets
- ☐ Seven Sets
- ☐ One Reproducible Set

Additional Sets _____ $_____
    ($40 each)

Mirror-Reverse Sets _____ $_____
    ($50 surcharge)

Itemized Materials List $_____
Only available for plans with prefixes AH, AHP, APS*, AX*, B*, BOD, C, CAR, CC, CDG*, CPS, DD*, DW, E, G, GSA, H, HFL, HOM, I*, IDG, J, K, L, LMB*, LRD, NW*, P, PH, R, S, SG, SUN, THD, U, UDA, UDG, VL, WH, YS.
*Not available on all plans. Please call before ordering.

Description of Materials $_____
Only for plans with prefixes AHP, C, DW, H, J, K, P, PH, SUL, VL, YS.

Typical How-To Diagrams $_____
- ☐ Plumbing ☐ Wiring ☐ Solar Heating ☐ Foundation & Framing Conversion

SUBTOTAL $_____

SALES TAX Minnesota residents add 6.5% $_____

SHIPPING & HANDLING $_____

GRAND TOTAL $_____

- ☐ Check/money order enclosed (in U.S. funds) payable to HomeStyles
- ☐ VISA   ☐ MasterCard   ☐ AmEx   ☐ Discover

Credit Card # _____ **Exp. Date** _____

Signature _____

Name _____

Address _____

City _____ **State** ____ **Country** _____

Zip _____ **Daytime Phone** (____) _____

☐ Please check if you are a contractor.

Mail form to: Sunset/HomeStyles
                    P.O. Box 75488
                    St. Paul, MN 55175-0488

Or fax to: (612) 602-5002

FOR FASTER SERVICE CALL 1-800-820-1283

SS01

Photo courtesy of Breland & Farmer Designers, Inc.

Three-Bedroom Home Features Screened-In Porch

- This classic story-and-a-half design encompasses a thoroughly modern interior on a compact foundation area.
- Living and dining rooms flow together, yet are divided by a screened porch which provides more space in nice weather.
- Deluxe master bedroom is larger than you might expect in a home this size, and includes a big walk-in closet and a dressing area.
- The large kitchen includes abundant counter space, and adjoins a roomy utility area.
- The upstairs includes two nice-sized bedrooms and a convenient bath.

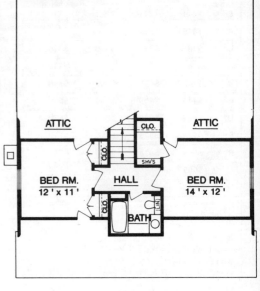

UPPER FLOOR

Plan E-1626

Bedrooms: 3	**Baths:** 2

Space:
Upper floor:	464 sq. ft.
Main floor:	1,136 sq. ft.

Total living area:	1,600 sq. ft.
Porches:	393 sq. ft.
Garage:	462 sq. ft.
Storage:	11 sq. ft.

Exterior Wall Framing:	2x6

Foundation options:
Crawlspace.
Slab.
(Foundation & framing conversion diagram available — see order form.)

Blueprint Price Code:	B

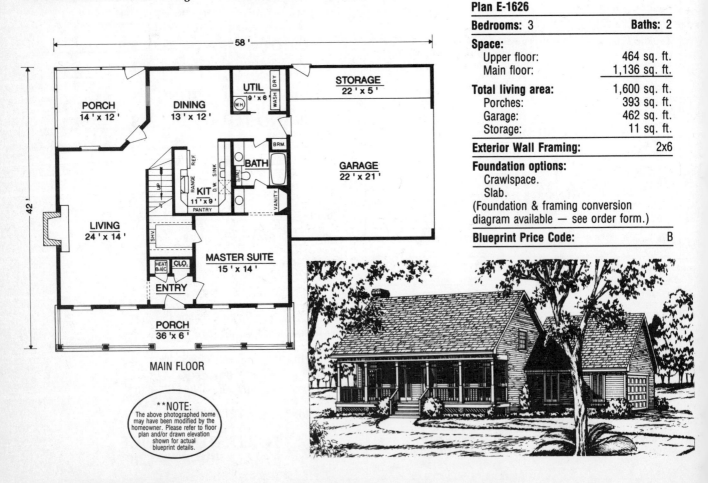

MAIN FLOOR

NOTE:
The above photographed home may have been modified by the homeowner. Please refer to floor plan and/or drawn elevation shown for actual blueprint details.

TO ORDER THIS BLUEPRINT, CALL TOLL-FREE 1-800-547-5570 (prices and details on pp. 12-15.)

Plan E-1626

Great Starter Home

With under 1,200 sq. ft., this plan presents an excellent alternative to expensive housing. Moreover, this attractive design demonstrates that you don't have to sacrifice style for economy.

The exterior is characterized by multi-paned, bay windows for eye-catching street appeal.

The living room adjoins the dining room to create shared visual space for a more expansive feeling.

A pantry and handy eating counter highlight the efficient U-shaped kitchen. You'll also find a convenient half bath situated discreetly around the corner.

All three bedrooms are sequestered upstairs. Note the walk-in closet in the master bedroom. It includes mirrored sliding doors and a private vanity. Access to the main bathroom is possible through a pocket door.

This is a great starter home for young families.

Main floor:	546 sq. ft.
Upper floor:	647 sq. ft.
Total living area:	1,193 sq. ft.
(Not counting garage)	

PLAN R-2114
WITHOUT BASEMENT
(CRAWLSPACE FOUNDATION)

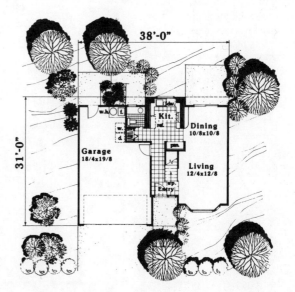

Blueprint Price Code A

Plan R-2114

TO ORDER THIS BLUEPRINT, CALL TOLL-FREE 1-800-547-5570
(prices and details on pp. 12-15.)

Small Home has Big Impact

- Small in area but big on function, this angled, three-bedroom ranch glows with charm.
- The central foyer neatly channels traffic to the bedroom wing, the formal areas to the rear and the kitchen and family room to the left.
- Highlighted by a sloped ceiling and a stone fireplace, the living and dining rooms combine for a dramatic setting that overlooks a backyard terrace.
- The family room and kitchen also flow together smoothly for a casual family atmosphere.
- Two skylit bathrooms and three bedrooms are secluded to the right for quiet.

Plan K-696-T

Bedrooms: 3	Baths: 2 ½
Space:	
Main floor	1,272 sq. ft.
Total Living Area	**1,272 sq. ft.**
Basement	1,232 sq. ft.
Garage	509 sq. ft.
Exterior Wall Framing	2x4 or 2x6

Foundation options:

Standard Basement

Slab

(Foundation & framing conversion diagram available—see order form.)

Blueprint Price Code	**A**

TO ORDER THIS BLUEPRINT,
CALL TOLL-FREE 1-800-547-5570
(prices and details on pp. 12-15.)

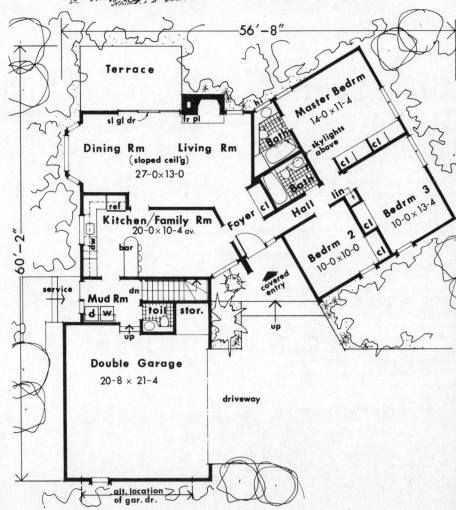

Plan K-696-T

Cozy Home for Retirees or New Families

Total living area: 1,283 sq. ft.
(Not counting basement or garage)

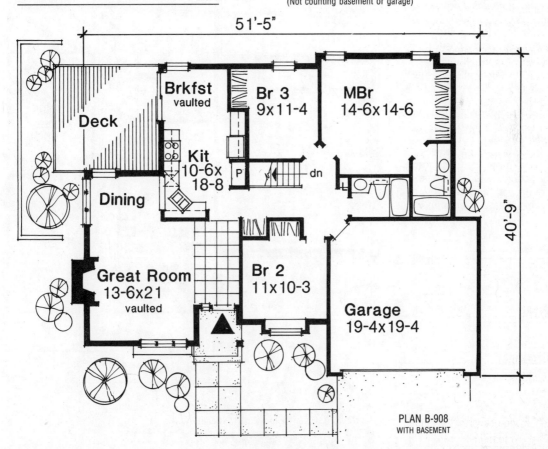

51'-5"

40'-9"

Deck

Brkfst
vaulted

Br 3
9x11-4

MBr
14-6x14-6

Kit
10-6x
18-8

P

dn

Dining

Great Room
13-6x21
vaulted

Br 2
11x10-3

Garage
19-4x19-4

PLAN B-908
WITH BASEMENT

Blueprint Price Code A

Plan B-908

TO ORDER THIS BLUEPRINT,
CALL TOLL-FREE 1-800-547-5570
(prices and details on pp. 12-15.)

Cozy & Compact

- While relatively compact and simple in construction, this plan offers many of the features desired by home builders today.
- The master suite includes a private bath and large closets.
- The living room is spacious, and adjoins the dining room to create abundant space for entertaining.
- The kitchen includes a handy breakfast counter bar, a pantry and a utility area for laundry chores.
- Two secondary bedrooms are roomy, boast large closets and have easy access through a central hallway to a full bath. Also note that the hallway can be closed off from the living room.
- The two-car garage includes storage space and offers easy access to the kitchen, making it easy to bring in the groceries.

Plan E-1204

Bedrooms: 3	Baths: 2
Space:	
Main floor	1,288 sq. ft.
Total Living Area	**1,288 sq. ft.**
Garage	441 sq. ft.
Storage (in garage)	60 sq. ft.
Exterior Wall Framing	2x4

Foundation options:

Crawlspace

Slab

(Foundation & framing conversion diagram available—see order form.)

Blueprint Price Code	**A**

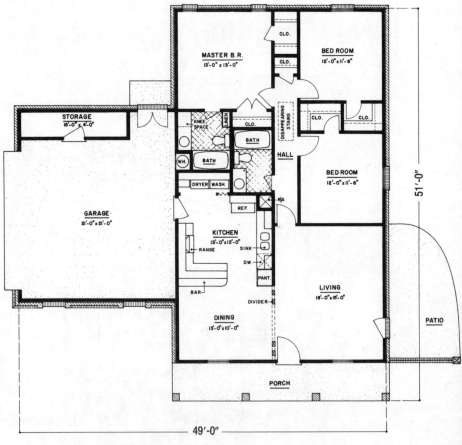

Plan E-1204

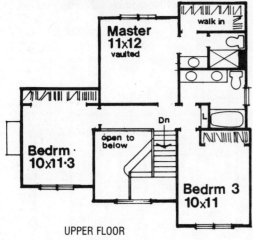

Master
11x12
vaulted

walk in

Bedrm
10x11·3

open to below

Dn

Bedrm 3
10x11

UPPER FLOOR

Delightful, Open Spaces

- A lot of room is offered in this compact but open three-bedroom home.
- The volume entry opens to a spacious living room with a fireplace, an open stairway to the upper level and windows that overlook the front porch and the rear patio.
- Between the living room and kitchen is a dining area with sliders that access the patio.
- Near the kitchen and garage entrance are handy laundry facilities and a powder room.
- The upper-level hallway connects the three bedrooms and overlooks the foyer below. At the center is a vaulted master bedroom with a private bath and a walk-in closet.
- Two secondary bedrooms share a second bath.

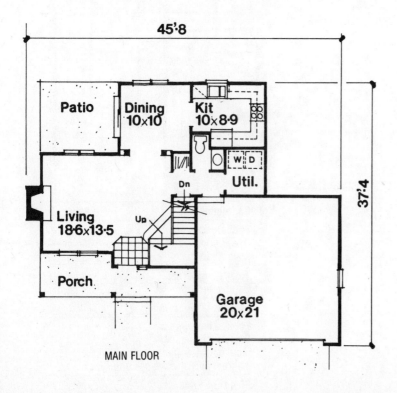

45'·8

Patio

Dining
10x10

Kit
10x8·9

Living
18·6x13·5

Up

Dn

W D

Util.

Porch

Garage
20x21

37'·4

MAIN FLOOR

Plan AG-1201	
Bedrooms: 3	Baths: 2 ½
Space:	
Upper floor	668 sq. ft.
Main floor	620 sq. ft.
Total Living Area	**1,288 sq. ft.**
Basement	620 sq. ft.
Garage	420 sq. ft.
Exterior Wall Framing	2x4
Foundation options:	
Standard Basement	
(Foundation & framing conversion diagram available—see order form.)	
Blueprint Price Code	**A**

Plan AG-1201

Massive, Windowed Great Room

- This attractive, open design can function as a cabin, mountain retreat or permanent residence.
- The kitchen and Great Room merge to form a large family activity area; an open balcony loft above offers an elevated view of the massive front window wall.
- A third sleeping room upstairs could be split into two smaller bedrooms.
- The main level of the home is entered via a split-landing deck off the Great Room.

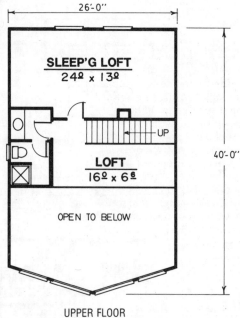

UPPER FLOOR

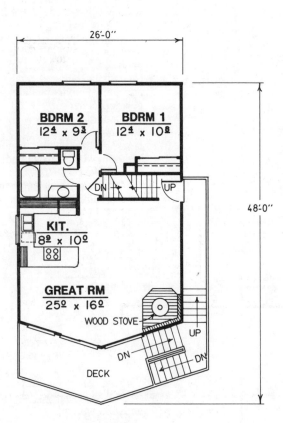

MAIN FLOOR

Plan I-1354-B

Bedrooms: 2-3	Baths: 2
Space:	
Upper floor:	366 sq. ft.
Main floor:	988 sq. ft.
Total living area:	1,354 sq. ft.
Garage and basement:	1,000 sq. ft.
Exterior Wall Framing:	2x6

Foundation options:
Standard basement.
(Foundation & framing conversion diagram available — see order form.)

Blueprint Price Code:	A

Plan I-1354-B

Open Plan in Traditional Design

- This modest-sized design is popular for its simple yet stylish exterior, making it suitable for either country or urban settings.
- A covered front porch and gabled roof extension accent the facade while providing sheltered space for outdoor relaxing.
- Inside, the living room with a cathedral ceiling and fireplace is combined with an open dining area and kitchen with island to create one large gathering spot for family and guests.

- The master bedroom features a private bath, large closet and ample sleeping area.
- Two other bedrooms share a second full bath.
- A convenient utility area and walk-in pantry are found in the passageway to the carport; also note the large outdoor storage closet.

Plan J-86155

Bedrooms: 3	Baths: 2
Total living area:	1,385 sq. ft.
Basement:	1,385 sq. ft.
Carport:	380 sq. ft.
Exterior Wall Framing:	2x4

Foundation options:
Standard basement.
Crawlspace.
Slab.
(Foundation & framing conversion diagram available — see order form.)

Blueprint Price Code: A

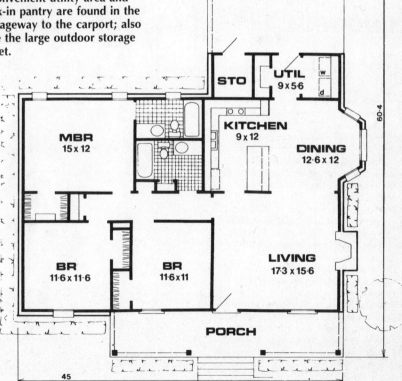

Plan J-86155

Economy and Beauty

Measuring in at only 1,410 sq. ft., this home will be very economical to build. What you'll also discover are beautiful arched windows which highlight the exterior, underscoring the fact that small doesn't mean you have to settle for less design quality.

The traffic plan is efficiently laid out to maximize the usable living area. Accented by a fireplace, the living room flows into the dining room to increase the visual feeling of spaciousness.

The practical U-shaped kitchen includes a handy pantry and opens to the nook for informal dining.

Upstairs, the master bedroom includes a convenient walk-in closet brightened by an illuminating skylight and a convenient vanity. Notice how the main bath adjoins the master bedroom via a pocket door for easy accessibility.

PLAN R-2099
WITHOUT BASEMENT
(CRAWLSPACE FOUNDATION)

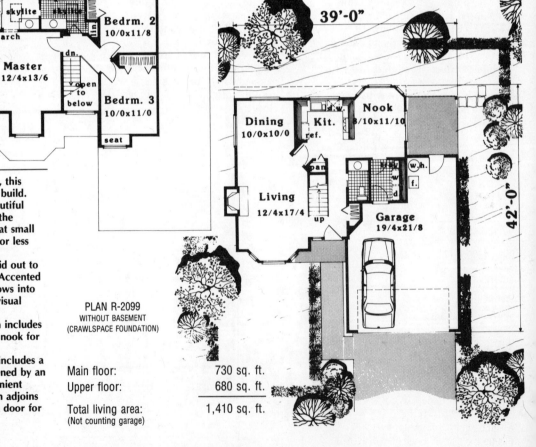

Main floor:	730 sq. ft.
Upper floor:	680 sq. ft.
Total living area: (Not counting garage)	1,410 sq. ft.

TO ORDER THIS BLUEPRINT, CALL TOLL-FREE 1-800-547-5570
(prices and details on pp. 12-15.)

Blueprint Price Code A
Plan R-2099

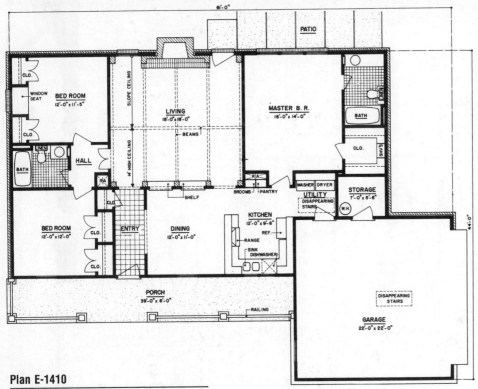

Vaulted Ceiling in Living Room

- This home packs a lot of grace and space into 1,418 square feet.
- Note the large living room with its beamed, vaulted ceiling and massive fireplace.
- The formal dining room lies off the foyer, and adjoins the efficient kitchen, which also includes a pantry and utility area.
- The master suite features a large walk-in closet and roomy master bath.
- At the other end of the home, two secondary bedrooms with abundant closet space share another full bath.
- The house-spanning porch invites guests to come in for a relaxing visit.

Plan E-1410

Bedrooms: 3	Baths: 2

Space:

Total living area:	1,418 sq. ft.
Garage:	484 sq. ft.
Storage:	38 sq. ft.
Porch:	238 sq. ft.

Exterior Wall Framing:	2x4

Foundation options:
Crawlspace.
Slab.
(Foundation & framing conversion diagram available — see order form.)

Blueprint Price Code:	A

Plan E-1410

Appealing and Affordable

- This affordable 1,428-sq.-ft. home has an exterior available in a choice of brick, stucco or siding.
- Its simple yet appealing interior design offers three bedrooms, two full baths and open living spaces.
- The spacious living room at the center of the home has a vaulted ceiling and a rear fireplace flanked by windows.
- A spacious bay with French doors to a rear patio highlights the adjoining dining room.
- A large, sunny eat-in kitchen has generous counter space and a handy washer/dryer closet near the garage entrance.
- The master bedroom features a dramatic corner window and a private, vaulted bath with luxury tub.

Plan APS-1413

Bedrooms: 3	Baths: 2
Space:	
Main floor	1,428 sq. ft.
Total Living Area	**1,428 sq. ft.**
Garage	387 sq. ft.
Exterior Wall Framing	2x4

Foundation options:

Slab

(Foundation & framing conversion diagram available—see order form.)

Blueprint Price Code   A

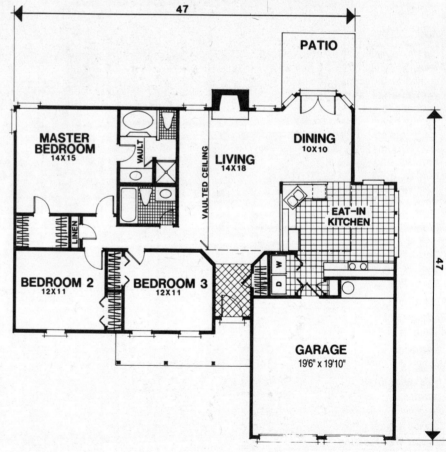

TO ORDER THIS BLUEPRINT,
CALL TOLL-FREE 1-800-547-5570
(prices and details on pp. 12-15.)

Plan APS-1413

Neatly Arranged

- Four bedrooms and generous-sized living areas are found in this compact home.
- Off the foyer and open to the upper level, a skylighted living room with cathedral ceiling and front view merges with a formal dining room for a dramatic setting.
- A large bayed kitchen and a family room join at the rear of the home. The family room features a large masonry fireplace and sliding glass doors for outdoor access. The kitchen has a handy pantry and a laundry closet just steps away.
- The large master bedroom is privately hidden on the main level. It offers a dressing area and a skylighted bath.
- Three additional bedrooms and a second full bath share the upper level.

Plan AX-8817-A

Bedrooms: 4	Baths: 2 ½
Space:	
Upper floor	600 sq. ft.
Main floor	856 sq. ft.
Total Living Area	**1,456 sq. ft.**
Basement	856 sq. ft.
Garage	240 sq. ft.
Optional two-car garage	413 sq. ft.
Exterior Wall Framing	**2x4**

Foundation options:

Standard Basement

Slab

(Foundation & framing conversion diagram available — see order form.)

Blueprint Price Code	**A**

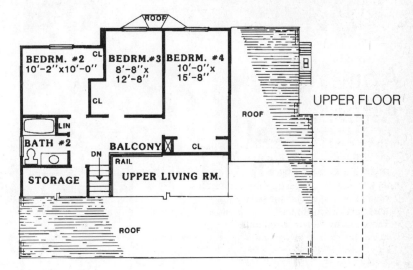

UPPER FLOOR

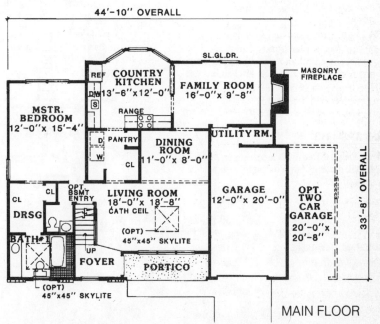

MAIN FLOOR

Plan AX-8817-A

Economical and Functional

Economically structured and architecturally refined, this L-shaped four-bedroom ranch is finished in horizontal wood siding. Optional skylights at the entry and reception hall brighten the interiors. Living and dining rooms, with sloped ceiling, open onto one another in a scheme that exaggerates the size of each.

An energy-efficient brick fireplace graces the living room. Sliding glass doors lead into a large rear terrace.

Family room and kitchen offer a dinette corner for casual meals. The kitchen is centrally located to serve the dinette and the formal dining room. A nearby mudroom includes a washroom and laundry facilities.

Four bedrooms are isolated in a wing of their own. The master bedroom is luxuriously treated with a private terrace and a tiled bathroom, complete with a whirlpool tub.

Total living area:	1,458 sq. ft.
(Not counting garage)	
Basement (optional):	1,512 sq. ft.
Garage, mudroom, etc.:	561 sq. ft.

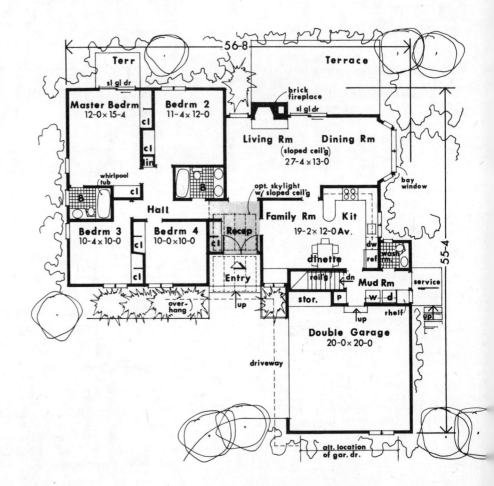

Blueprint Price Code A

Plan K-659-U

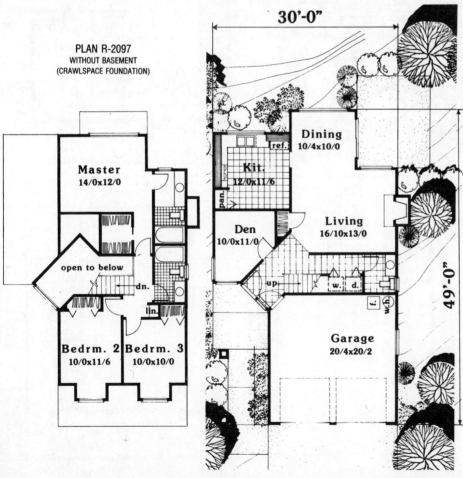

PLAN R-2097
WITHOUT BASEMENT
(CRAWLSPACE FOUNDATION)

30'-0"

49'-0"

Master
14/0x12/0

open to below

dn.

lin.

Bedrm. 2
10/0x11/6

Bedrm. 3
10/0x10/0

Dining
10/4x10/0

ref.

Kit.
12/0x11/6

pan.

Den
10/0x11/0

Living
16/10x13/0

up

w. d.

f.

w.h.

Garage
20/4x20/2

Good Looks and Efficiency

This two-story contemporary home combines both good looks and efficiency. Together they make this home a sure winner.

You'd have to look long and hard for a home under 1,500 sq. ft., such as this, that has more pizzazz or amenities.

Visitors are greeted by a dramatic entry with illuminating clerestory window and overhead balcony. A vaulted den is located directly off the entry for easy access and boasts corner windows for plenty of natural light.

The cozy country kitchen to the rear of the house includes a large pantry and extra room for a breakfast table.

The spacious walk-in closet featured in the master bedroom, upstairs, frees up additional wall space in the room itself for furniture arrangement.

This home measures only 30' in width, making it ideally suited for a narrow lot.

Main floor:	768 sq. ft.
Upper floor:	698 sq. ft.
Total living area: (Not counting garage)	1,466 sq. ft.

Blueprint Price Code A

Plan R-2097

Comfortable and Affordable

- This plan proves that comfort and affordability can go hand in hand.
- The home's square shape and simple lines make it easier to build, but it's far from plain. In fact, the optional elevations shown here are just two examples of the customizing touches that are possible.
- The gabled roofline and covered front porch with decorative railings render a warm, appealing look. Inside, the floor plan is generous without being wasteful.
- The large living room with fireplace is open to the dining room, maximizing space. The dining room, in turn, flows into the kitchen and dinette. A pocket door leads to a mud room, half-bath and laundry area, all of which are also accessible from the garage.

Elevation A

- The three bedrooms on the second floor share a full bath that has a private entrance from the master bedroom.
- The full basement provides more possibilities for comfortable, cost-efficient family living.

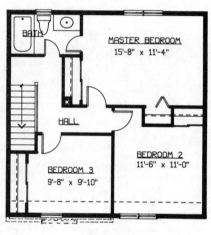

UPPER FLOOR

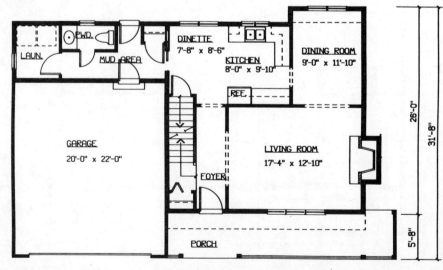

Elevation B

Plan GL-1473	
Bedrooms: 3	**Baths:** 1 ½
Space:	
Upper floor	676 sq. ft.
Main floor	797 sq. ft.
Total Living Area	**1,473 sq. ft.**
Basement	797 sq. ft.
Garage	440 sq. ft.
Exterior Wall Framing	2x6
Foundation options:	
Standard Basement	
(Foundation & framing conversion diagram available—see order form.)	
Blueprint Price Code	**A**

MAIN FLOOR

TO ORDER THIS BLUEPRINT,
CALL TOLL-FREE 1-800-547-5570
(prices and details on pp. 12-15.)

Plan GL-1473

Compact, Cozy, Inviting

- Liberal-sized living room is centrally located and features corner fireplace and sloped ceilings.
- Separate two-car garage is included with plan.
- Two-bedroom loft overlooks living room and entryway below.
- Full-width porches, both front and rear, invite guests and family alike for leisure time rest and relaxation.

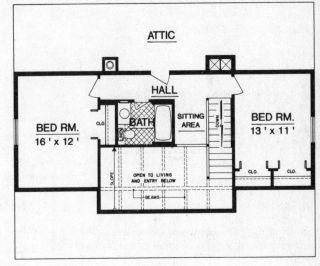

ATTIC

HALL

BED RM.
16' x 12'

BATH

SITTING AREA

BED RM.
13' x 11'

OPEN TO LIVING AND ENTRY BELOW

BEAMS

UPPER FLOOR

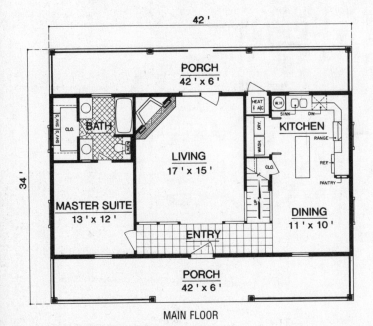

42'

PORCH
42' x 6'

BATH

KITCHEN

LIVING
17' x 15'

RANGE

REF

PANTRY

MASTER SUITE
13' x 12'

DINING
11' x 10'

ENTRY

PORCH
42' x 6'

34'

MAIN FLOOR

Plan E-1421

Bedrooms: 3	Baths: 2
Space:	
Upper floor:	561 sq. ft.
Main floor:	924 sq. ft.
Total living area:	1,485 sq. ft.
Basement:	approx. 924 sq. ft.
Porches:	504 sq. ft.
Exterior Wall Framing:	2x6

Foundation options:
Standard basement.
Crawlspace.
Slab.
(Foundation & framing conversion diagram available — see order form.)

Blueprint Price Code:	A

TO ORDER THIS BLUEPRINT, CALL TOLL-FREE 1-800-547-5570
(prices and details on pp. 12-15.)

Plan E-1421

Cottage in the Country

- A nostalgic cottage exterior look would be appealing whether built in the country or the suburbs.
- The interior offers excitement and efficiency in its 1,497 sq. ft.
- A formal living room and interesting octagonal dining room greet guests from the entry.
- The kitchen overlooks the family room with cathedral ceiling, fireplace, and sliders to a covered patio.
- The master suite includes a vaulted ceiling, walk-in closet and private bath.

Plan Q-1497-1A

Bedrooms: 3	Baths: 2
Space:	
Total living area:	1,497 sq. ft.
Garage:	383 sq. ft.
Exterior Wall Framing:	2x4
Foundation options:	
Slab.	
(Foundation & framing conversion diagram available — see order form.)	
Blueprint Price Code:	A

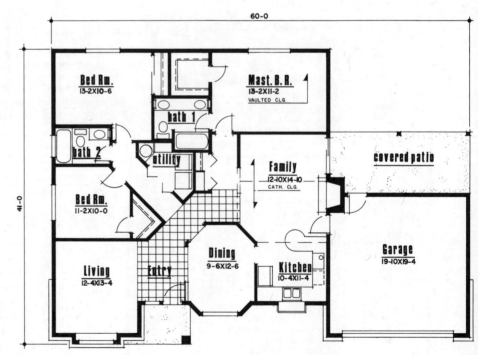

Plan Q-1497-1A

Traditional Flavor for Modern Plan

First floor: 817 sq. ft.
Second floor: 699 sq. ft.

Total living area: 1,516 sq. ft.
(Not counting basement or garage)

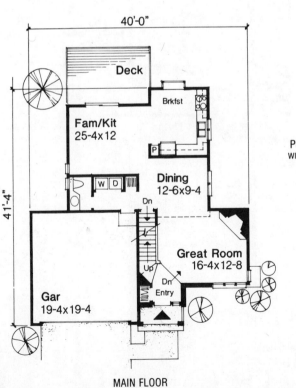

40'-0"

41'-4"

Deck

Brkfst

Fam/Kit
25-4x12

P

Dining
12-6x9-4

W D

Dn

Up

Dn
Entry

Great Room
16-4x12-8

Gar
19-4x19-4

MAIN FLOOR
817 SQ. FT.

PLAN B-901
WITH BASEMENT

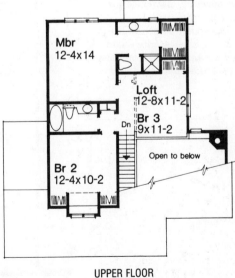

Mbr
12-4x14

Loft
12-8x11-2

Br 3
9x11-2

Dn

Open to below

Br 2
12-4x10-2

UPPER FLOOR
699 SQ. FT.

Blueprint Price Code B
Plan B-901

TO ORDER THIS BLUEPRINT,
CALL TOLL-FREE 1-800-547-5570
(prices and details on pp. 12-15.)

Open Plan Includes Circular Dining Room

- Innovative architectural features and a functional, light-filled floor plan are the hallmarks of this attractive design.
- The facade is graced by a stone chimney and a circular glass bay which houses the spectacular dining room with its domed ceiling.
- A bright, sunny kitchen is set up for efficient operation and adjoins a dinette area which echoes the circular shape of the formal dining room.
- The living room features a stone fireplace, and opens to the dining room to make a great space for entertaining.
- The bedrooms are zoned to the left, with the master suite including a private bath, large walk-in closet and access to an outdoor terrace.

Plan K-663-N

Bedrooms: 3	Baths: 2
Space:	
Total living area:	1,560 sq. ft.
Basement:	1,645 sq. ft.
Garage:	453 sq. ft.
Mudroom & stairs:	122 sq. ft.
Exterior Wall Framing:	2x4/2x6

Foundation options:
Standard basement.
Slab.
(Foundation & framing conversion diagram available — see order form.)

Blueprint Price Code:	B

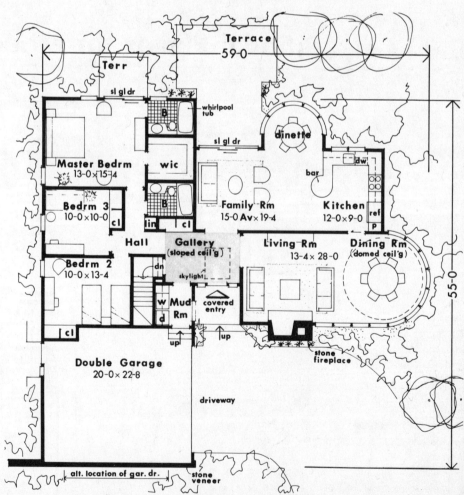

Plan K-663-N

Exciting Hot Tub Deck

- The elegant exterior of this two-story conceals an equally exciting interior floor plan.
- Older couples or young professionals starting out will enjoy this stylish, smaller home.
- The spacious living and dining room combination features a dramatic cathedral ceiling, fireplace and access to the rear patio.
- The adjoining kitchen has a lovely front window wall and counter and/or eating bar.
- Also on the main floor is an exciting master suite with large luxury bath and adjoining hot tub deck.

Plan NW-249

Bedrooms: 3	Baths: 2
Space:	
Upper floor	459 sq. ft.
Main floor	1,106 sq. ft.
Total Living Area	**1,565 sq. ft.**
Garage	556 sq. ft.
Exterior Wall Framing	2x6

Foundation options:

Crawlspace

(Foundation & framing conversion diagram available—see order form.)

Blueprint Price Code	**B**

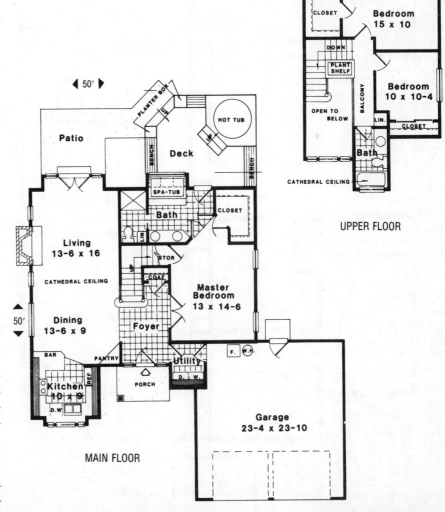

UPPER FLOOR

MAIN FLOOR

Plan NW-249

TO ORDER THIS BLUEPRINT,
CALL TOLL-FREE 1-800-547-5570
(prices and details on pp. 12-15.)

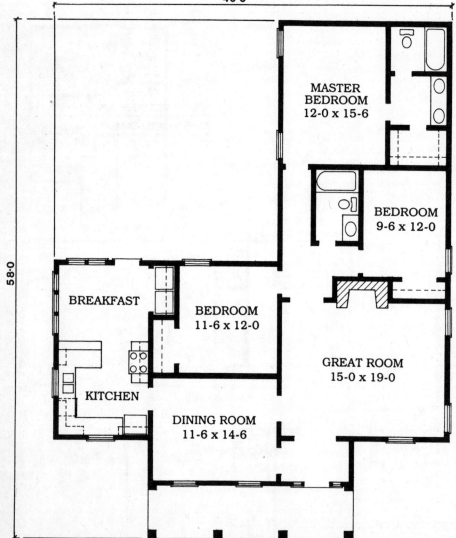

Charming and Efficient

- The facade of this charming home is highlighted by a porch and eye-catching entryway.
- Inside, the foyer leads into a spacious dining room and exceptionally grand Great Room warmed by a fireplace.
- A large, sunny kitchen opens to a brightly lit breakfast area that also houses a convenient washer and dryer.
- The three bedrooms are spaced apart from each other to provide privacy and quiet.
- The master suite is located at the rear of the home for additional privacy; it has a personal bath with twin vanities and a walk-in closet.

Plan V-1580-LC

Bedrooms: 3	Baths: 2
Space:	
Main floor	1,580 sq. ft.
Total Living Area	**1,580 sq. ft.**
Exterior Wall Framing	2x6

Foundation options:
Crawlspace
(Foundation & framing conversion diagram available—see order form.)

Blueprint Price Code	B

Plan V-1580-LC

Tradition Updated

- Traditional lines, materials, and even a front porch create a nostalgic exterior appeal.
- The interior breaks the traditional mold, however. You won't find the small, boxy, low ceilinged rooms of older homes here. Rather, all of the living areas blow open with dramatic cathedral ceilings with skylights.

- The formal living/dining spaces flow together oriented to the front. The family room shares a three-sided fireplace with the living room.
- The island kitchen opens to a spacious breakfast room.
- The three bedrooms share two full baths in the sleeping wing of the plan.

Plan AX-90303-A

Bedrooms: 3	Baths: 2

Space:	
Total living area:	1,615 sq. ft.
Optional basement:	1,615 sq. ft.
Garage:	412 sq. ft.

Exterior Wall Framing:	2x4

Foundation options:
Standard basement.
Crawlspace.
(Foundation & framing conversion diagram available — see order form.)

Blueprint Price Code:	B

Floor Plan

72'-4" OVERALL

32'-4" OVERALL

PATIO

SL GL DR

SKYLITE

CL W D

LAUN RM

UTIL RM

DW S

CATH CEIL
BRKFST RM
8'-6" x 11'-4"

CATH CEIL
KITCHEN
9'-6" x 13'-4"
SKYLITE

REF

CATH CEIL
FAMILY RM
15'-0" x 13'-4"
SKYLITE

MSTR BATH

BATH #2

WICL

MSTR BEDRM
15'-0" x 13'-4"

CL CL

FIREPLACE

TWO CAR GARAGE
20'-0" x 20'-0"

CATH CEIL
DINING RM
10'-2" x 12'-4"

CATH CEIL
LIVING RM
12'-6" x 13'-4"

LIN

CL

FOYER

BEDRM #3
10'-0" x 9'-8"

BEDRM #2
11'-4" x 11'-0"

PORCH

UP

Plan AX-90303-A

TO ORDER THIS BLUEPRINT, CALL TOLL-FREE 1-800-547-5570
(prices and details on pp. 12-15.)

Eye-Catching Design For Scenic Site

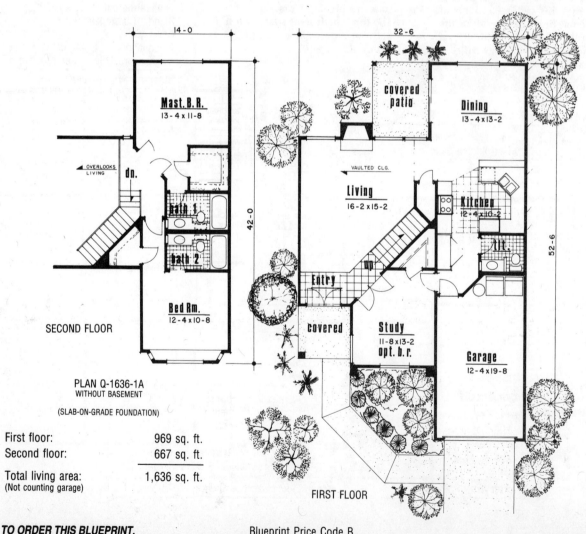

14 - 0

Mast. B.R.
13 - 4 x 11-8

OVERLOOKS LIVING

dn.

42 - 0

Bath 1

Bath 2

Bed Rm.
12 - 4 x 10-8

SECOND FLOOR

PLAN Q-1636-1A
WITHOUT BASEMENT

(SLAB-ON-GRADE FOUNDATION)

32 - 6

covered patio

Dining
13 - 4 x 13-2

VAULTED CLG.

Living
16 - 2 x 15-2

Kitchen
12 - 4 x 10-2

52 - 6

Entry

up

covered

Study
11 - 8 x 13-2
opt. b.r.

Garage
12 - 4 x 19-8

FIRST FLOOR

First floor:	969 sq. ft.
Second floor:	667 sq. ft.
Total living area: (Not counting garage)	1,636 sq. ft.

TO ORDER THIS BLUEPRINT,
CALL TOLL-FREE 1-800-547-5570
(prices and details on pp. 12-15.)

Blueprint Price Code B

Plan Q-1636-1A

Great Room Featured

- In this rustic design, the centrally located Great Room features a cathedral ceiling with exposed wood beams. Living and dining areas are separated by a massive fireplace.
- The isolated master suite features a walk-in closet and compartmentalized bath.
- The galley type kitchen is between the breakfast room and formal dining area. A large utility room and storage room complete the garage area.
- On the opposite side of the Great Room are two additional bedrooms and a second full bath.

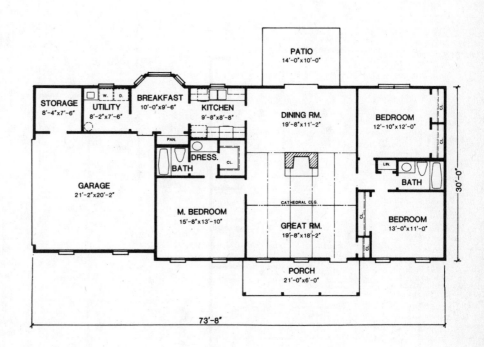

Plan C-8460

Bedrooms: 3	Baths: 2

Space:

Total living area:	1,670 sq. ft.
Basement:	approx. 1,600 sq. ft.
Garage:	427 sq. ft.
Storage:	63 sq. ft.
Exterior Wall Framing:	2x4

Foundation options:
Standard basement.
Crawlspace.
Slab.
(Foundation & framing conversion diagram available — see order form)

Blueprint Price Code: B

TO ORDER THIS BLUEPRINT,
CALL TOLL-FREE 1-800-547-5570
(prices and details on pp. 12-15.)

Plan C-8460

PLAN R-2133
WITHOUT BASEMENT
(CRAWLSPACE FOUNDATION)

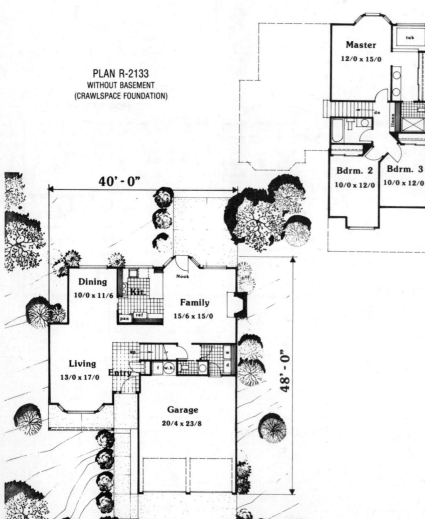

Master
12/0 x 15/0

tub

Bdrm. 2
10/0 x 12/0

Bdrm. 3
10/0 x 12/0

40' - 0"

48' - 0"

Dining
10/0 x 11/6

Kit.

Nook

pan   ref

Family
15/6 x 15/0

Living
13/0 x 17/0

Entry

Garage
20/4 x 23/8

Comfortable in Any Setting

Successfully combining a welcoming country porch, large bay window and beveled cedar siding, the facade of this cozy two-story home favorably complements the interior room arrangement.

The large family room with its masonry fireplace will warm the hearts of all who enter the room. Homemaker tasks will be lightened by the open kitchen arrangement which includes a corner pantry, various built-ins and a windowed octagonal projection effectively unifying this informal portion of the home. Not to be overlooked are the separate laundry, half-bath and storage tucked under the stairway, all carefully located between the family room and garage.

The second floor includes a master suite in addition to the two secondary bedrooms. The spacious master suite boasts a beautiful windowed projection as well as a magnificant bath arrangement including a spa tub, double vanity, large linen closet and a wall-spanning, three-doored wardrobe.

At only 40' in width, the design of this comfortable family home offers a roomy coziness in a modest square footage.

Main floor:	930 sq. ft.
Upper floor:	770 sq. ft.
Total living area: (Not counting garage)	1,700 sq. ft.

Blueprint Price Code B
Plan R-2133

Designed for Livability

- As you enter this excitingly spacious traditional home you see through the extensive windows to the back yard.
- This four-bedroom home was designed for livability of the maturing family with the separation of the master suite.
- The formal dining room expands spatially to the living room while being framed by the column and plant shelves.
- The bay that creates the morning room and sitting area for the master suite also adds excitement to this plan, both inside and out.
- The master bath offers an exciting oval tub under glass and separate shower, as well as a spacious walk-in closet and dressing area.

Plan DD-1696		
Bedrooms: 4		**Baths:** 2
Space:		
Main floor		1,748 sq. ft.
Total Living Area		**1,748 sq. ft.**
Basement		1,748 sq. ft.
Garage		393 sq. ft.
Exterior Wall Framing		2x4
Foundation options:		
Basement		
Crawlspace		
Slab		
(Foundation & framing conversion diagram available—see order form.)		
Blueprint Price Code		B

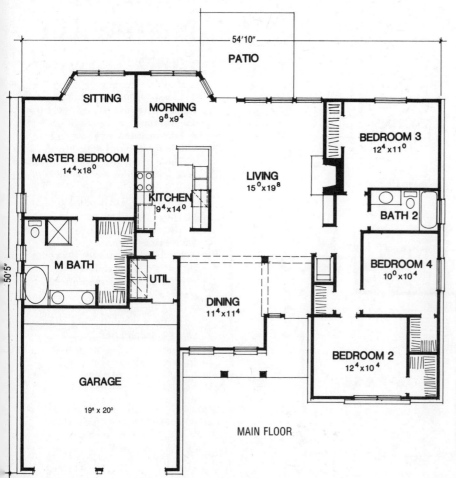

MAIN FLOOR

Plan DD-1696

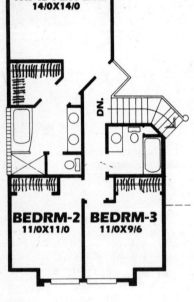

MASTER BR.
14/0X14/0

DN.

BEDRM-2
11/0X11/0

BEDRM-3
11/0X9/6

UPPER FLOOR

An Impressive Facade for a Narrow Lot Plan

- Classic architectural lines set this relatively modest home apart from the ordinary.
- Low-maintenance stucco exterior will keep its good looks for decades.
- The entry leads past a convenient powder room to the angled stairway or into the living room.
- The sunny, U-shaped kitchen provides abundant counter space.
- The roomy living room includes a fireplace.
- Upstairs, the master bedroom suite includes a large walk-in closet plus a private bath with separate tub and shower.
- Two secondary bedrooms have large front windows, big closets and share a second bath.

FAM. RM.
13/0X17/6

LIVING
17/6X15/0

DINING

KITCHEN
10/0X15/6

UP

DN.

GARAGE
21/0X21/0

50' 0

32' 0

MAIN FLOOR

Plan SD-9003

Bedrooms: 3	Baths: 2½
Space:	
Upper floor:	821 sq. ft.
Main floor:	930 sq. ft.
Total living area:	1,751 sq. ft.
Basement:	930 sq. ft.
Garage:	441 sq. ft.
Exterior Wall Framing:	2x6

Foundation options:
Standard basement.
Crawlspace.
(Foundation & framing conversion diagram available — see order form.)

Blueprint Price Code: B

Plan SD-9003

Efficient Dining-Kitchen-Nook Combination

- Here's a four-bedroom design that is beautiful in its simplicity and ease of construction.
- All on one floor, it offers ample space for both family life and entertaining.
- A huge living room soars aloft with vaulted, beamed ceilings and features a massive fireplace to give a Great Room feel to the area.
- The roomy, efficient kitchen is flanked by a sunny informal eating area protruding into the back yard and a front-facing formal dining room that is right off the elegant foyer.
- A deluxe master suite includes a dressing room, large closet and private bath.
- The three secondary bedrooms are larger than average and also offer ample closet space.
- Convenient storage and utility areas are segmented off the two-car garage.

Plan E-1702

Bedrooms: 4	Baths: 2

Space:	
Total living area:	1,751 sq. ft.
Porch:	64 sq. ft.
Garage:	484 sq. ft.
Storage:	105 sq. ft.

Exterior Wall Framing:	2x4

Foundation options:
Crawlspace.
Slab.
(Foundation & framing conversion diagram available — see order form)

Blueprint Price Code:	B

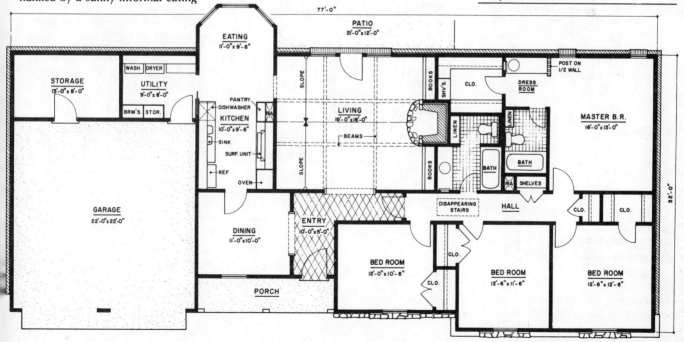

Plan E-1702

Panoramic Rear View

- This rustic but elegant country home offers an open, airy interior.
- At the center of the floor plan is a spacious living room with a sloped ceiling, fireplace and an all-glass circular wall giving a panoramic view of the backyard.
- The adjoining dining room shares the sloped ceiling and offers sliders to the rear terrace.
- The bright kitchen has a large window, an optional skylight and a counter bar that separates it from the bayed dinette.
- The bedroom wing includes two secondary bedrooms and a large, bayed master bedroom with dual walk-in closets and a private bath with a sloped ceiling and a garden whirlpool tub.

Plan K-685-DA	
Bedrooms: 3	Baths: 2 ½
Space:	
Main floor	1,760 sq. ft.
Total Living Area	**1,760 sq. ft.**
Basement	1,700 sq. ft.
Garage	482 sq. ft.
Exterior Wall Framing	2x4 or 2x6
Foundation options:	
Standard Basement	
Slab	
(Foundation & framing conversion diagram available—see order form.)	
Blueprint Price Code	B

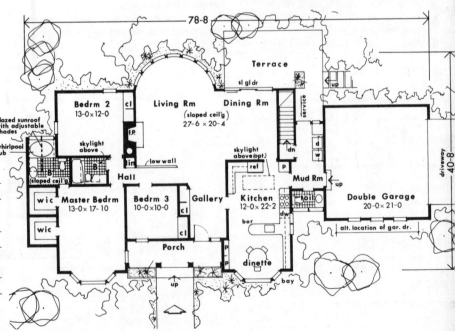

Plan K-685-DA

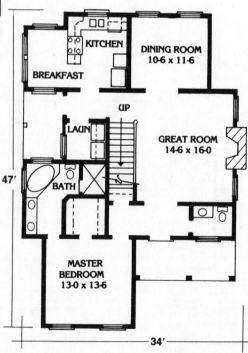

an V-1797

edrooms: 4	Baths: 2½

pace:
Upper floor:	675 sq. ft.
Main floor:	1,122 sq. ft.
tal living area:	1,797 sq. ft.

terior Wall Framing:	2x6

eiling Heights:
Upper floor:	8'
Main floor:	9'

oundation options:
 Crawlspace only.
oundation & framing conversion
agram available — see order form.)

lueprint Price Code:	B

An Aura of Quiet Peace

- This charming design exudes an aura of the peace and quiet of simpler times.
- Note the inviting side porch off the kitchen and laundry area which tempt the owners to a bit of rest between chores.
- An inviting front porch leads to an expansive Great Room and to the dining room beyond.
- The master suite, downstairs, faces the front of the home, and includes an impressive bath with oval corner tub and separate shower.
- Upstairs, three secondary bedrooms share another full bath.
- The fourth bedroom, on the right, could be finished later or converted to other uses.

Plan V-1797

Classic Country-Style

- At the center of this rustic country home is an enormous living room with vaulted ceilings, a massive stone fireplace and entrance to a rear porch.
- The adjoining eating area and kitchen provide plenty of room for dining and meal preparation. A sloped ceiling with false beams, porch overlook, pantry, spice cabinet and counter bar are some

attractions found here.
- Formal dining and entertaining can take place in the dining room off the entry.
- For privacy, you'll find the secluded master suite rewarding; it offers a private bath with dressing area, walk-in closet and isolated toilet and tub.
- The two additional bedrooms also have abundant walk-in closet space.

Plan E-1808	
Bedrooms: 3	**Baths:** 2
Space:	
Main floor	1,800 sq. ft.
Total Living Area	**1,800 sq. ft.**
Garage and storage	605 sq. ft.
Porches	354 sq. ft.
Exterior Wall Framing	2x4
Foundation options:	
Crawlspace	
Slab	
(Foundation & framing conversion diagram available—see order form.)	
Blueprint Price Code	B

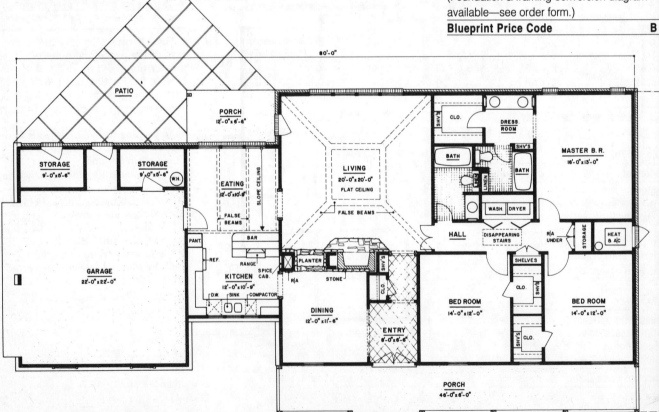

Plan E-1808

Luxury-Filled One-Story

- Interesting roof angles and refined window treatments make this handsome one-story home stand out in any neighborhood.

- Luxurious features abound within, starting with the raised-ceiling reception hall. The adjacent living room is open to the formal dining room and boasts cathedral ceilings, a central fireplace and lots of glass.

The combination kitchen, dinette and family room is flooded with light to create a warm, bright atmosphere. The bay-windowed dinette overlooks the rear terrace, with access through patio doors in the family room. A built-in entertainment center adds more versatility to the family room area.

The master bedroom suite is magnificent, featuring a double-door entry, sliders to a private terrace, a large walk-in closet and a great master bath. Another full bath, brightened by a skylight, is convenient to both of the secondary bedrooms as well as to the mud room. The efficient air-locked mud room provides access to the garage and the optional basement.

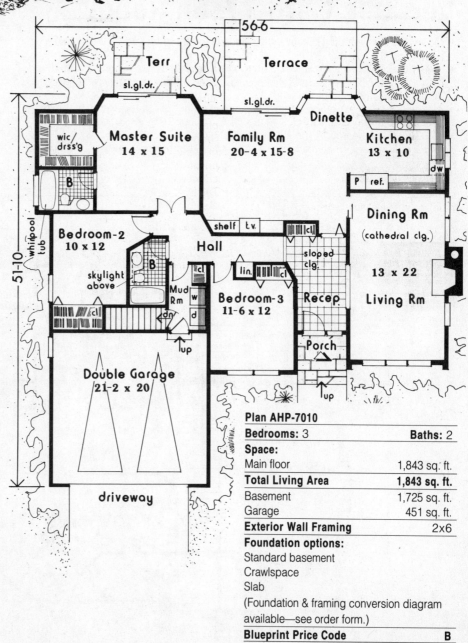

Plan AHP-7010	
Bedrooms: 3	**Baths:** 2
Space:	
Main floor	1,843 sq. ft.
Total Living Area	**1,843 sq. ft.**
Basement	1,725 sq. ft.
Garage	451 sq. ft.
Exterior Wall Framing	2x6
Foundation options:	
Standard basement	
Crawlspace	
Slab	
(Foundation & framing conversion diagram available—see order form.)	
Blueprint Price Code	B

Plan AHP-7010

Versatile Garden/Sun Room

- A curved front-wrapping porch borders an octagonal dining area in this country home.
- Both the dining area and kitchen open to the Great Room, at the center of the floor plan; it features a rear fireplace, sloped ceiling and adjoining garden or sun room, also accessed through the garage.
- A generous-sized master bedroom is positioned at the rear of the home, with private luxury bath and walk-in closet.
- Two secondary bedrooms share a second full bath.
- Bonus attic space can be made into a game room, hobby area, study or additional bedrooms.

Plan DD-1852

Bedrooms: 3	Baths: 2
Space:	
Main floor	1,852 sq. ft.
Total Living Area	**1,852 sq. ft.**
Basement	1,852 sq. ft.
Garage	528 sq. ft.
Exterior Wall Framing	2x4

Foundation options:

Standard Basement
Crawlspace
Slab
(Foundation & framing conversion diagram available—see order form.)

Blueprint Price Code	E

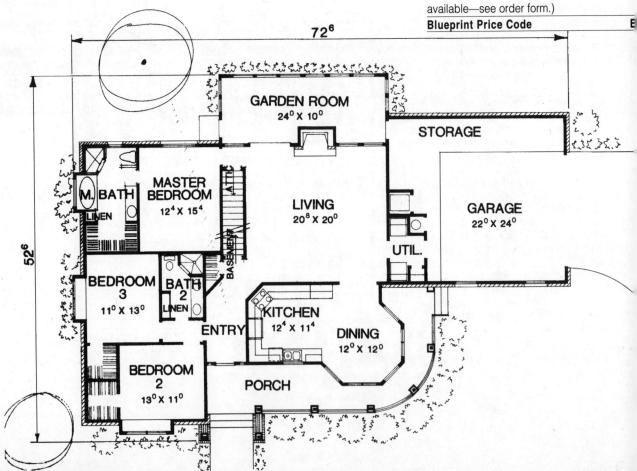

Plan DD-1852

Rustic Comfort

- While rustic in exterior appearance, this home is completely modern inside and loaded with the amenities preferred by today's builders.
- A large living room is made to seem immense by use of 16' ceilings, and an impressive fireplace and hearth dominate one end of the room.
- A formal dining room adds to the spaciousness, since it is separated from the living room only by a divider and a 6" step.
- The large U-shaped kitchen is adjoined by a convenient sewing and utility area, which in turn leads to the garage. A storage area is included in the garage, along with a built-in workbench.

- The sumptuous master suite features a sitting area, enormous walk-in closet and deluxe private bath.
- The two secondary bedrooms share another full bath and are zoned for privacy.

Plan E-1607	
Bedrooms: 3	Baths: 2

Space:

Total living area:	1,600 sq. ft.
Basement:	approx. 1,600 sq. ft.
Garage:	484 sq. ft.
Storage:	132 sq. ft.
Porch:	295 sq. ft.

Exterior Wall Framing:	2x6

Foundation options:
Standard basement.
Crawlspace.
Slab.
(Foundation & framing conversion diagram available — see order form)

Blueprint Price Code:	B

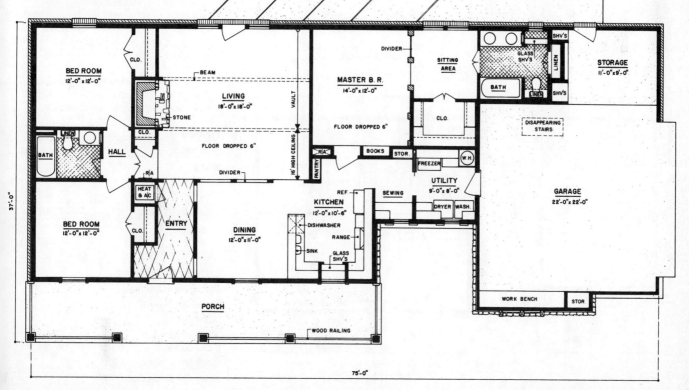

Plan E-1607

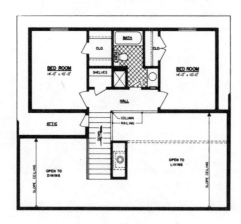

UPPER FLOOR

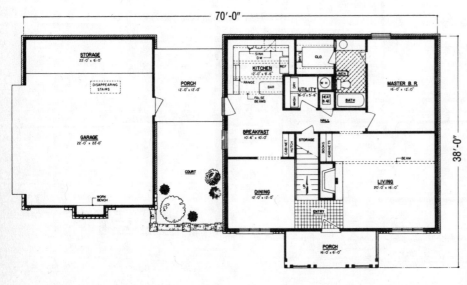

MAIN FLOOR

The Solid Look of Stone

- This traditional design offers a touch of Tudor along with the solid, stable look of a stone facade.
- An especially interesting feature is the courtyard/porch combination between the garage and the house.
- A main-floor master bedroom features a private bath and large walk-in closet.
- The living room is spacious and boasts an impressive fireplace and hearth, along with a vaulted ceiling.
- A formal dining room with a vaulted ceiling adjoins a roomy breakfast area, which in turn leads to an efficient and attractive kitchen with a beamed ceiling.
- Upstairs, two bedrooms share a full bath and a balcony hallway which overlooks the living room below.

Plan E-1620

Bedrooms: 3	Baths: 2
Space:	
Upper floor	448 sq. ft.
Main floor	1,152 sq. ft.
Total Living Area	**1,600 sq. ft.**
Basement	1,152 sq. ft.
Garage	484 sq. ft.
Storage (in garage)	132 sq. ft.
Exterior Wall Framing	2x6

Foundation options:
Standard basement
Crawlspace
Slab
(Foundation & framing conversion diagram available—see order form.)

Blueprint Price Code	B

Plan E-1620

Warmth and Charm

- Two fireplaces combined with careful blending of wood and stone give this home a warm and charming look.
- The large living room offers a sloped, beamed ceiling and a large fireplace, and is open to the dining room to create one large space for entertaining.
- The roomy kitchen/utility area provides abundant space for cooking and other household chores.
- The master suite boasts a sloped ceiling, a large fireplace, a dressing room with walk-in closet and private access to the main-floor bath.
- Two upstairs bedrooms, each with double closets, share another full bath.

Plan E-1613

Bedrooms: 3	Baths: 2
Space:	
Upper floor	472 sq. ft.
Main floor	1,144 sq. ft.
Total Living Area	**1,616 sq. ft.**
Basement	1,144 sq. ft.
Garage	484 sq. ft.
Storage	133 sq. ft.
Porches	116 sq. ft.
Exterior Wall Framing	2x6

Foundation options:
Standard Basement
Crawlspace
Slab
(Foundation & framing conversion diagram available—see order form.)

Blueprint Price Code	**B**

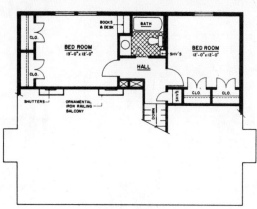

UPPER FLOOR

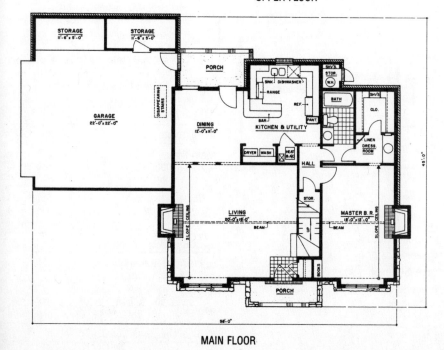

MAIN FLOOR

Plan E-1613

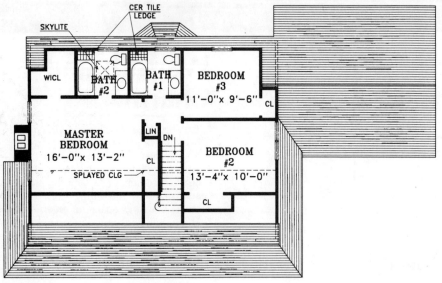

SKYLITE · CER TILE LEDGE

WICL · BATH #2 · BATH #1 · BEDROOM #3 11'-0"x 9'-6" CL

MASTER BEDROOM 16'-0"x 13'-2" · LIN · DN · BEDROOM #2 13'-4"x 10'-0" CL

SPLAYED CLG · CL

UPPER FLOOR

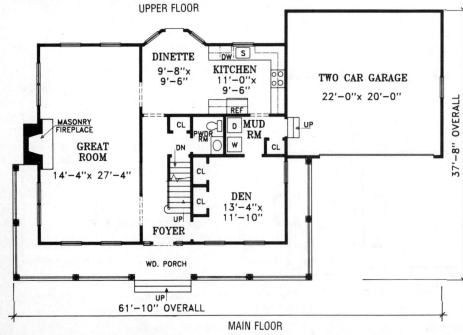

DINETTE 9'-8"x 9'-6" · DW · S · KITCHEN 11'-0"x 9'-6" · TWO CAR GARAGE 22'-0"x 20'-0"

MASONRY FIREPLACE · CL · REF · 37'-8" OVERALL

GREAT ROOM 14'-4"x 27'-4" · PWDR RM · D · MUD RM · W · CL · UP

DN · CL

UP · DEN 13'-4"x 11'-10"

FOYER

WD. PORCH

UP · 61'-10" OVERALL

MAIN FLOOR

Quaint
Country Design

- The renewed "country" look is evident in this simply designed two-story with wrap-around front porch.
- Functional living areas flank the entryway and stairs.
- A beautiful and spacious Great Room, with masonry fireplace and wrap-around windows, is to the left, and a nice-sized den which could serve as a library, office, guest room or fourth bedroom is to the right.
- The kitchen is a lovely space with two separate areas, an efficient work area and a distinct bay windowed dining area with center door leading to the rear yard.
- The second floor includes a master bedroom with full private bath and two large closets, plus two secondary bedrooms.

Plan AX-89311

Bedrooms: 3	Baths: 2½

Space:	
Upper floor:	736 sq. ft.
Main floor:	1,021 sq. ft.

Total living area:	**1,757 sq. ft.**
Basement:	approx. 1,021 sq. ft.
Garage:	440 sq. ft.

Exterior Wall Framing:	2x4

Foundation options:
Standard basement.
Slab.
(Foundation & framing conversion diagram available — see order form.)

Blueprint Price Code:	B

TO ORDER THIS BLUEPRINT, CALL TOLL-FREE 1-800-547-5570 (prices and details on pp. 12-15.)

Plan AX-89311

Open Planning in a Classic Style

Exterior walls are 2x6 construction.
Specify crawlspace or slab foundation.

UPPER LEVEL

PLAN E-1708
WITHOUT BASEMENT

Living area:	1,717 sq. ft.
Porches:	131 sq. ft.
Garage & Storage:	556 sq. ft.
Total:	2,404 sq. ft.

LOWER LEVEL

ELEVATION A

Compact Victorian

- This compact Victorian design incorporates four bedrooms and three full baths into a home that's only 30 feet wide.
- The upstairs master suite includes a deluxe bath and a bayed sitting area.
- The roomy parlor includes a fireplace, and the formal dining room has a beautiful bay window.
- The downstairs bedroom, with its adjoining full bath, makes a great office or guest bedroom.
- Please specify attached garage if desired.

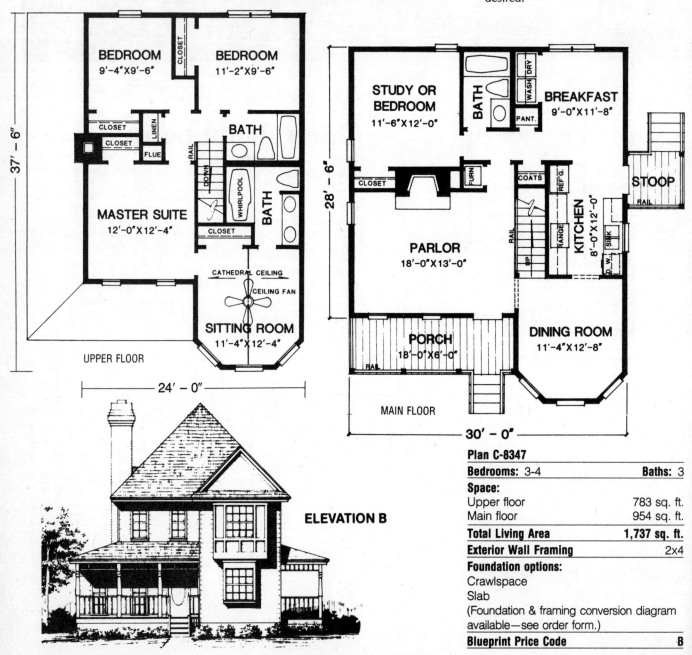

BEDROOM 9'-4"X9'-6"
BEDROOM 11'-2"X9'-6"
CLOSET
CLOSET
CLOSET
LINEN
FLUE
BATH
RAIL
DOWN
WHIRLPOOL
BATH
MASTER SUITE 12'-0"X12'-4"
CLOSET
CATHEDRAL CEILING
CEILING FAN
SITTING ROOM 11'-4"X12'-4"

UPPER FLOOR

37' – 6"
24' – 0"

STUDY OR BEDROOM 11'-6"X12'-0"
BATH
WASH DRY
BREAKFAST 9'-0"X11'-8"
PANT.
CLOSET
FURN.
COATS
REF'G.
STOOP
RAIL
PARLOR 18'-0"X13'-0"
RAIL
RANGE
KITCHEN 8'-0"X12'-0"
D.W. SINK
UP
PORCH 18'-0"X6'-0"
RAIL
DINING ROOM 11'-4"X12'-8"

MAIN FLOOR

28' – 6"
30' – 0"

ELEVATION B

Plan C-8347	
Bedrooms: 3-4	**Baths: 3**
Space:	
Upper floor	783 sq. ft.
Main floor	954 sq. ft.
Total Living Area	**1,737 sq. ft.**
Exterior Wall Framing	2x4

Foundation options:
Crawlspace
Slab
(Foundation & framing conversion diagram available—see order form.)

Blueprint Price Code	**B**

Plan C-8347

Expandable Traditional

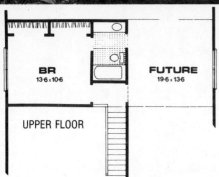

BR 13·6 x 10·6

FUTURE 19·6 x 13·6

UPPER FLOOR

- This homey traditional will be at home in any neighborhood, rural or urban.
- A gracious porch leads into the large living room which features a cozy fireplace.
- A sunny breakfast nook provides space for family and guest dining.

- The galley-type kitchen opens onto a back porch.
- The master suite is generously sized and exhibits a raised ceiling; a private bath and large closet are also part of the master suite.
- A second bedroom, another bath and convenient utility areas complete the first floor.
- Upstairs, you'll find a third bath and third bedroom, plus a large space that could be finished in the future for any number of purposes.

PORCH

BR 11·6 x 10·3

MBR 16·6 x 13
RAISED CEILING

KIT 10 x 8

BKFST 13 x 11

UTIL

GARAGE 19·3 x 19·3

LIVING 15·6 x 15

PORCH 20 x 6

MAIN FLOOR

50·4

40

Plan J-8636

Bedrooms: 3	Baths: 3
Space:	
Upper floor:	270 sq. ft.
Main floor:	1,253 sq. ft.
Bonus area:	270 sq. ft.
Total living area:	1,793 sq. ft.
Basement:	1,287 sq. ft.
Garage:	390 sq. ft.
Porches:	155 sq. ft.
Exterior Wall Framing:	2x4

Foundation options:
Standard basement.
Crawlspace.
Slab.
(Foundation & framing conversion diagram available — see order form.)

| **Blueprint Price Code:** | B |

Plan J-8636

REAR VIEW

Bungalow Style for Today

- Many of the features of the once-popular bungalow are preserved and improved upon in this plan.
- A special touch is the pergola — the wooden trelliswork attached to the porch roof and supported by tapered columns.
- The spacious foyer has doors opening from both the porch and the opposing garage.
- The sunken living room is separated from the dining room by a custom-designed handrail.
- French doors close off the den or third bedroom from the living room.
- The expansive kitchen features an island work center, a pantry, a bay window with built-in desk, and access to the rear deck.
- The master suite has numerous frills.

Plans H-1459-1 & -1A

Bedrooms: 2	Baths: 2
Space:	
Upper floor	658 sq. ft.
Main floor	1,201 sq. ft.
Total Living Area	**1,859 sq. ft.**
Basement	630 sq. ft.
Garage	280 sq. ft.
Exterior Wall Framing	2x6

Foundation options:

Partial Basement

Crawlspace

(Foundation & framing conversion diagram available—see order form.)

Blueprint Price Code	B

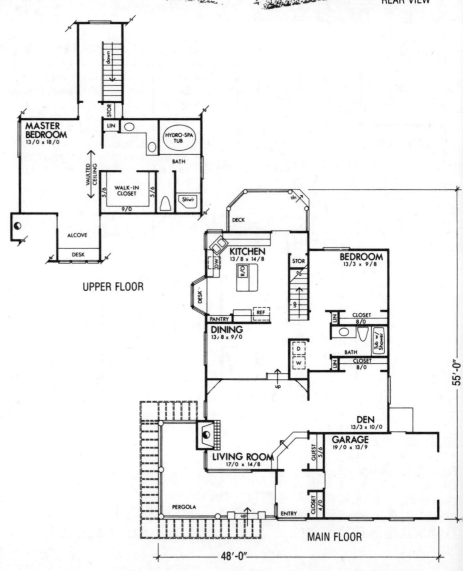

UPPER FLOOR

MAIN FLOOR

TO ORDER THIS BLUEPRINT, CALL TOLL-FREE 1-800-547-5570 (prices and details on pp. 12-15.)

Plans H-1459-1 & -1A

Raised Interest

- The raised living and deck areas of this design take full advantage of surrounding views. A sloping lot can be accommodated with the shown lower level retaining wall.
- The lower level foyer feels high and is bright with a two-and-a-half-story opening lighting the stairwell.
- A two-car tuck-under garage and two bedroom suites complete the lower level.
- At the top of the stairs, guests are wowed with a view into the Grand Room, with high vaulted ceiling, fireplace and atrium doors and windows overlooking the main deck.
- The kitchen incorporates a sunny good morning room.
- The master suite dazzles with a vaulted ceiling, plant shelves, a private deck and a splashy master bath.

MAIN FLOOR

Plan EOF-44

Bedrooms: 4	Baths: 2
Living Area:	
Main floor	1,256 sq. ft.
Daylight basement	541 sq. ft.
Total Living Area:	**1,797 sq. ft.**
Garage	460 sq. ft.
Exterior Wall Framing:	2x4

Foundation Options:
Daylight basement
(Typical foundation & framing conversion diagram available—see order form.)

BLUEPRINT PRICE CODE:	B

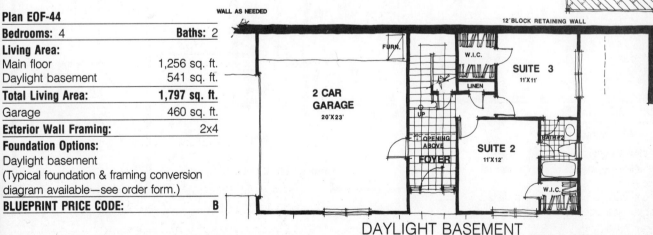

DAYLIGHT BASEMENT

Plan EOF-44

TO ORDER THIS BLUEPRINT,
CALL TOLL-FREE 1-800-547-5570
(prices and details on pp. 12-15.)

Two-Story Traditional Design

AREAS

Living-Lower	1251 sq. ft.
Living-Upper	576 sq. ft.
Living-Total	1827 sq. ft.
Porches	477 sq. ft.
Sun Garden	80 sq. ft.
Total	2384 sq. ft.

THIS PLAN INCLUDES A SEPARATE GARAGE PLAN FEATURING A 22' x 22' DOUBLE GARAGE AND A 4' x 14' STORAGE AREA.

PLAN E-1814
(WITHOUT BASEMENT)

Exterior walls are 2x6 construction.
Specify crawlspace or slab foundation.

MAIN FLOOR

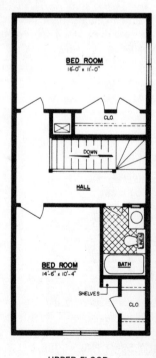

UPPER FLOOR

Blueprint Price Code B
Plan E-1814

Queen Anne with Contemporary Interior

This gracious home offers numerous features for convenience and charm:
- 1,864 sq. ft. of living area.
- 2 bedrooms, plus den.
- Traditional exterior style.
- 30' wide at first floor, 32' wide at second floor.
- Versatile kitchen with range/oven/eating bar combination.
- Practical spice cabinet, pantry and nook.
- Sunken living room with vaulted ceiling, fireplace, French doors, wet bar and built-in shelves.
- Dramatic open staircase.
- Interesting entry open to bridge above.
- 2½ baths.
- Cozy loft open to living area.
- Spacious and elegant master bedroom with bay window, walk-in closet, separate shower, double-sink vanity and window overlooking living/loft area.
- Energy-efficient specifications throughout, including 2x6 wall framing.

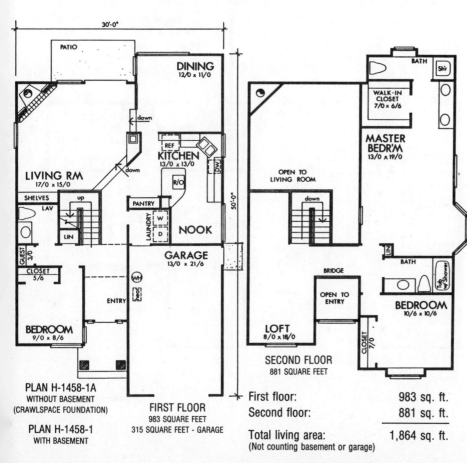

PLAN H-1458-1A
WITHOUT BASEMENT
(CRAWLSPACE FOUNDATION)

PLAN H-1458-1
WITH BASEMENT

FIRST FLOOR
983 SQUARE FEET
315 SQUARE FEET - GARAGE

SECOND FLOOR
881 SQUARE FEET

First floor: 983 sq. ft.
Second floor: 881 sq. ft.
Total living area: 1,864 sq. ft.
(Not counting basement or garage)

Blueprint Price Code B

Plans H-1458-1 & 1A

Great Bedroom/Bath Combination

- Dining room has view of entry and living room through surrounding arched openings.
- Living room features 12' ceilings, fireplace, and a view to the outdoor patio.
- Kitchen has attached eating area with sloped ceilings.
- Tray ceiling adorns the master suite; attached bath has skylight and marble enclosed tub.

Plan E-1830

Bedrooms: 3	Baths: 2

Space:

Total living area:	1,868 sq. ft.
Garage and storage:	616 sq. ft.
Porch:	68 sq. ft.

Exterior Wall Framing:	2x6

Foundation options:
Crawlspace.
Slab.
(Foundation & framing conversion diagram available — see order form.)

Blueprint Price Code:	B

Plan E-1830

Affordable Country-Style

- This charming country-inspired home is economical to build and requires only a small lot.
- The powder room and guest closet are conveniently located near the foyer, as well as a large combination living/dining room with walk-in bay window.
- A low partition visually separates the kitchen and adjacent family room, which features angled fireplace, cathedral ceiling with skylight, and sliding glass doors open to the rear yard.
- The second floor features an optional loft or fourth bedroom.

Plan AX-8923-A

Bedrooms: 3-4	Baths: 2½
Space:	
Upper floor:	853 sq. ft.
Main floor:	1,082 sq. ft.
Total living area:	1,935 sq. ft.
Basement:	approx. 1,082 sq. ft.
Garage:	420 sq. ft.
Exterior Wall Framing:	2x4

Foundation options:
Standard basement.
Slab.
(Foundation & framing conversion diagram available — see order form.)

Blueprint Price Code:	B

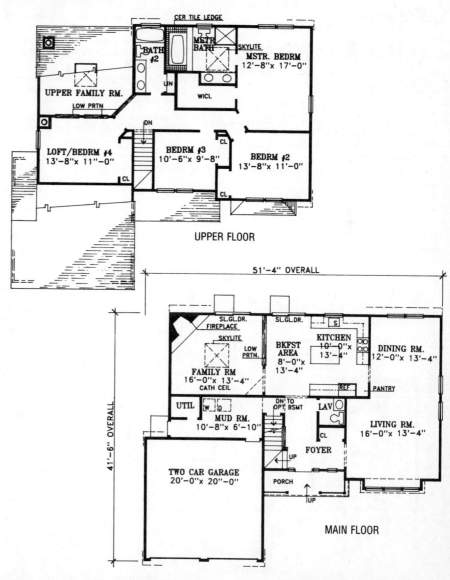

UPPER FLOOR

MAIN FLOOR

Plan AX-8923-A

Farmhouse with Victorian Touch

- Scalloped shingles and horizontal siding accented by detailed brackets define the Victorian exterior. The sides and rear of the home are brick.
- Both the master bedroom and guest bedroom are located on the lower level. A third bedroom and game room is located on the upper level. The game room doubles as a fourth bedroom when needed.
- Both the living room and dining room feature ceilings open to the upper level game room.
- The master suite is spacious and has an adjoining bath with twin vanities, angled tub and large walk-in closet.
- Typical ceilings heights are 8'.
- This home is energy efficient.

PLAN E-1910
WITHOUT BASEMENT

Exterior walls are 2x6 construction.
Specify crawlspace or slab foundation.

Heated area:	1,974 sq. ft.
Unheated area:	821 sq. ft.
Total area:	2,795 sq. ft.

LOWER LEVEL
FLOOR PLAN

UPPER LEVEL
FLOOR PLAN

Blueprint Price Code B
Plan E-1910

Classic Homestead

SECOND FLOOR

- WALK IN CLOSET
- LAV
- W.C.
- BEDROOM 11'-0"×11'-5"
- CLOSET
- CLOSET
- BEDROOM 10'-0"×11'-5"
- LINEN
- sh'w'r
- BEDROOM 13'-0"×15'-0"
- down
- BEDROOM 10'-0"×11'-5"
- BATH
- LAV
- W.C.
- CLOSET

Plans H-3678-3 & H-3678-3A

Bedrooms: 4	Baths: 2½

Finished space:

Upper floor:	960 sq. ft.
Main floor:	1,036 sq. ft.

Total living area:	**1,996 sq. ft.**
Basement:	900 sq. ft.
Garage:	413 sq. ft.

Features:
Spacious living room and large family room.
Convenient nook/kitchen/laundry arrangement.
Inviting porch and roomy entry area.

Exterior Wall Framing:	**2x4**

Foundation options: (Specify)
Standard Basement: Plan H-3678-3
Crawlspace: Plan H-3678-3A
(Foundation & framing conversion diagram available — see order form.)

Blueprint Price Code:
Without finished basement design: B
With finished basement design: D

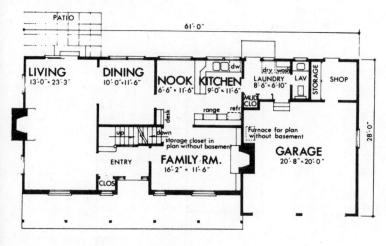

FIRST FLOOR

- PATIO
- 61'-0"
- LIVING 13'-0"×23'-3"
- DINING 10'-0"×11'-6"
- NOOK 6'-6"×11'-6"
- KITCHEN 9'-0"×11'-6"
- dw
- dry wash
- LAUNDRY 8'-6"×6'-10"
- LAV
- STORAGE
- SHOP
- desk
- range
- refr
- MUD CLO
- up
- down
- storage closet in plan without basement
- furnace for plan without basement
- ENTRY
- FAMILY RM. 16'-2"×11'-6"
- CLOS
- GARAGE 20'-8"×20'-0"
- 28'-0"

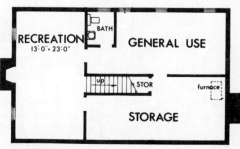

BASEMENT

- RECREATION 13'-0"×23'-0"
- BATH
- GENERAL USE
- up
- STOR
- furnace
- STORAGE

Plans H-3678-3 & -3A

Functional, Nostalgic Home Offers Choices in Floor Plans

- Your choice of first- and second-floor room arrangements and foundation plans is required when ordering this design.
- Pick from a family room/kitchen combination with a separate living room, or an expansive living/dining room adjoining a kitchen and nook with either two or three bedrooms.
- In both cases, front entry parlor has an open stairway brightened by a round glass window.
- 8' wide front porch connects with a covered walk to a detached double-car garage.

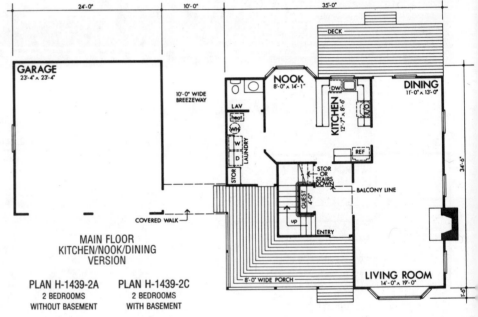

MAIN FLOOR
KITCHEN/NOOK/DINING
VERSION

PLAN H-1439-2A
2 BEDROOMS
WITHOUT BASEMENT

PLAN H-1439-2C
2 BEDROOMS
WITH BASEMENT

PLAN H-1439-3A
3 BEDROOMS
WITHOUT BASEMENT

PLAN H-1439-3C
3 BEDROOMS
WITH BASEMENT

(See facing page for alternate main floor)

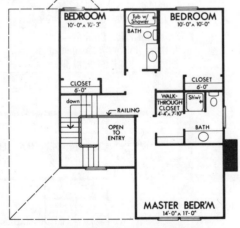

SECOND FLOOR - THREE BEDROOMS
678 SQUARE FEET

SECOND FLOOR - TWO BEDROOMS
678 SQUARE FEET

Plans H-1439-2A, -2C, -3A & -3C

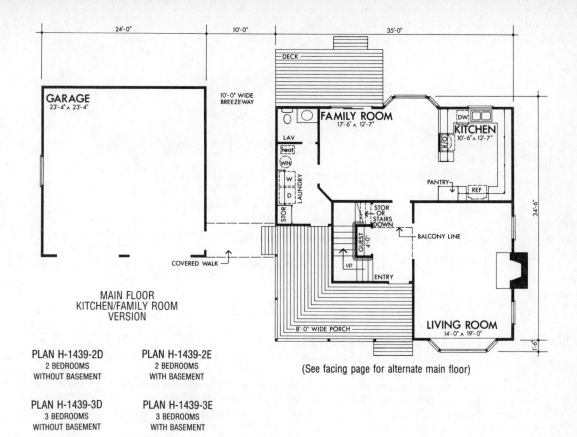

MAIN FLOOR
KITCHEN/FAMILY ROOM
VERSION

PLAN H-1439-2D
2 BEDROOMS
WITHOUT BASEMENT

PLAN H-1439-2E
2 BEDROOMS
WITH BASEMENT

PLAN H-1439-3D
3 BEDROOMS
WITHOUT BASEMENT

PLAN H-1439-3E
3 BEDROOMS
WITH BASEMENT

(See facing page for alternate main floor)

Plans H-1439-2A, -2C, -3A & -3C
Plans H-1439-2D, -2E, -3D & -3E

Bedrooms: 2-3	Baths: 2½
Space:	
Upper floor:	678 sq. ft.
Main floor:	940 sq. ft.
Total living area:	1,618 sq. ft.
Basement:	approx. 940 sq. ft.
Garage:	544 sq. ft.
Exterior Wall Framing:	2x6

Foundation options:
Standard basement (Plans H-1439-2C, -3C, -2E & -3E).
Crawlspace (Plans H-1439-2A, -3A, -2D & -3D).
(Foundation & framing conversion diagram available — see order form.)

Blueprint Price Code: B

SECOND FLOOR — THREE BEDROOMS
678 SQUARE FEET

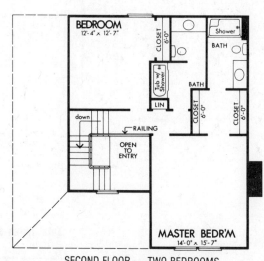

SECOND FLOOR — TWO BEDROOMS
678 SQUARE FEET

Plans H-1439-2D, -2E, -3D & -3E

Maximum Appeal

- At an economical 1,873 sq. ft., this home projects tremendous street appeal with its interesting roof line and multi-paned windows.
- An extended ledge wraps around the exterior of the living room and can be used as a flower shelf.
- The entry opens to a tray-ceilinged living-dining room, perfect for large formal groups.
- The kitchen is highlighted by a sunny garden window and opens to the alcove nook and family room with fireplace.
- The stairway landing off the entry is accented by a tall arched window.
- Upstairs, skylights brighten the main bathroom and the exciting vaulted master bath.
- Don't miss the built-in bookshelves and corner windows located in the master bedroom.

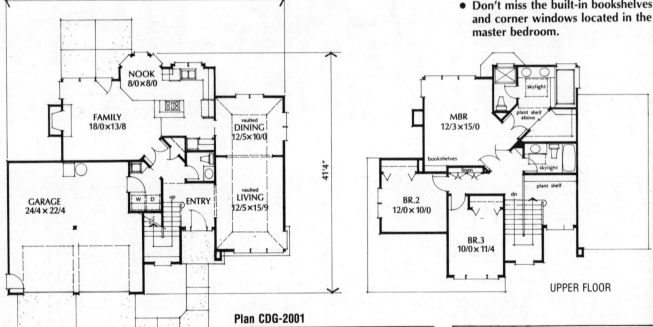

Plan CDG-2001

Bedrooms: 3	Baths: 2½

Space:	
Upper floor:	860 sq. ft.
Main floor:	1,013 sq. ft.

Total living area:	1,873 sq. ft.
Garage:	543 sq. ft.

Exterior Wall Framing:	2x4

Ceiling Heights:	
Upper floor:	8'
Main floor:	9'

Foundation options:
Crawlspace.
(Foundation & framing conversion diagram available — see order form.)

Blueprint Price Code:	B

Plan CDG-2001

Sun-Filled Living Areas

- A decorative front porch highlights the exterior of this two-story traditional.
- Inside, a compact but comfortable floor plan flows from the dramatic two-story foyer.
- A sun-filled living room and bayed breakfast area stretch across the rear of the home. An open railing between the two areas allows the corner fireplace in the living room to be seen from both the nook and the full-featured island kitchen.
- The focal-point dining room offers an elegant, octagonal-shaped tray ceiling.
- A pantry, a built-in work desk and a handy half-bath and laundry room are located between the kitchen and the garage entrance.
- A lovely bay window, a huge walk-in closet and a private bath with dressing area, twin vanities and lavish garden tub are offered in the master bedroom on the upper level. Three extra bedrooms and a second bath complete the design.

Plan OH-135

Bedrooms: 4	Baths: 2 ½
Space:	
Upper floor	935 sq. ft.
Main floor	923 sq. ft.
Total Living Area	**1,858 sq. ft.**
Basement	923 sq. ft.
Garage	400 sq. ft.
Exterior Wall Framing	2x4

Foundation options:

Standard Basement

(Foundation & framing conversion diagram available—see order form.)

Blueprint Price Code	B

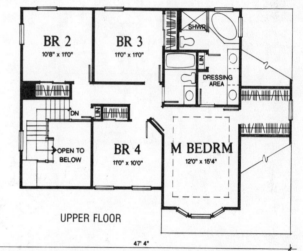

UPPER FLOOR

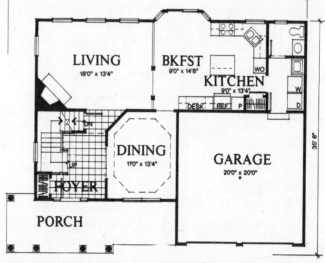

MAIN FLOOR

Plan OH-135

TO ORDER THIS BLUEPRINT, CALL TOLL-FREE 1-800-547-5570

(prices and details on pp. 12-15.)

Nicely Sized and Styled

- Eye-catching entry columns and varying rooflines accent this versatile two-story.
- The vaulted entry and living room are open to the upper level. Decorative columns, a lovely corner window and a front window seat are found in the living room, which is open to the hall and the stairway.
- The roomy kitchen and breakfast area at the rear of the home offers a pantry and a bayed window that overlooks a rear patio. There is easy access to the formal dining room and to the casual family room through a handy pass-through.
- Sliders in the family room open to the patio; an optional fireplace may also be added.
- A convenient main-floor laundry room is located near the garage access.
- All four bedrooms are found on the upper level, the master with a private bath.

UPPER FLOOR

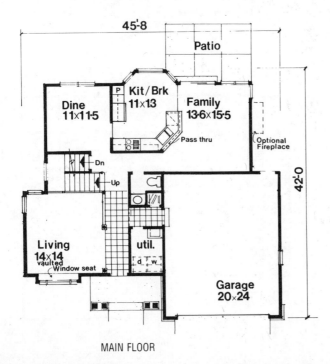

MAIN FLOOR

Plan AG-1801	
Bedrooms: 4	Baths: 2 ½
Space:	
Upper floor	890 sq. ft.
Main floor	980 sq. ft.
Total Living Area	**1,870 sq. ft.**
Basement	980 sq. ft.
Garage	480 sq. ft.
Exterior Wall Framing	2x6
Foundation options:	
Standard Basement	
(Foundation & framing conversion diagram available—see order form.)	
Blueprint Price Code	B

Plan AG-1801

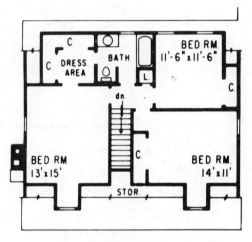

SECOND FLOOR

Cozy
Cape Cod

First floor:	1,068 sq. ft.
Second floor:	804 sq. ft.
Total living area: (Not counting basement or garage)	**1,872 sq. ft.**

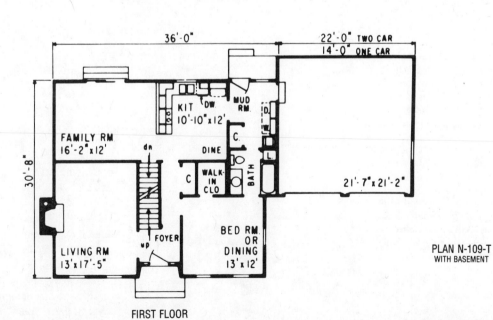

PLAN N-109-T
WITH BASEMENT

FIRST FLOOR

Distinctive One-Story Design

- Angles and curves define the exterior of this distinctive home. A hipped roof with deep overhangs caps the main part of the house. A gabled roof provides contrast and emphasizes the picture window with charming planter box.
- A trellised walkway leads to the double-door entry. The foyer is brightened by a half-round roof window that accentuates the semi-circular ceiling.
- The living room, straight ahead, is highlighted by a cathedral ceiling and a fireplace framed by angled glass walls. A French door opens to a large backyard terrace.
- The dining room is open to the living room, but a lower ceiling in the dining room helps visually separate the two rooms.
- A large combination family room, dinette and kitchen is adjacent to the formal living areas. The family room has sliding glass doors to the terrace, the dinette is distinguished by a bayed eating alcove, and the kitchen has a snack bar.
- Convenient to the family living areas are a spacious laundry room, a mud room and a utility area with a pantry closet plus two additional closets.
- The sleeping wing is well isolated from the activity areas. The spacious master bedroom includes twin closets plus a large walk-in closet. The private bath features an oversized whirlpool tub and double-bowl vanity.
- The two smaller bedrooms also have double closets and share a second bath with dual sinks.

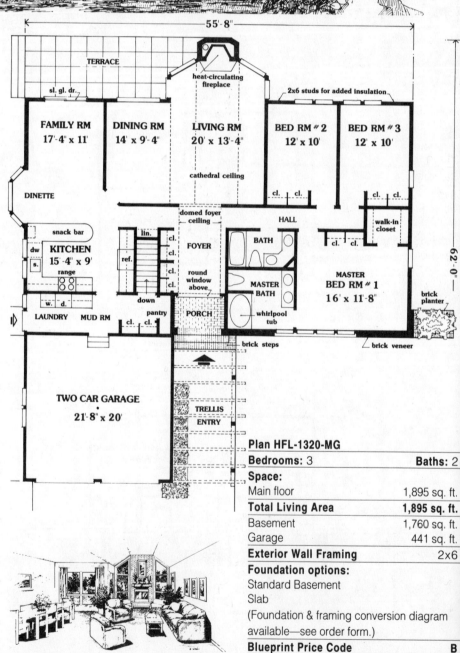

Plan HFL-1320-MG	
Bedrooms: 3	**Baths:** 2
Space:	
Main floor	1,895 sq. ft.
Total Living Area	**1,895 sq. ft.**
Basement	1,760 sq. ft.
Garage	441 sq. ft.
Exterior Wall Framing	2x6

Foundation options:
Standard Basement
Slab
(Foundation & framing conversion diagram available—see order form.)

Blueprint Price Code	B

Plan HFL-1320-MG

Plan M-2214

Bedrooms: 4	Baths: 2½

Space:

Upper floor:	940 sq. ft.
Main floor:	964 sq. ft.
Total living area:	**1,904 sq. ft.**
Basement:	approx. 964 sq. ft.
Garage:	440 sq. ft.

Exterior Wall Framing:	2x4

Foundation options:
Standard basement only.
(Foundation & framing conversion
diagram available — see order form.)

Blueprint Price Code:	B

Traditional Saltbox Roofline

- This classic saltbox exterior offers an open, flexible interior, with well-planned space for the large, busy family.
- The spacious living room includes an impressive fireplace and sliding doors to a screened porch at the rear of the home.
- The large, open-design kitchen blends in with the family room to create a delightful space for food preparation and family life.
- A formal dining room is found at the right as you enter the foyer.
- Upstairs, a deluxe master suite includes a private bath and large closet.
- Three secondary bedrooms share a second upstairs bath.
- Note the convenient washer/dryer area and half-bath off the kitchen.

UPPER FLOOR

35

26

Bed Rm. 10x12
Bed Rm. 10x9
M. Bed Rm. 12x17
Bed Rm. 13x12
dn

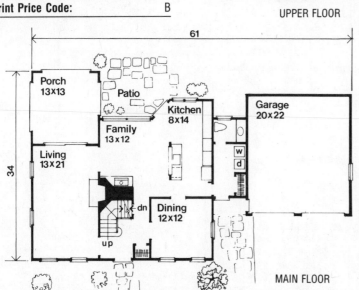

MAIN FLOOR

61

34

Porch 13x13
Patio
Kitchen 8x14
Garage 20x22
Family 13x12
Living 13x21
w
d
dn
Dining 12x12
up

Plan M-2214

Living Room Looks Out over Patio

- At the center of this stylish ranch is a spacious living room with a grand fireplace, a 10-ft. ceiling and a spectacular rear window wall that overlooks a large patio.
- Decorative columns define the separation of the living room and the entry and formal dining room.
- The walk-through kitchen has a pantry and a separate range and oven. An eating bar is shared with the large adjoining morning room, which has direct access to the patio.
- Separated from the secondary bedrooms by closets and two baths, the master bedroom is quiet and oriented to the rear. The master bath offers separate vanities, an enormous walk-in closet and a separate tub and shower.

Plan DD-1916

Bedrooms: 3	Baths: 2

Living Area:

Main floor	1,927 sq. ft.
Total Living Area:	**1,927 sq. ft.**
Standard basement	1,927 sq. ft.
Garage	428 sq. ft.
Exterior Wall Framing:	2x4

Foundation Options:

Standard basement
Crawlspace
Slab
(Typical foundation & framing conversion diagram available—see order form.)

BLUEPRINT PRICE CODE:	**B**

*TO ORDER THIS BLUEPRINT,
CALL TOLL-FREE 1-800-547-5570*

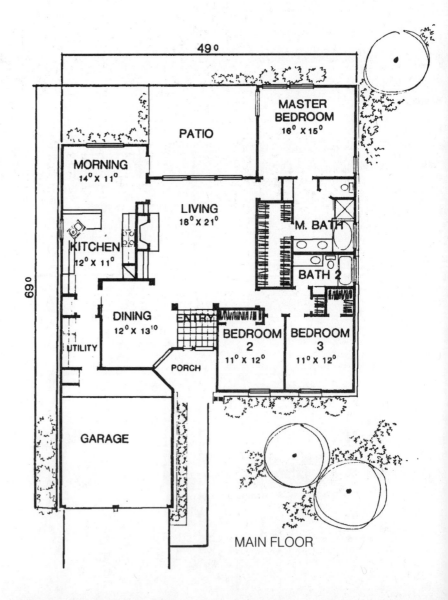

Plan DD-1916

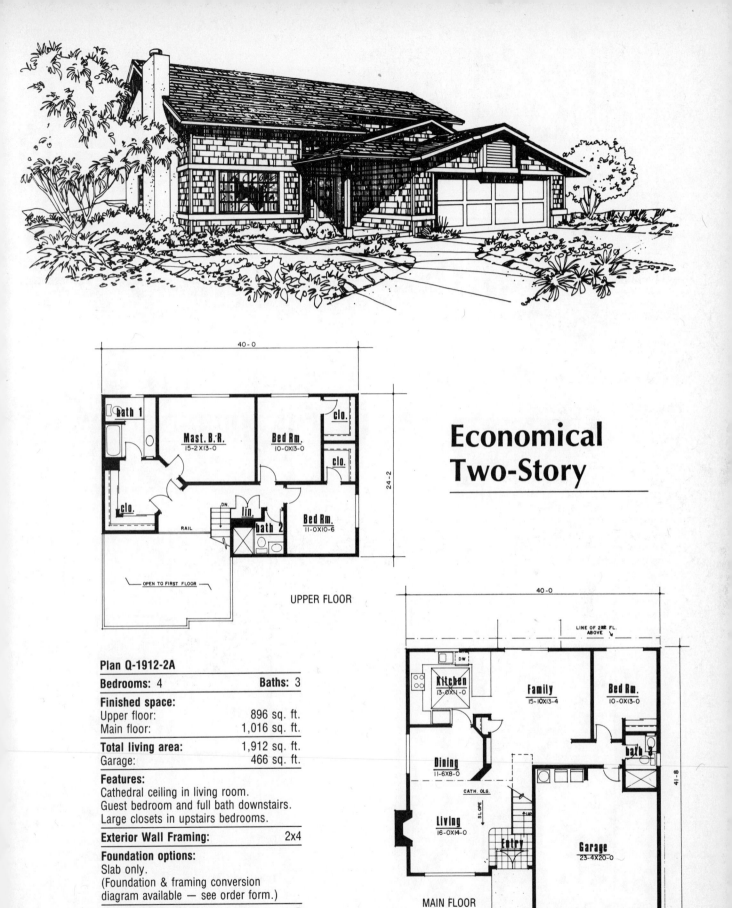

40 - 0

Bath 1

Mast. B.R.
15-2 X13-0

Bed Rm.
10-0X13-0

clo.

clo.

24 - 2

clo.

DN

lin.

RAIL

bath 2

Bed Rm.
11-0X10-6

OPEN TO FIRST FLOOR

UPPER FLOOR

Economical Two-Story

Plan Q-1912-2A

Bedrooms: 4	Baths: 3

Finished space:

Upper floor:	896 sq. ft.
Main floor:	1,016 sq. ft.

Total living area:	1,912 sq. ft.
Garage:	466 sq. ft.

Features:
Cathedral ceiling in living room.
Guest bedroom and full bath downstairs.
Large closets in upstairs bedrooms.

Exterior Wall Framing:	2x4

Foundation options:
Slab only.
(Foundation & framing conversion
diagram available — see order form.)

Blueprint Price Code:	B

40 - 0

LINE OF 2ᴺᴰ FL. ABOVE

DW

Kitchen
13-0XN-0

Family
15-10X13-4

Bed Rm.
10-0X13-0

bath

41 - 8

Dining
11-6X8-0

CATH. CLG.

SLOPE

UP

Living
16-0X14-0

Entry

Garage
23-4X20-0

MAIN FLOOR

Plan Q-1912-2A

TO ORDER THIS BLUEPRINT,
CALL TOLL-FREE 1-800-547-5570
(prices and details on pp. 12-15.) **73**

Southwest Design
Fits Long, Narrow Lot

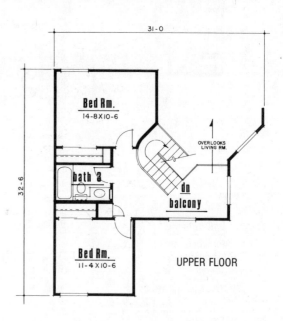

MAIN FLOOR

31-0

covered patio

Family
12-8x17-0

Kitchen
10-8x9-0

CATH CLG   CATH CLG

Dining
10-8x7-8

Mast. B.R.
15-0x14-8

Living
15-4x12-4

VAULTED CLG.

up

Entry

bath 1

bath 2

Study / opt. b.r.
10-8x10-6

CLOSET

utility

Garage
19-4x20-2

70-0

UPPER FLOOR

31-0

Bed Rm.
14-8X10-6

OVERLOOKS LIVING RM.

bath 3

dn
balcony

Bed Rm.
11-4X10-6

32-6

PLAN Q-1915-1A
WITHOUT BASEMENT
(SLAB-ON-GRADE FOUNDATION)

First floor:	1,400 sq. ft.
Second floor:	515 sq. ft.
Total living area: (Not counting garage)	1,915 sq. ft.

Blueprint Price Code B
Plan Q-1915-1A

41'

BREAKFAST

KITCHEN

DINING ROOM
11-6 x 11-6

BATH

GREAT ROOM
15-0 x 17-6

MASTER BEDROOM
12-6 x 13-6

UP

36'

MAIN FLOOR

BATH

BEDROOM
11-0 x 12-6

DOWN

BEDROOM
11-0 x 13-6

BEDROOM
11-0 x 13-6

UPPER FLOOR

Distinction and Serenity

- The elegant facade of this design promises a home of distinction and serenity.
- A generously sized Great Room, complete with fireplace, leads into a formal dining room.
- The kitchen is also large and flows into a sunny, bay-windowed breakfast nook.
- A magnificent downstairs master suite includes a superb bath with separate tub and shower, two vanities and a large closet.
- The main floor also includes a convenient laundry area (off the breakfast nook) and a powder room off the center hall.
- Upstairs, you will find three more bedrooms and another full bath. (The fourth bedroom, with the dormer, could be finished at a later date, or used for a study or play room.)

Plan V-1918	
Bedrooms: 4	Baths: 2½
Space:	
Upper floor:	790 sq. ft.
Main floor:	1,128 sq. ft.
Total living area:	1,918 sq. ft.
Exterior Wall Framing:	2x6

Ceiling Heights:	
Upper floor:	8'
Main floor:	9'

Foundation options:
Crawlspace only.
(Foundation & framing conversion diagram available — see order form.)

Blueprint Price Code: B

Plan V-1918

New-Age Victorian

- A modern-day interior floor plan combines with a historical exterior to make this Victorian a sure hit with today's families.
- The turret, so dominant on the outside, becomes a focal point inside as well.
- All of the rooms radiate from the octagonal foyer. The huge Great Room with a fireplace is directly opposite a charming formal dining room with window alcove.
- The kitchen, bay-windowed breakfast room and the laundry room are tucked behind the foyer, separated from the formal living areas by a powder room, a short hallway and the stairway to the upper level.
- The second-floor landing repeats the shape of the foyer and features an oval window.
- The master bedroom suite far exceeds anything imaginable during the Victorian era. It includes a walk-in closet, dressing area with dual vanities, separate shower and romantic step-up spa tub set into a bay window.
- The two remaining bedroms share another full bath.
- In keeping with the grandeur of Victorian times, both floors feature 9-ft. ceilings.

BEDROOM
9-6 X 11-0

MASTER BEDROOM
14-6 X 15-0

DOWN

BEDROOM
11-6 X 12-6

UPPER FLOOR

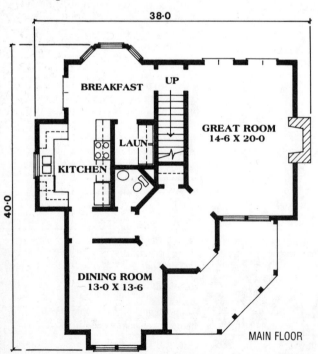

38-0

BREAKFAST

UP

GREAT ROOM
14-6 X 20-0

LAUN

KITCHEN

40-0

DINING ROOM
13-0 X 13-6

MAIN FLOOR

Plan V-1947	
Bedrooms: 3-4	**Baths:** 2 ½
Space:	
Upper floor	948 sq. ft.
Main floor	999 sq. ft.
Total Living Area	**1,947 sq. ft.**
Exterior Wall Framing	2x6
Foundation options:	
Crawlspace (Foundation & framing conversion diagram available—see order form.)	
Blueprint Price Code	B

TO ORDER THIS BLUEPRINT,
CALL TOLL-FREE 1-800-547-5570

76 (prices and details on pp. 12-15.)

Plan V-1947

Details Make the Difference

- The gable windows outlined with bold detailing add definition to this striking transitional home. The covered front porch softens the home's look and gives it a welcoming look.
- The floor plan includes both a formal living and dining room, plus an informal family room, breakfast room and kitchen area.
- The dining room features a tray ceiling, while the living room has vaulted ceilings. French doors, flanked by built-in shelves, open to the family room.
- The family room has a fireplace and sliding doors to the patio. The breakfast room is highlighted by the bay-windowed eating area on one side and built-in shelves on the other.

- The kitchen includes a countertop island, and a utility room and a half-bath are close by.
- The second-story balcony overlooks the vaulted entry with overhead plant shelf.
- The master suite offers all the modern amenities, including a spa tub. The two remaining bedrooms are well proportioned and share another full bath.

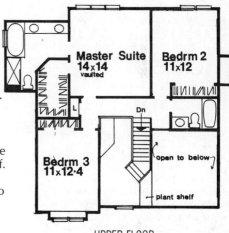

UPPER FLOOR

Plan AG-1901

Bedrooms: 3-4	Baths: 2 ½
Space:	
Upper floor	820 sq. ft.
Main floor	1,152 sq. ft.
Total Living Area	**1,972 sq. ft.**
Basement	1,152 sq. ft.
Garage	420 sq. ft.
Exterior Wall Framing	**2x6**

Foundation options:

Standard basement

(Foundation & framing conversion diagram available—see order form.)

Blueprint Price Code	**B**

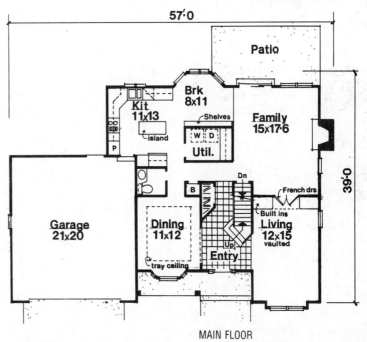

MAIN FLOOR

Plan AG-1901

Colonial with Modern Interior

This house is thoroughly Colonial outside, but inside are all the space-saving, energy-conserving details of contemporary living. The family room has a cozy fireplace as its hub and an exit, via sliding glass doors, to the terrace. The kitchen is located to easily serve the several dining and snacking areas.

The second floor offers privacy for the four bedrooms and two baths.

First floor:	983 sq. ft.
Second floor:	990 sq. ft.
Total living area:	1,973 sq. ft.
(Not counting basement or garage)	
Basement (opt.):	983 sq. ft.
Gar., Mud Rm, Etc.:	562 sq. ft.

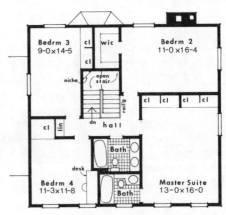

SECOND FLOOR

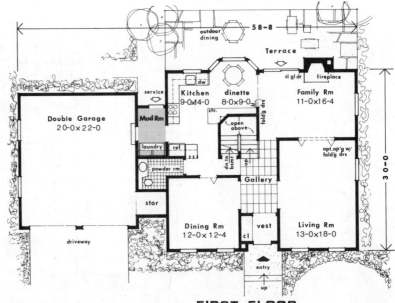

FIRST FLOOR

(prices and details on pp. 12-15.)

TO ORDER THIS BLUEPRINT,
CALL TOLL-FREE 1-800-547-5570

Blueprint Price Code B

Plan K-274-M

A Shape that's Easy to Build

- The basic rectangular shape of this two-story makes it economical to build. All four bedrooms are located on the upper level.
- The main-floor central hallway is decorated by an open stairway; it is flanked by a dining room and a formal living room with an attractive fireplace that can be seen from the foyer. Sliding glass doors at the rear overlook the back porch.
- A brilliant family room, bayed dinette and kitchen combine at the rear for an open, yet intimate, atmosphere. A wood-beam ceiling adds a homey touch.
- Main-floor laundry facilities, a half-bath and a handy service porch are located near the garage access.

Plan HFL-1070-RQ

Bedrooms: 4	Baths: 2 ½
Space:	
Upper floor	1,013 sq. ft.
Main floor	983 sq. ft.
Total Living Area	**1,996 sq. ft.**
Basement	889 sq. ft.
Garage	403 sq. ft.
Exterior Wall Framing	**2x6**

Foundation options:

Standard Basement

Slab

(Foundation & framing conversion diagram available—see order form.)

Blueprint Price Code	**B**

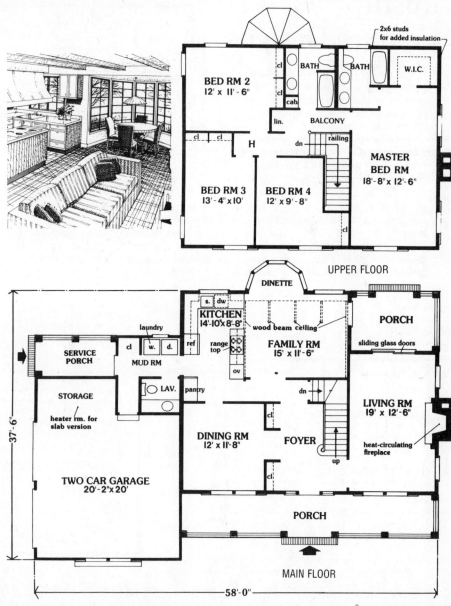

UPPER FLOOR

MAIN FLOOR

Plan HFL-1070-RQ

Rustic Country Design

- A welcoming front porch, window shutters and a bay window on the exterior of this rustic design are complemented by a comfortable, informal interior.
- A spacious country kitchen includes a bay-windowed breakfast area, center work island and abundant counter and cabinet space.
- Note the large utility room in the garage entry area.
- The large Great Room includes an impressive fireplace and another informal eating area with double doors opening to a deck, patio or screened porch. Also note the half-bath.

- The main floor master suite features a walk-in closet and compartmentalized private bath.
- Upstairs, you will find two more bedrooms, another full bath and a large storage area.

UPPER FLOOR

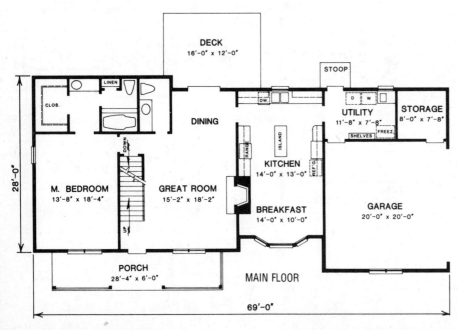

MAIN FLOOR

Plan C-8476

Bedrooms: 3	**Baths: 2½**

Space:	
Upper floor:	720 sq. ft.
Main floor:	1,277 sq. ft.
Total living area:	**1,997 sq. ft.**
Basement:	approx. 1,200 sq. ft.
Garage:	400 sq. ft.
Storage:	(in garage) 61 sq. ft.
Exterior Wall Framing:	2x4

Foundation options:
Daylight basement.
Standard basement.
Crawlspace.
Slab.
(Foundation & framing conversion diagram available — see order form.)

Blueprint Price Code:	B

TO ORDER THIS BLUEPRINT, CALL TOLL-FREE 1-800-547-5570
(prices and details on pp. 12-15.)

80

Plan C-8476

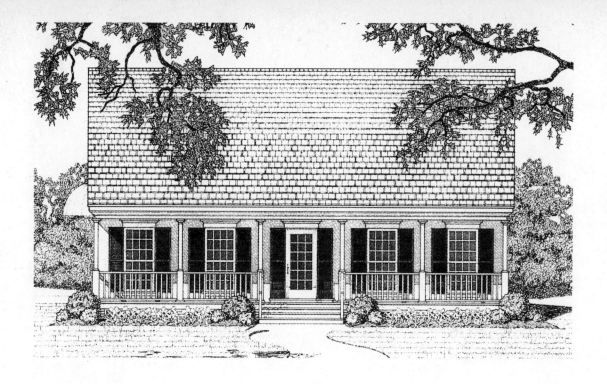

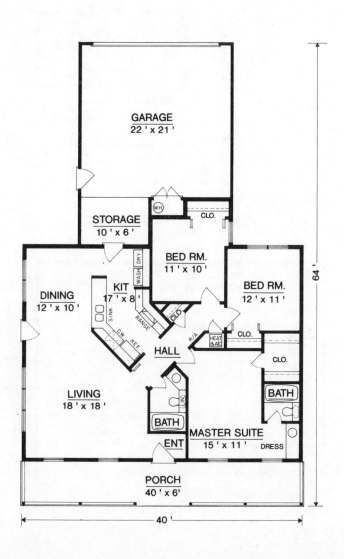

GARAGE
22' x 21'

STORAGE
10' x 6'

WH.

CLO.

BED RM.
11' x 10'

BED RM.
12' x 11'

DINING
12' x 10'

WASH DRY

KIT
17' x 8'

SINK
RANGE

CLO.

CLO.

HALL

DW. REF

R/A

HEAT & AC

CLO.

LIVING
18' x 18'

BATH

LIN.

BATH

MASTER SUITE
15' x 11'

DRESS

ENT

CLO.

PORCH
40' x 6'

64'

40'

Cozy Veranda Invites Visitors

- Large covered front porch has detailed columns and railings.
- Compact size fits small lots, yet facade gives illusion of larger home.
- Space-saving angular design minimizes hallway space.
- Master suite features walk-in closet, private bath, and separate dressing and sink area.

Plan E-1217

Bedrooms: 3	Baths: 2
Space:	
Total living area:	1,266 sq. ft.
Garage and storage:	550 sq. ft.
Exterior Wall Framing:	2x6

Foundation options:
Crawlspace.
Slab.
(Foundation & framing conversion diagram available — see order form.)

Blueprint Price Code:	A

Plan E-1217

Compact and Expandable

- Its compact 1,430 square-foot design and economical use of space make this home perfect for the first time buyer.
- Grouped together on the first floor are the living room, dining room and kitchen, all under a vaulted ceiling; the living room boasts a huge corner fireplace.
- An unfinished room opposite the utility area can be finished as your budget allows.
- A mid-sized master bedroom on the upper level has a front window view, walk-in closet, and private bath.
- Two additional bedrooms share a second full bath.

Plan NW-754-E

Bedrooms: 3	Baths: 2 ½
Space:	
Upper floor	624 sq. ft.
Main floor	806 sq. ft.
Total Living Area	**1,430 sq. ft.**
Garage	398 sq. ft.
Exterior Wall Framing	**2x6**
Foundation options:	
Crawlspace & Slab Combination	
(Foundation & framing conversion diagram	
available—see order form.)	
Blueprint Price Code	**A**

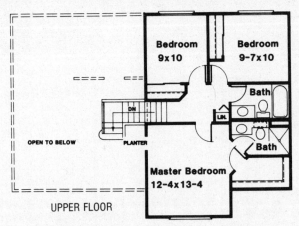

UPPER FLOOR

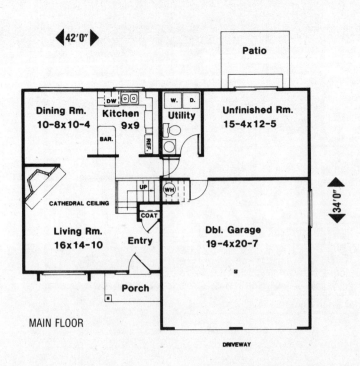

MAIN FLOOR

Plan NW-754-E

The Solid Look of Permanence

- Exterior design lends an air of quality and elegance which is carried on throughout the home.
- Large, centered living room decor includes 10' ceilings, detailed fireplace, and ceiling fans.
- Side porch can be entered through living/dining area.
- Minimum halls generate maximum living space.
- Secluded master suite has romantic sitting area and designer bath.

Plan E-1435

Bedrooms: 3	Baths: 2

Space:
Total living area:	1,442 sq. ft.
Garage and storage:	516 sq. ft.
Porches:	128 sq. ft.

Exterior Wall Framing:	2x4

Foundation options:
Crawlspace.
Slab.
(Foundation & framing conversion diagram available — see order form.)

Blueprint Price Code:	A

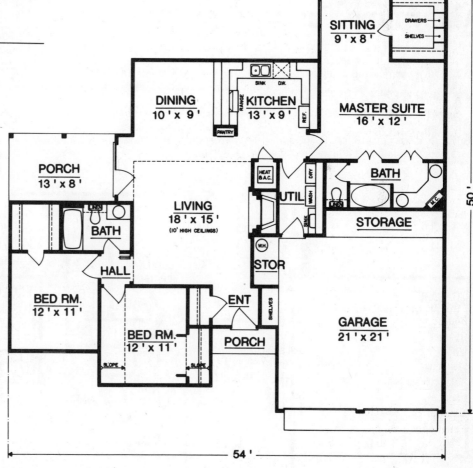

Plan E-1435

Charming Family Home

- Relatively modest in size, this plan offers plenty of living space, an attractive exterior and an efficient floor plan.
- A central foyer directs traffic to the Great Room, kitchen or bedroom hallway.
- The spacious Great Room features a cathedral ceiling and a large fireplace,

and also offers easy access to the outdoors.
- The kitchen features a large counter island, a breakfast nook and a cathedral ceiling.
- The master bedroom includes a private bath and walk-in closet.
- Two additional bedrooms share another full bath.

Plan N-1220	
Bedrooms: 3	Baths: 2
Living Area:	
Main floor	1,540 sq. ft.
Total Living Area:	**1,540 sq. ft.**
Standard basement	1,540 sq. ft.
Garage	462 sq. ft.
Exterior Wall Framing:	2x4
Foundation Options:	
Standard basement	
Crawlspace	
Slab	
(Typical foundation & framing conversion diagram available—see order form.)	
BLUEPRINT PRICE CODE:	B

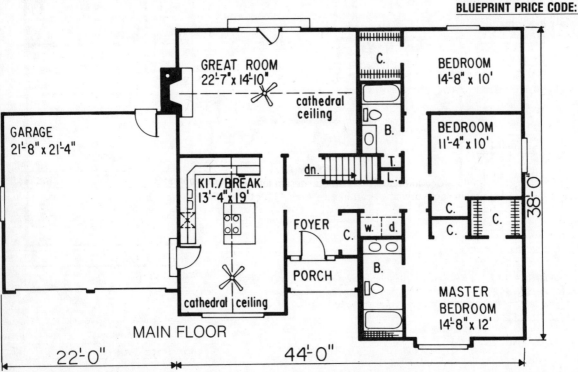

MAIN FLOOR

TO ORDER THIS BLUEPRINT, CALL TOLL-FREE 1-800-547-5570
(prices and details on pp. 12-15.)

Plan N-1220

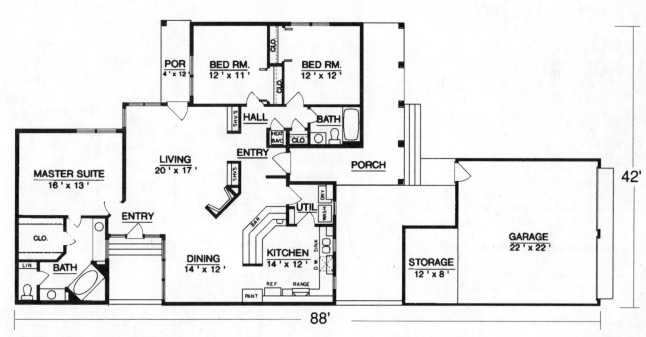

Nice & Narrow

Fun and functional covered porches in the front and rear of this unique design let the owners enjoy outdoor views and maintain some privacy, even in a narrow, 42-foot wide plan.

Central and open are the spacious living room with angled fireplace, dining room, and kitchen with open counter/wet bar.

The plan includes front and side entries which overlook porches, and the living room offers another covered porch facing the back yard.

The secluded master bedroom suite has a private bath with angled tub, walk-in closet and separate vanities.

Two additional bedrooms are well separated from the master suite for privacy, and share a second full bath.

Plan E-1511	
Bedrooms: 3	Baths: 2
Space:	
Total Living Area	**1,599 sq. ft.**
Garage	484 sq. ft.
Storage	96 sq. ft.
Exterior Wall Framing	2x6
Foundation options:	
Crawlspace	
Slab	
(Foundation & framing conversion diagram available—see order form.)	
Blueprint Price Code	B

Plan E-1511

Efficient Three-Bedroom

- This modest-sized, but open and efficient floor plan is perfect for young or starting families.
- A formal dining room with front corner window and vaulted living room flank the foyer.
- The vaulted family room at the rear has decorative entry columns and an attached rear deck seen through sliders; the room is open to a generous-sized kitchen with handy pantry.
- Secluded at the rear corner of the home is the master suite with private bath, featuring dual vanities. Washer and dryer are close by.
- Two secondary bedrooms occupy the opposite end, separated by a second bath.

Plan B-90005

Bedrooms: 3	Baths: 2
Space:	
Main floor	1,636 sq. ft.
Total Living Area	**1,636 sq. ft.**
Basement	1,636 sq. ft.
Garage	374 sq. ft.
Exterior Wall Framing	2x4
Foundation options:	
Standard Basement	
(Foundation & framing conversion diagram available—see order form.)	
Blueprint Price Code	**B**

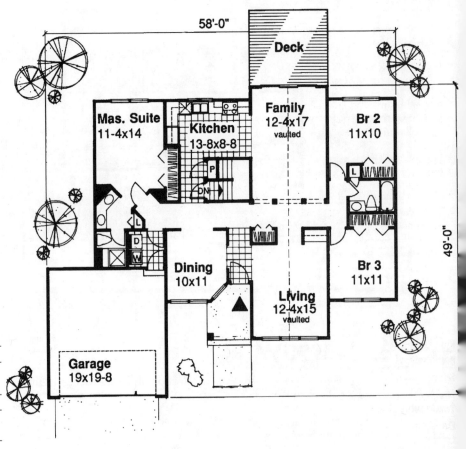

58'-0"

Deck

Mas. Suite
11-4x14

Kitchen
13-8x8-8

Family
12-4x17
vaulted

Br 2
11x10

P

DN

Dining
10x11

Living
12-4x15
vaulted

Br 3
11x11

Garage
19x19-8

49'-0"

Plan B-90005

Angled, Vaulted Kitchen

- A corner fireplace and angled wall in the vaulted living room and bordering kitchen add interest to the interior of this medium-sized three-bedroom.
- The living room is open to the adjoining vaulted dining room, allowing a clear view of the rear deck and yard.
- Uniquely shaped and also oriented to the rear, the vaulted kitchen with eating bar and pantry joins a sunny breakfast nook with private access to the deck.
- The sleeping wing offers a generous-sized master bedroom with a nice bath for two; a step-up tub, separate shower, large walk-in closet and twin vanities make it ideal for two.
- Two secondary bedrooms share the rest of the plan with a second bath and laundry room.

Plan U-90-102

Bedrooms: 3	Baths: 2
Space:	
Main floor	1,689 sq. ft.
Total Living Area	**1,689 sq. ft.**
Basement	1,689 sq. ft.
Garage	576 sq. ft.
Exterior Wall Framing	2x4

Foundation options:

Daylight Basement

Standard Basement

Crawlspace

Slab

(Foundation & framing conversion diagram available—see order form.)

Blueprint Price Code	**B**

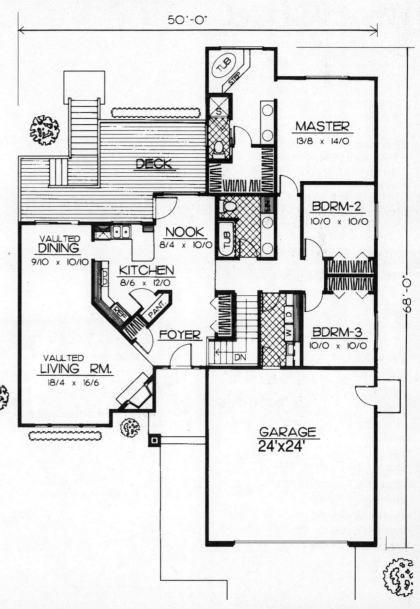

Plan U-90-102

CALL TOLL-FREE 1-800-547-5570
(prices and details on pp. 12-15.) **87**

What You See is What You Get

- Open, family living is brought to mind in looking at this two-story's exterior; inside you'll find it is indeed the case.
- The family dining, cooking and relaxing areas are open to one another at the rear of the home; an informal dinette opens to an optional rear porch or patio.
- A half-wall is the only division between the kitchen and adjoining family room, which houses a large fireplace and plenty of room to relax.
- Off the foyer, the formal living room overlooks the inviting front porch.
- Upstairs you'll find a generous master bedroom with dual closets and a private bath.
- Two secondary bedrooms share a hall bath.

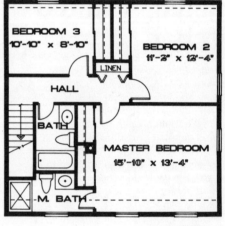

UPPER FLOOR

Plan GL-1700	
Bedrooms: 3	**Baths:** 2 ½
Space:	
Upper floor	756 sq. ft.
Main floor	944 sq. ft.
Total Living Area	**1,700 sq. ft.**
Basement	944 sq. ft.
Garage	484 sq. ft.
Exterior Wall Framing	2x6
Foundation options:	
Standard Basement	
(Foundation & framing conversion diagram available—see order form.)	
Blueprint Price Code	**B**

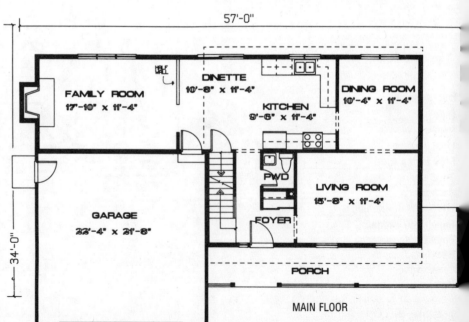

MAIN FLOOR

TO ORDER THIS BLUEPRINT,
CALL TOLL-FREE 1-800-547-5570

88 (prices and details on pp. 12-15.)

Plan GL-1700

Spacious "Gathering Room"

- This highly traditional design offers a charming exterior and highly functional and modern interior.
- A vaulted foyer leads to a formal dining room on the left or a sitting room on the right.
- An efficient kitchen, with pantry, opens to a spacious "gathering room" which features a fireplace and built-in bookshelves. A sunny breakfast nook is off to the rear and opens to a patio or deck.
- Upstairs, a master suite features a large walk-in closet and a private bath.
- Two other bedrooms share another full bath, and there is also a roomy linen closet in the hallway.
- A breezeway connecting the garage to the house offers convenient space for a laundry facility.

Plan S-4859

Bedrooms: 3	Baths: 2 ½
Space:	
Upper floor	763 sq. ft.
Main floor	988 sq. ft.
Total Living Area	**1,751 sq. ft.**
Basement	988 sq. ft.
Garage	484 sq. ft.
Exterior Wall Framing	2x6

Foundation options:

Standard Basement

Crawlspace

(Foundation & framing conversion diagram available—see order form.)

Blueprint Price Code	**B**

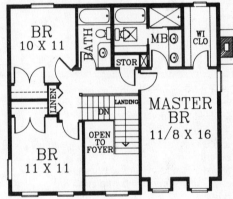

UPPER FLOOR

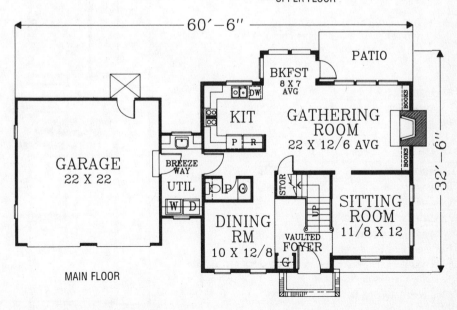

MAIN FLOOR

Plan S-4859

(prices and details on pp. 12-15.)

TO ORDER THIS BLUEPRINT, CALL TOLL-FREE 1-800-547-5570

Story-and-a-Half Fits on Narrow Lot

- This traditional plan has a thoroughly modern interior, with plenty of space for family and guests.
- The living and dining rooms flow together to make a large open space for entertaining.
- More private family gatherings are easily accommodated in a sunny dinette.
- Note the mudroom and half-bath in the garage entry area.
- The master suite is downstairs, with two secondary bedrooms and another full bath on the upper level.

Plan A-2272-DS

Bedrooms: 3	Baths: 2½
Space:	
Upper floor	509 sq. ft.
Main floor	1,252 sq. ft.
Total Living Area	**1,761 sq. ft.**
Basement	approx. 1,200 sq. ft.
Garage	440 sq. ft.
Exterior Wall Framing	2x6

Foundation options:
Standard Basement
(Foundation & framing conversion diagram available—see order form.)

Blueprint Price Code	**B**

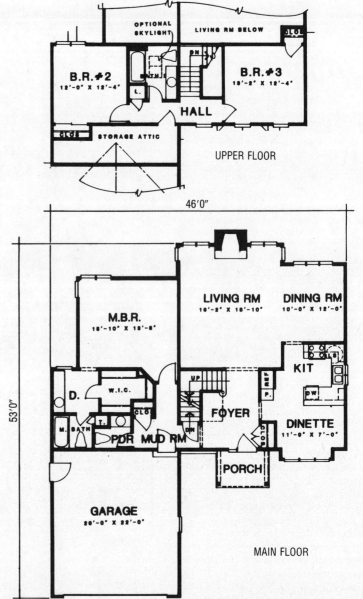

UPPER FLOOR

MAIN FLOOR

TO ORDER THIS BLUEPRINT,
CALL TOLL-FREE 1-800-547-5570
(prices and details on pp. 12-15.)

Plan A-2272-DS

A Personality of Its Own

- With this unique design you can build a dream home that will truly stand out from all the rest. Victorian flourishes give the exterior lots of curb appeal and a look that says "home." The front gable is the center of attention, with its decorative spire and ornate window. An oval, leaded glass window in the front door and sidelights make the entry just as inviting.

- An immense Great Room with fireplace is the focal point of the interior. Space is maximized by eliminating seldom-used formal living areas. The Great Room combines with the dining room and kitchen to create one huge, very livable area for family and guests. Bay windows and a sliding glass door in the dining room enhance the bright, open floor plan.

- The kitchen includes a breakfast bar and is convenient to the laundry room and a half-bath off the rear entrance.

- The first-floor master suite with a large walk-in closet is another bonus feature. The master bath is highlighted by a relaxing tub situated in a secluded bay. A separate shower and extra-large vanity are other appreciated features.

- Three good-sized bedrooms are on the second floor. A compartmentalized bath alleviates morning rush-hour traffic.

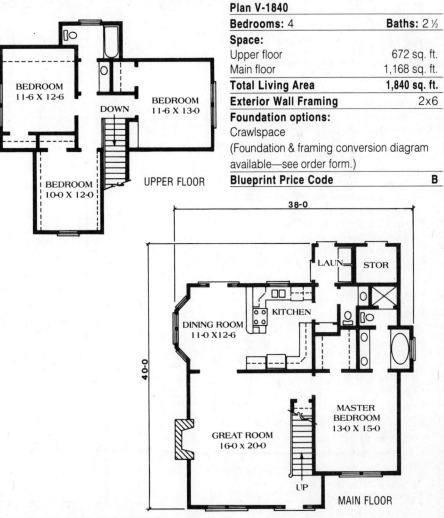

Plan V-1840

Bedrooms: 4	**Baths:** 2 ½
Space:	
Upper floor	672 sq. ft.
Main floor	1,168 sq. ft.
Total Living Area	**1,840 sq. ft.**
Exterior Wall Framing	2x6

Foundation options:

Crawlspace
(Foundation & framing conversion diagram available—see order form.)

Blueprint Price Code	B

Plan V-1840

Great Room, Loft Featured

- Decorative stone accents the facade of this exciting yet economical home.
- Today's family will enjoy the large vaulted Great Room at the rear; it boasts a center fireplace and a sliding glass door to the backyard.
- The second-story loft overlooks the Great Room for a dramatic effect.
- The roomy island kitchen can be accessed from both the Great Room and the formal dining room, which features a cathedral ceiling.
- The kitchen is located to allow the cook to enjoy the fireplace and participate in the on-going family activities in the Great Room.
- The convenient main-floor laundry facilities and a half-bath are situated near the garage entrance.
- Secluded to the rear is a spacious master bedroom with dressing area, dual closets and a private bath.

Plan A-2184-DS

Bedrooms: 2-3	**Baths:** 2 ½
Space:	
Upper floor	502 sq. ft.
Main floor	1,348 sq. ft.
Total Living Area	**1,850 sq. ft.**
Basement	1,348 sq. ft.
Garage	528 sq. ft.
Exterior Wall Framing	2x6

Foundation options:

Standard Basement

(Foundation & framing conversion diagram available—see order form.)

Blueprint Price Code	B

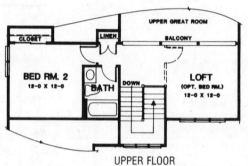

UPPER FLOOR

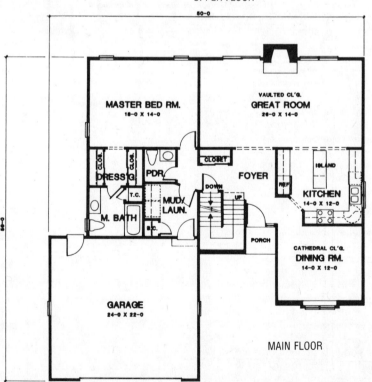

MAIN FLOOR

Plan A-2184-DS

Efficient Yet Exciting One-Story

- A narrow, 45-foot width allows this plan to be built in almost any urban or suburban lot.
- The view from the entry includes the sunken living room to the right, with vaulted ceiling and bow window plus a long view straight ahead through the vaulted family room to the rear yard.
- The kitchen is well situated between the formal dining room, with a view into the living room, and the family room with fireplace.
- The sleeping wing of the plan, to the left of the entry, includes three bedrooms and two full baths. The master suite offers a vaulted ceiling, walk-in closet, and private bath with separate shower and spa tub.

Plan I-1871-A

Bedrooms: 3	Baths: 2
Space:	
Main floor	1,871 sq. ft.
Total Living Area	**1,871 sq. ft.**
Garage	371 sq. ft.
Exterior Wall Framing	2x6
Foundation options:	
Crawlspace	
(Foundation & framing conversion diagram available—see order form.)	
Blueprint Price Code	B

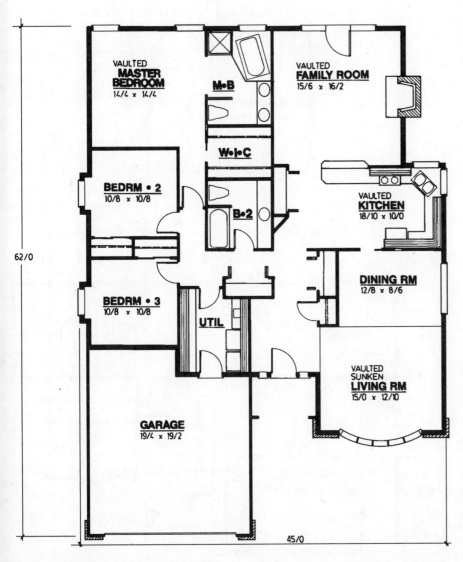

VAULTED MASTER BEDROOM
14/4 x 14/4

M•B

VAULTED FAMILY ROOM
15/6 x 16/2

W•I•C

BEDRM • 2
10/8 x 10/8

B•2

VAULTED KITCHEN
18/10 x 10/0

BEDRM • 3
10/8 x 10/8

UTIL

DINING RM
12/8 x 8/6

GARAGE
19/4 x 19/2

VAULTED SUNKEN LIVING RM
15/0 x 12/10

62/0

45/0

Plan I-1871-A

Simple Elegance

- This simple, yet elegant exterior houses an interior that is efficient and functional.
- Four bedrooms, lots of closet space, two full baths upstairs and a powder room on the main level leave little to complain about in the efficiency department.
- Flowing together at the rear of the home are the family activity areas; only a half-wall separates the large family room from the adjoining dinette and kitchen. The formal dining room joins the kitchen on the opposite side.
- An optional fireplace can add drama to the formal living room at the front of the home.
- Two mid-sized bedrooms, a spacious master bedroom and a large, fourth bedroom share the upper level with two full baths.

Plan GL-1926

Bedrooms: 4	Baths: 2 ½
Space:	
Upper floor	972 sq. ft.
Main floor	954 sq. ft.
Total Living Area	**1,926 sq. ft.**
Basement	954 sq. ft.
Garage	484 sq. ft.
Exterior Wall Framing	**2x6**
Foundation options:	

Standard Basement
(Foundation & framing conversion diagram available—see order form.)

Blueprint Price Code	**B**

***TO ORDER THIS BLUEPRINT,
CALL TOLL-FREE 1-800-547-5570***

(prices and details on pp. 12-15.)

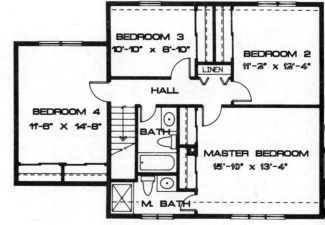

UPPER FLOOR

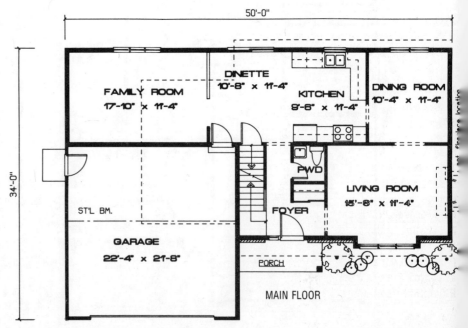

MAIN FLOOR

Plan GL-1926

Family Room is Bright, Warm

- This stately New England colonial shows off a columned front porch and eye-catching elliptical window.
- Inside, formal living and dining rooms combine for gracious entertaining.
- The roomy island kitchen and breakfast area overlook an attached rear deck and an adjoining bayed family room, accented with cathedral ceiling, skylights and fireplace.
- The second-floor master suite uses closet space to separate it from a private bath; dual vanities and a separate tub and shower are nice extras.
- Generous closet space is also allotted the three additional bedrooms, which share a second bath on this level.

Plan OH-108	
Bedrooms: 4	**Baths: 2 ½**
Space:	
Upper floor	968 sq. ft.
Main floor	1,000 sq. ft.
Total Living Area	**1,968 sq. ft.**
Basement	1,000 sq. ft.
Garage	400 sq. ft.
Exterior Wall Framing	2x4
Foundation options:	
Standard Basement	
(Foundation & framing conversion diagram available—see order form.)	
Blueprint Price Code	**B**

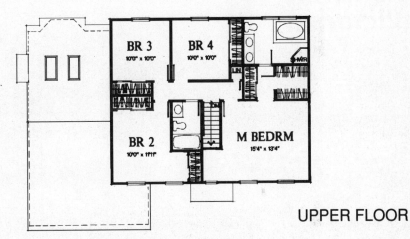

UPPER FLOOR

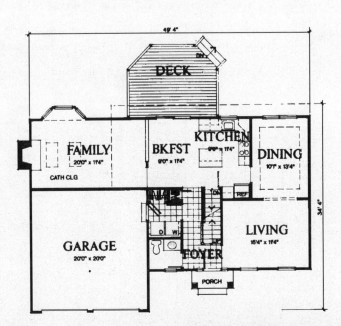

MAIN FLOOR

Plan OH-108

*TO ORDER THIS BLUEPRINT,
CALL TOLL-FREE 1-800-547-5570*
(prices and details on pp. 12-15.)

Romantic Victorian

- This plan proves the romance of Victorian styling can be achieved without sacrificing modern lifestyles.
- The exterior is classic, while the interior admirably meets the needs of today's families.
- While the home totals just over 2,000 sq. ft., it includes many features found in larger homes — such as a bright, airy formal dining room, a roomy foyer and a large family room.
- The living room is especially large for a home of this total size and features a massive fireplace.
- Upstairs, a majestic master suite includes tower windows and access to a private deck. Two other bedrooms share a double-vanity bath.

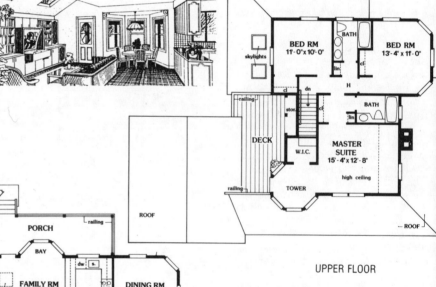

UPPER FLOOR

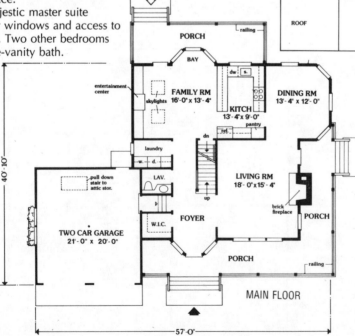

MAIN FLOOR

Plan HFL-1050-MD

Bedrooms: 3		Baths: 2½
Space:		
Upper floor		896 sq. ft
Main floor		1,110 sq. ft
Total Living Area		**2,006 sq. ft**
Basement		967 sq. ft
Garage		420 sq. ft
Exterior Wall Framing		2x6

Foundation options:
Standard Basement
(Foundation & framing conversion diagram available—see order form.)

Blueprint Price Code

TO ORDER THIS BLUEPRINT, CALL TOLL-FREE 1-800-547-5570 (prices and details on pp. 12-15.)

Plan HFL-1050-MD

Farmhouse with Modern Touch

- This classic center-hall design features an All-American Farmhouse exterior wrapped around a super-modern interior.
- A large family room features a built-in entertainment center and adjoins a convenient dinette for quick family meals.
- The spacious living and dining rooms adjoin to provide abundant space for large gatherings.

- An inviting porch leads into a roomy foyer which highlights a curved staircase.
- The second floor features a deluxe master suite and three secondary bedrooms.

VIEW INTO LIVING ROOM FROM FOYER.

UPPER FLOOR

BED RM 4
10' x 10'

DRESS RM.

BED RM 3
12'-6"x11'-4"

vanity

BATH

HALL

LIN.

dn

BED RM 2
12'-6" x 11'-4"

rail

open

cl

MASTER BED RM
16'-8"x 11'-4"

BATH

MAIN FLOOR

60'-0"

35'-6"

TERRACE

sliding glass doors

sliding glass doors

service entry

s.   dw

range

MUD RM

cl

DINING RM
12'-6"x11'-6"

KITCHEN
10'-8" x 10'

ref.

DINETTE
8'-8" x 8'-8"

LAUNDRY
d.   w.

TWO CAR GARAGE
21'-4" x 19'-8"

heat-circulating fireplace

LAV.

dn

railing

open

FAMILY RM
16' x 12'-2"(avg.)

entertainment center

LIVING RM
19'-8"x 12'-6"

FOYER

up

cl

high ceiling

PORCH

Plan HFL-1040-MB

Bedrooms: 4	Baths: 2½
Space:	
Upper floor	936 sq. ft.
Main floor	1,094 sq. ft.
Total Living Area	**2,030 sq. ft.**
Basement	1,022 sq. ft.
Garage	420 sq. ft.
Exterior Wall Framing	2x6

Foundation options:
Standard Basement
Slab
(Foundation & framing conversion diagram available—see order form.)

Blueprint Price Code	C

Plan HFL-1040-MB

TO ORDER THIS BLUEPRINT,
CALL TOLL-FREE 1-800-547-5570
(prices and details on pp. 12-15.)

A Cape Cod with Volume

- Spectacular value underscores this transitional Cape Cod design.
- An elegant and spacious atmosphere is created with a vaulted foyer and arched openings to the adjoining vaulted living room and dining room with coved ceiling.
- Casual family interaction is possible with the combination family room, bayed nook and roomy, open kitchen.
- The pantry and laundry room are conveniently located near the garage entrance.
- Upstairs you'll find a spacious master bedroom with private luxury bath and two additional bedrooms which share a second full bath.

Plan CDG-2033	
Bedrooms: 3	**Baths: 2½**
Space:	
Upper floor	863 sq. ft.
Main floor	1,193 sq. ft.
Total Living Area	**2,056 sq. ft.**
Garage	421 sq. ft.
Exterior Wall Framing	2x4
Foundation options:	
Crawlspace	
(Foundation & framing conversion diagram available—see order form.)	
Blueprint Price Code	**C**

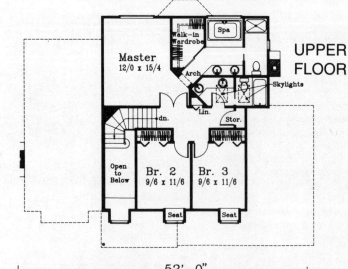

UPPER FLOOR

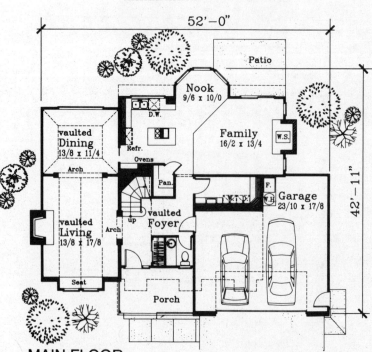

MAIN FLOOR

Plan CDG-2033

Victorian Exterior, Modern Interior

- This classic exterior is built around an interior that offers all the amenities wanted by today's families.
- A Great Room provides ample space for large gatherings and multiple family activities.
- A formal dining room is available for special occasions, and a casual breakfast nook serves everyday dining needs.
- A deluxe main-floor master suite features a cathedral ceiling.
- Upstairs, two secondary bedrooms share a full bath and a balcony overlooking the Great Room below.

Plan DW-2112

Bedrooms: 3	Baths: 2½
Space:	
Upper floor	514 sq. ft.
Main floor	1,598 sq. ft.
Total Living Area	**2,112 sq. ft.**
Basement	1,598 sq. ft.
Exterior Wall Framing	2x4

Foundation options:
Standard Basement
Crawlspace
Slab
(Foundation & framing conversion diagram available—see order form.)

Blueprint Price Code	C

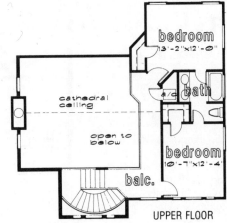

UPPER FLOOR

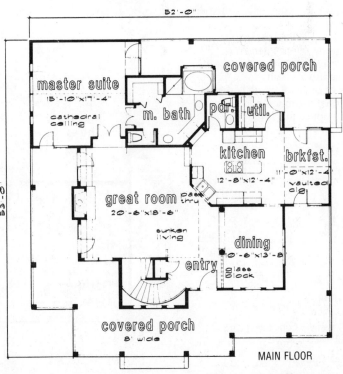

MAIN FLOOR

Plan DW-2112

Volume with Expansion Option

- Vertical siding, multiple roof peaks and a contrasting stone exterior give this two-story a soaring and stately appearance.
- Volume continues to the interior as well with a loft overlooking the foyer and vaulted family room below.
- A fireplace, corner windows and sliders to a rear deck are found in the family room, which merges to the breakfast area.
- The formal dining room and living room with front window seat join to the right of the foyer.
- The upper level offers a generous vaulted master bedroom with walk-in closet and a private bath.
- A loft area or optional fourth bedroom, two additional bedrooms and a second full bath complete this level.

Plan B-90025

Bedrooms: 3-4	Baths: 2 ½
Space:	
Upper floor	1,055 sq. ft.
Main floor	1,068 sq. ft.
Total Living Area	**2,123 sq. ft.**
Basement	1,068 sq. ft.
Garage	377 sq. ft.
Exterior Wall Framing	2x6

Foundation options:

Standard Basement

(Foundation & framing conversion diagram available—see order form.)

Blueprint Price Code	**C**

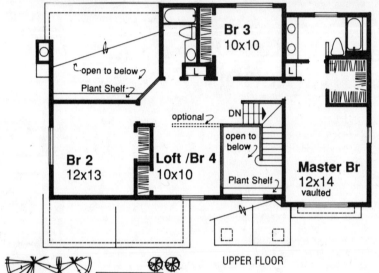

UPPER FLOOR

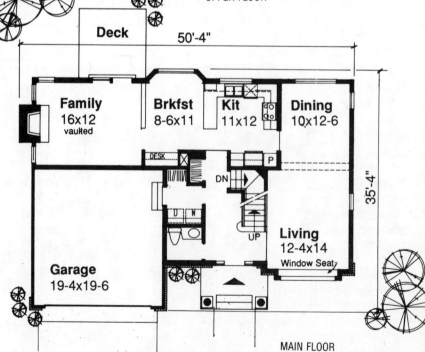

MAIN FLOOR

Plan B-90025

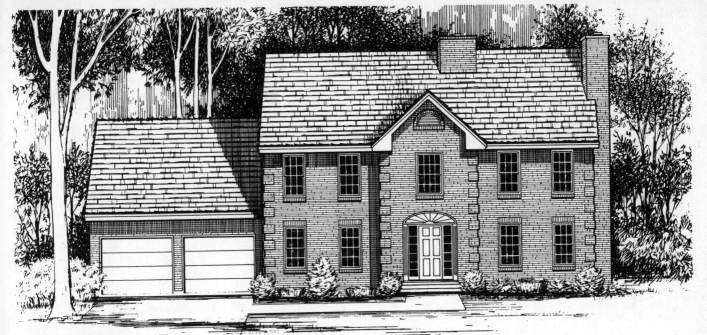

Dignified Family Home

- This dignified and stately home features an open floor plan and a basic design that can take advantage of a shallow lot.
- An enormous activity area is positioned to the left of a roomy foyer, and adjoins a casual dining room across a half-wall.
- The L-shaped kitchen boasts a counter island, and conveniently serves both the nook and the formal dining room.
- The living room features a fireplace.
- On the upper floor, a deluxe master bedroom suite includes a large walk-in closet and a private bath with shower and tub.
- Three secondary bedrooms share another full bath, and a ''future room'' over the garage offers potential for multi-use space.

Plan N-1339

Bedrooms: 4	Baths: 2½
Living Area:	
Upper floor	1,389 sq. ft.
Main floor	1,389 sq. ft.
Bonus area	241 sq. ft.
Total Living Area:	**3,019 sq. ft.**
Standard basement	1,389 sq. ft.
Garage	528 sq. ft.
Exterior Wall Framing:	2x4

Foundation Options:
Standard basement
Slab
(Typical foundation & framing conversion diagram available—see order form.)

BLUEPRINT PRICE CODE: E

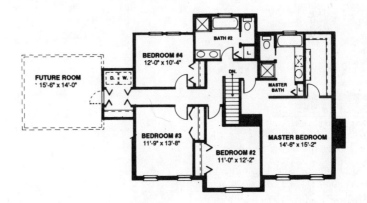

UPPER FLOOR

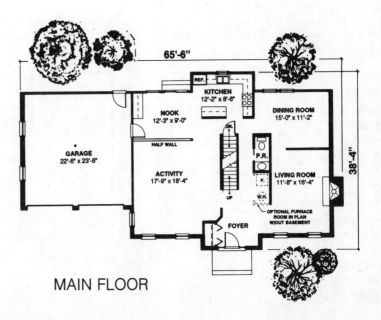

MAIN FLOOR

Plan N-1339

Sunroom Adds Glamour

- A beautiful sunken sunroom adds an extra touch of glamour to this gracious home.
- A cathedral ceiling ushers you into the large entry, and sloped ceilings grace the activity area, kitchen and sunroom.
- The open activity area includes a wet bar, a fireplace and easy access to the kitchen, sunroom and dining area.
- The master bedroom includes two large walk-in closets and a luxurious bath featuring a raised Roman tub and a compartmented shower.

Plan N-1274

Bedrooms: 3		**Baths:** 2½
Living Area:		
Main floor		2,180 sq. ft.
Total Living Area:		**2,180 sq. ft.**
Standard basement		1,940 sq. ft.
Garage		523 sq. ft.
Exterior Wall Framing:		2x4

Foundation Options:

Standard basement

Slab

(Typical foundation & framing conversion diagram available—see order form.)

BLUEPRINT PRICE CODE:	C

TO ORDER THIS BLUEPRINT,
CALL TOLL-FREE 1-800-547-5570

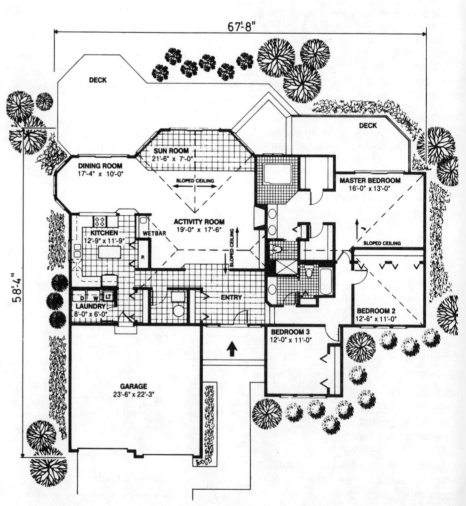

Plan N-1274

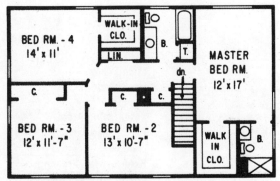

UPPER FLOOR

BED RM. - 4
14' x 11'

WALK-IN CLO.

LIN.

B.

T.

MASTER BED RM.
12' x 17'

dn.

C.

C.

C.

BED RM. - 3
12' x 11'-7"

BED RM. - 2
13' x 10'-7"

WALK IN CLO.

B.

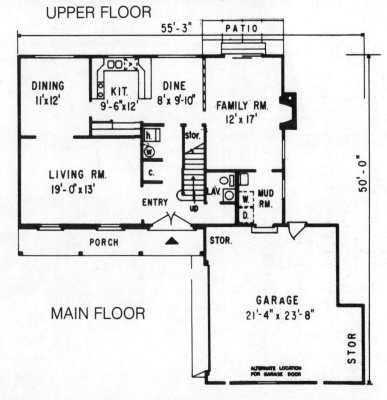

MAIN FLOOR

55'-3"

PATIO

DINING
11' x 12'

KIT.
9'-6" x 12'

DINE
8' x 9'-10'

FAMILY RM.
12' x 17'

h.

stor.

W

LIVING RM.
19'-0" x 13'

C.

ENTRY

UP

LAV.

W. D.

MUD RM.

50'-0"

PORCH

STOR.

GARAGE
21'-4" x 23'-8"

STOR

ALTERNATE LOCATION FOR GARAGE DOOR

Simple Lines, Easy Comfort

- With its simple lines, this plan offers the potential of economical space for today's busy families.
- An inviting front porch offers a welcoming touch, and leads visitors into a central entry area.
- The main floor features abundant space for guests, with its large living room and formal dining room.
- For more casual family living, note the large family room, the informal dining area and the U-shaped kitchen.
- The second-floor master bedroom includes a large walk-in closet and a private bath.
- Three other bedrooms share another full bath, and bedroom #4 includes a large walk-in closet.

Plan N-1077

Bedrooms: 4	**Baths:** 2½

Living Area:

Upper floor	1,092 sq. ft.
Main floor	1,104 sq. ft.
Total Living Area:	**2,196 sq. ft.**
Standard basement	1,100 sq. ft.
Garage	505 sq. ft.

Exterior Wall Framing:	2x4

Foundation Options:
Standard basement
Slab
(Typical foundation & framing conversion diagram available—see order form.)

BLUEPRINT PRICE CODE:	C

TO ORDER THIS BLUEPRINT,
CALL TOLL-FREE 1-800-547-5570
(prices and details on pp. 12-15.) **103**

Plan N-1077

Family Activity Loft

- This beautiful contemporary home was designed with spaciousness in mind.
- Located at the center of the home is an imposing sunken Great Room with a sloped ceiling, a magnificent fireplace and a spectacular view of the outdoors.
- An open railing divides the Great Room from the dining room and kitchen.

- Located in the right wing of the home is the master bedroom suite with its large walk-in closet and private bath. An adjoining second bath services the two front bedrooms.
- A large loft area that overlooks the Great Room would be ideal for a family recreation room.

Plan N-1102	
Bedrooms: 3-4	**Baths: 2½**
Living Area:	
Upper floor	400 sq. ft.
Main floor	1,898 sq. ft.
Total Living Area:	**2,298 sq. ft.**
Partial basement	836 sq. ft.
Garage	455 sq. ft.
Exterior Wall Framing:	2x4
Foundation Options:	
Partial basement	
Crawlspace	
(Typical foundation & framing conversion diagram available—see order form.)	
BLUEPRINT PRICE CODE:	C

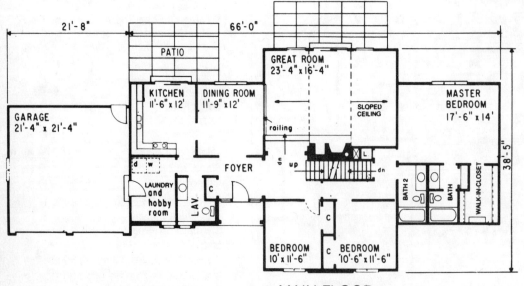

MAIN FLOOR

UPPER FLOOR

Plan N-1102

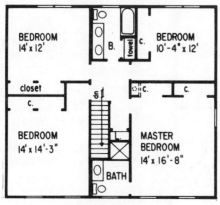

UPPER FLOOR

Stately Comfort

- The exterior of this Colonial design features traditional double-hung, multi-paned windows and horizontal siding.
- Inside, the living room is isolated from the rest of the main floor to allow for more formal entertaining, and a formal dining room is also included.
- The large family room/breakfast nook/kitchen area provides abundant space for family living.
- The master suite includes a private bath and two closets.
- Three other bedrooms share a full bath with double sinks.

Plan N-1209

Bedrooms: 4	Baths: 2½
Living Area:	
Upper floor	1,152 sq. ft.
Main floor	1,152 sq. ft.
Total Living Area:	**2,304 sq. ft.**
Standard basement	1,152 sq. ft.
Garage	505 sq. ft.
Exterior Wall Framing:	2x4

Foundation Options:
Standard basement
Slab
(Typical foundation & framing conversion diagram available—see order form.)

BLUEPRINT PRICE CODE: C

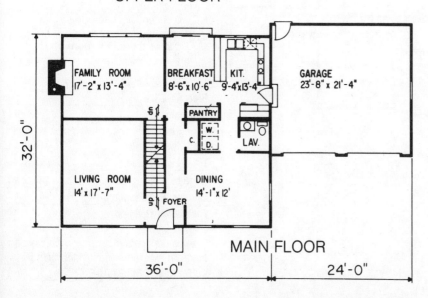

MAIN FLOOR

Plan N-1209

Elegant and Stylish

- An elegant brick exterior sets the tone for this stylish design.
- A raised foyer leads visitors to a formal dining room with a coffered ceiling or to a spacious living room.
- A double-sided fireplace is shared between the living room and the game room, which both feature cathedral ceilings.
- The large kitchen includes a work island, a pantry and abundant counter space.
- A magnificent master suite includes a luxurious master bath, two large closets and a multi-sided, multi-windowed sleeping area.
- Two secondary bedrooms share another full bath with two sinks.
- Also note the utility room off the breakfast nook.

Plan KY-2328

Bedrooms: 3	Baths:
Living Area:	
Main floor	2,328 sq. ft
Total Living Area:	**2,328 sq. f**
Garage	460 sq. f
Exterior Wall Framing:	2x

Foundation Options:

Slab
(Typical foundation & framing conversion diagram available—see order form.)

BLUEPRINT PRICE CODE:

60'-7"

74'-7"

game rm.
cath. clg.
16' x 19'

living rm.
cath. clg.
16' x 19'

master
suite
coff. clg.
16' x 16'

wetbar

double
sided
fireplace

pantry

dining
coff. clg.
13' x 11'

entry
raised 6"
7' x 11'

bath

hall

linen

master
bath
cath. clg.

shower

ref.

oven

kitchen
cath. clg.
13' x 18'

cooktop

linen

coats

w/s

brm.
freezer

utility
5' x 9'

washer   dryer

breakfast
cath. clg.
12' x 11'

dw.

porch

bedrm. 3
cath. clg.
11' x 11'

bedrm. 2
10' x 13'

garage
20' x 23'

MAIN FLOOR

TO ORDER THIS BLUEPRINT,
CALL TOLL-FREE 1-800-547-5570

Plan KY-2328

Brilliant Columns

- Brilliant entry columns and a stucco exterior give this one-story a distinguished look.
- Inside, the foyer offers views to a personal study or home office, a formal living room and a raised dining area with wood columns.
- The equally spectacular family room has a 14' ceiling, a fireplace, built-in book storage, and arched windows at the rear that overlook the attached deck.
- A counter bar separates the open kitchen from the family room; the kitchen also offers a pantry and an adjoining breakfast area.
- The large master suite is secluded to the rear of the home; it has a bayed sitting area and a roomy, private bath.

Plan DW-2342

Bedrooms: 3-4	Baths: 2
Space:	
Main floor	2,342 sq. ft.
Total Living Area	**2,342 sq. ft.**
Basement	2,342 sq. ft.
Garage	460 sq. ft.
Exterior Wall Framing	2x4

Foundation options:
Standard Basement
Crawlspace
Slab
(Foundation & framing conversion diagram available—see order form.)

Blueprint Price Code	C

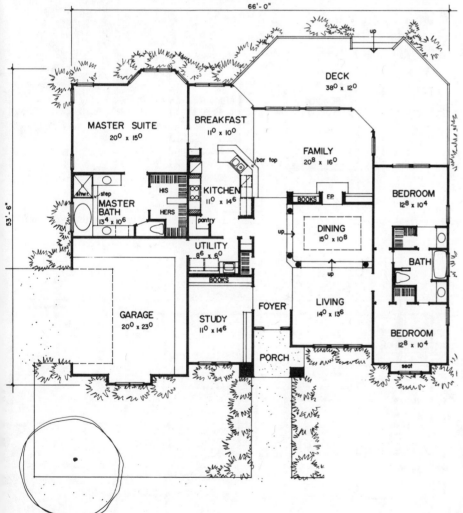

Plan DW-2342

Main-Floor Master Suite

- A traditional design with a contemporary interior, this home offers plenty of space and features for today's family.
- A large living room is brightened by a beautiful bay window.
- A spacious family room features an impressive fireplace.
- The kitchen/nook combination is roomy and efficient, with a pantry and an adjoining laundry and half-bath.
- The downstairs master suite is luxurious, with a private, skylighted bath and a large walk-in closet.
- Upstairs, three bedrooms share another full bath.

Plan N-1207

Bedrooms: 4	Baths: 2½
Living Area:	
Upper floor	727 sq. ft.
Main floor	1,633 sq. ft.
Total Living Area:	**2,360 sq. ft.**
Standard basement	1,633 sq. ft.
Garage	455 sq. ft.
Exterior Wall Framing:	2x4

Foundation Options:
Standard basement
Crawlspace
Slab
(Typical foundation & framing conversion diagram available—see order form.)

BLUEPRINT PRICE CODE: C

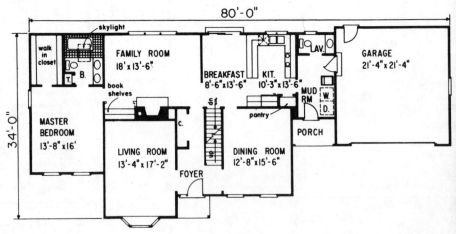

UPPER FLOOR

MAIN FLOOR

Plan N-1207

Grace, Refinement, Elegance

- An eye-catching exterior speaks of elegance and refinement, and an imaginative interior offers excitement and comfort.
  A splendid kitchen is flanked on the one hand by a bayed breakfast nook and on the other by a bright, spacious family center.
- The expansive living room boasts a fireplace and large windows to the rear porch, and the formal dining room offers space for elegant sit-down dinners.
  A luxurious master suite includes a huge deluxe bath and two large closets. The two secondary bedrooms and a study share another double bath. The study can serve as an office or fourth bedroom if needed.

Plan KY-2686

Bedrooms: 3-4	**Baths:** 2½

Living Area:
Main floor	2,686 sq. ft.
Total Living Area:	**2,686 sq. ft.**
Exterior Wall Framing:	2x4

Foundation Options:
Slab
(Typical foundation & framing conversion diagram available—see order form.)

BLUEPRINT PRICE CODE:	**D**

Plan KY-2686

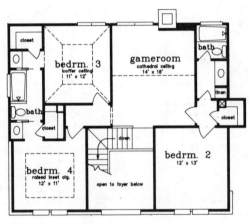

UPPER FLOOR

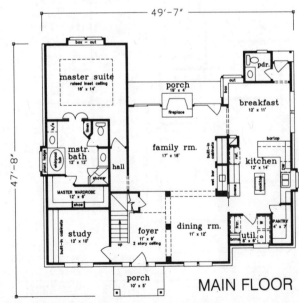

MAIN FLOOR

Impressive and Dignified

- This stately plan is equally impressive inside and out.
- A spacious foyer is flanked by a formal dining room on the right and a quiet study on the left.
- The large family room features a fireplace, a wet bar, built-in cabinets and easy access to a rear porch.
- A gorgeous kitchen features an island cooktop, a walk-in pantry and an eating bar connecting it to the adjoining breakfast nook.
- An opulent downstairs master suite includes a palatial bath plus an enormous walk-in closet.
- Upstairs, three bedrooms share two full baths and a large game room.

Plan KY-2743

Bedrooms: 4		**Baths:** 3½
Living Area:		
Upper floor		983 sq. f
Main floor		1,760 sq. f
Total Living Area:		**2,743 sq. f**
Exterior Wall Framing:		2x

Foundation Options:

Slab

(Typical foundation & framing conversion diagram available—see order form.)

BLUEPRINT PRICE CODE:

Plan KY-2743

Spacious Early American

- This is a classic example of a traditional style that has remained popular for generations.
- A basic rectangular shape, two stories and simple rooflines mean economy and ease of construction relative to the space enclosed.
- The main floor includes space for formal entertaining in the living and dining rooms.
- Casual family living is provided for in the large family room (with fireplace) and spacious kitchen/nook combination.
- Upstairs, a deluxe master suite includes a fine bath and large walk-in closet.
- Three other bedrooms share a second bath.
- A cozy side porch provides easy access to the mud room and laundry area.

Plan N-1208

Bedrooms: 4	Baths: 2½
Living Area:	
Upper floor	1,232 sq. ft.
Main floor	1,531 sq. ft.
Total Living Area:	**2,763 sq. ft.**
Standard basement	1,232 sq. ft.
Garage	668 sq. ft.
Exterior Wall Framing:	2x4

Foundation Options:
Standard basement
Crawlspace
Slab
(Typical foundation & framing conversion diagram available—see order form.)

BLUEPRINT PRICE CODE: D

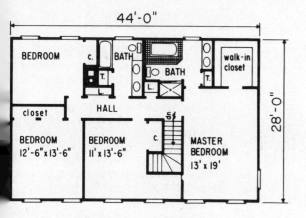

UPPER FLOOR

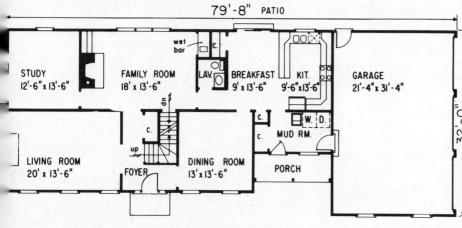

MAIN FLOOR

Plan N-1208

UPPER FLOOR

BEDROOM #2
12'-0" x 15'-6"

SITTING ROOM
11'-0" x 9'-0"

STAIR BALCONY

BEDROOM #3
12'-0" x 12'-0"

BALCONY

BATH 2

DN.

WALL CUTOUTS

HANDRAIL

MASTER BEDROOM
15'-1" x 12'-9"

OPEN BELOW TO DINING ROOM

PLANTER

OPEN BELOW TO FOYER

LIVING ROOM BELOW

COFFERED CEILING OPEN BELOW

MASTER BATH

MAIN FLOOR

70'-0"

64'-3"

FAMILY ROOM
17'-9" x 15'-7"

STAIR LANDING

DEN
14'-5" x 12'-0"

BREAKFAST
11'-0" x 12'-0"

POWDER ROOM

DN.

UP

COUNTER

KITCHEN
13'-10" x 12'-0"

REF.

DINING ROOM
14'-0" x 13'-0"

OPEN ABOVE

ENTRY
OPEN ABOVE

OPEN ABOVE

LIVING ROOM
17'-0" x 16'-0"

COVERED ABOVE

W. D. SHELVES

LAUNDRY

GARAGE
22'-0" x 24'-0"

Spacious Estate Home

- Abundant open ceilings are featured in this spacious estate home.
- The open-ceilinged entry foyer faces a spectacular wraparound stairway with full bay windows on the stair landing.
- In the left wing, you'll find a spacious family room, an open-ceilinged dining room, an L-shaped kitchen and a separate sunny breakfast room.
- Upstairs, a majestic master suite offers a deluxe private bath and a sitting area.
- Two secondary bedrooms share another full bath and balconies overlooking the foyer and the stairway.

Plan N-1315

Bedrooms: 3	Baths: 2½
Living Area:	
Upper floor	1,126 sq. ft.
Main floor	1,767 sq. ft.
Total Living Area:	**2,893 sq. ft.**
Standard basement	1,700 sq. ft.
Garage	528 sq. ft.
Exterior Wall Framing:	2x4

Foundation Options:
Standard basement
Slab
(Typical foundation & framing conversion diagram available—see order form.)

BLUEPRINT PRICE CODE: D

Plan N-1315

Time-Tested Traditional

- Tudor styling makes this design equally suited to a country acreage or city lot.
- Visitors are greeted by a generously sized foyer with a graceful staircase leading up to the second floor.
- Side-by-side fireplaces provide comfort to both the living room and the family room.
- The kitchen includes a pantry and adjoins a large breakfast nook. Also note the utility area and the bonus room off the kitchen.
- A majestic master suite includes a palatial bath and a huge walk-in closet. Three other bedrooms share a second full bath with two sinks.

Plan N-1239

Bedrooms: 4	**Baths:** 2½

Living Area:

Upper floor	1,386 sq. ft.
Main floor	1,731 sq. ft.
Total Living Area:	**3,117 sq. ft.**
Standard basement	1,700 sq. ft.
Garage	666 sq. ft.
Exterior Wall Framing:	2x4

Foundation Options:

Standard basement

(Typical foundation & framing conversion diagram available—see order form.)

BLUEPRINT PRICE CODE: E

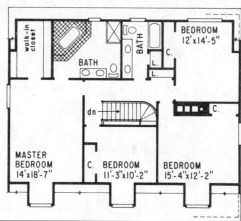

UPPER FLOOR

MAIN FLOOR

Plan N-1239

A Welcome Addition to Any Neighborhood

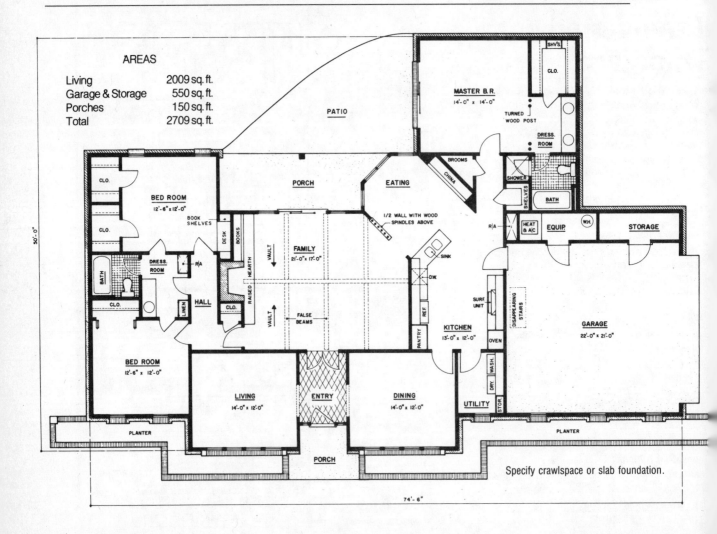

AREAS

Living	2009 sq. ft.
Garage & Storage	550 sq. ft.
Porches	150 sq. ft.
Total	2709 sq. ft.

SHV'S.

CLO.

MASTER B.R.
14'-0" x 14'-0"

TURNED
WOOD POST

DRESS.
ROOM

PATIO

BROOMS

CHINA

SHOWER

BATH

SHELVES

CLO.

BED ROOM
12'-6" x 12'-0"

BOOK
SHELVES

PORCH

EATING

1/2 WALL WITH WOOD
SPINDLES ABOVE

R|A

HEAT
& A/C

EQUIP

W.H.

STORAGE

DESK

BOOKS

VAULT

FAMILY
21'-0" x 17'-0"

SINK

DW.

BATH

DRESS.
ROOM

R|A

HALL

LINEN

CLO.

RAISED HEARTH

VAULT

FALSE
BEAMS

REF.

PANTRY

KITCHEN
13'-0" x 12'-0"

SURF.
UNIT

DISAPPEARING
STAIRS

GARAGE
22'-0" x 21'-0"

50'-0"

CLO.

BED ROOM
12'-6" x 12'-0"

LIVING
14'-0" x 12'-0"

ENTRY

DINING
14'-0" x 12'-0"

OVEN

UTILITY

WASH.

DRY.

STOR.

PLANTER

PORCH

PLANTER

Specify crawlspace or slab foundation.

74'-6"

Blueprint Price Code C

Plan E-2000

Design for Today

- Large kitchen includes island, desk and pantry.
- Splendid master suite includes bay window, large closet and deluxe, skylighted bath.
- Vaulted family room includes fireplace.
- Utility room is convenient to bedrooms and kitchen.

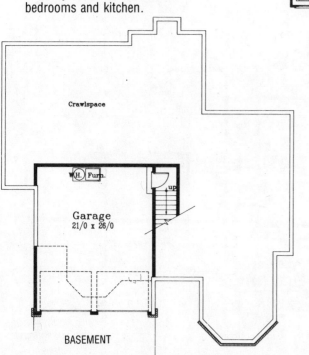

Crawlspace

Garage
21/0 x 26/0

W.H. Furn.

up

BASEMENT

53'-0"

55'-0"

BR. 2
12/0 x 11/8

Den/BR.3
10/4 x 11/8

Built-in

vaulted Family
13/6 x 15/6

Covered Patio

Skylight

Linen

Spa

Skylight

Walk-in

vaulted Master
15/0 x 17/0

Nook
8/6 x 13/0

D.W.

Refr

Desk Ovens

Pantry

dn
dn vaulted up
Entry
dn

Dining
11/0 x 12/0

vaulted/sunken Living
13/0 x 15/0

MAIN FLOOR

Plan CDG-4001

Bedrooms: 2-3	Baths: 2
Total living area:	2,022 sq. ft.
Garage:	546 sq. ft.
Exterior Wall Framing:	2x6

Foundation options:
  Crawlspace only.
  (Foundation & framing conversion diagram available — see order form.)

Blueprint Price Code: C

Plan CDG-4001

Colonial Design Alive with Solar Energy

This gracious colonial home combines traditional design with contemporary passive solar efficiency. Southern exposure at the rear provides maximum sunshine in the kitchen, dinette, family room, and cheerful sun room. Heat energy, accumulated in the insulated thermal flooring, is later released for night-time comfort. An air-lock vestibule, which minimizes heat loss, adds the elegance we associate with a center-hall colonial.

Upstairs, there are four comfortable bedrooms and two luxury baths — one accented by a whirlpool tub. Also, there is an electrically operated skylight that aids in natural cooling.

Total living area of the first floor, excluding sun room, comes to 1,030 sq. ft.; second floor adds 1,003 sq. ft. Garage, mud room, etc. are 500 sq. ft., and optional basement is 633 sq. ft.

Second floor plan

- glazed roof
- Bedrm 4 10-0 × 12-0
- Bath
- Master Bedrm 13-0 × 16-0
- whirlpool tub
- cl / cl / lin
- cl / cl / cl
- skylight above
- Gallery
- railg
- d
- walk-in-cl
- cl cl
- cl cl
- shelves
- open to below
- Bedrm 3 12-0 × 15-0
- Bath
- Bedrm 2 12-0 × 11-0
- upper part of portico

SECOND FLOOR
1003 SQUARE FEET

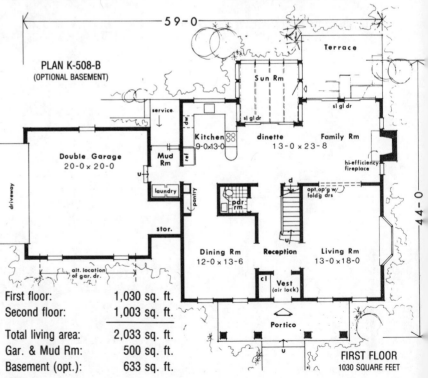

PLAN K-508-B
(OPTIONAL BASEMENT)

— 59-0 —

44-0

- Terrace
- Sun Rm
- service
- dw
- sl gl dr
- sl gl dr
- Double Garage 20-0 × 20-0
- Mud Rm
- ref
- Kitchen 9-0×13-0
- dinette 13-0 × 23-8
- Family Rm
- hi-efficiency fireplace
- laundry
- pantry
- pdr rm
- opt.op'g w/ fold'g drs
- d
- stor.
- Dining Rm 12-0×13-6
- Reception
- Living Rm 13-0 ×18-0
- alt. location of gar. dr.
- driveway
- cl
- Vest (air lock)
- Portico

FIRST FLOOR
1030 SQUARE FEET

First floor:	1,030 sq. ft.
Second floor:	1,003 sq. ft.
Total living area:	2,033 sq. ft.
Gar. & Mud Rm:	500 sq. ft.
Basement (opt.):	633 sq. ft.

Blueprint Price Code C

Plan K-508-B

Attractive, Open Floor Plan

- Two-story ceilings in the foyer and living room add an attractive spatial dimension to this versatile two-story, finished in stucco.
- The spacious living areas include a sunken, formal living room with a large fireplace, front-facing bay

window and entrance from both the foyer and dining room.
- The family room, 3 steps below the main level, offers a second fireplace and a view of the nook through an open railing.
- The kitchen includes an island

work area, corner window, pantry and sliding doors to the attached deck.
- The home accommodates a master bedroom and two secondary bedrooms on the second floor and a single bedroom on the main level.

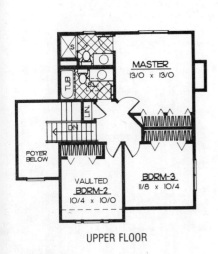

UPPER FLOOR

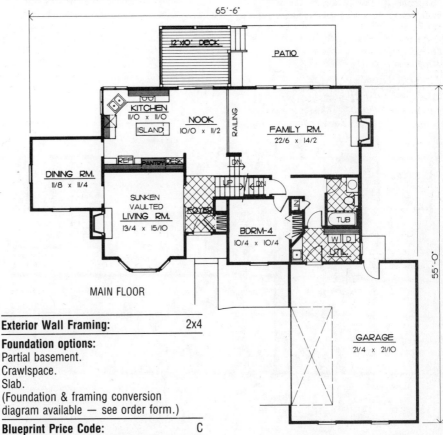

MAIN FLOOR

Plan U-89-403

Bedrooms: 4	Baths: 3

Space:

Upper floor:	656 sq. ft.
Main floor:	1,385 sq. ft.
Total living area:	**2,041 sq. ft.**
Basement:	704 sq. ft.
Garage:	466 sq. ft.

Exterior Wall Framing:	2x4

Foundation options:
Partial basement.
Crawlspace.
Slab.
(Foundation & framing conversion diagram available — see order form.)

Blueprint Price Code:	C

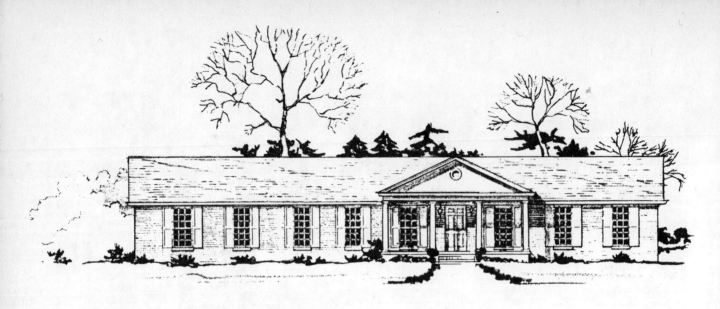

One-Story, Four-Bedroom Colonial

Here's gracious living at its best — North or South. Four bedrooms, two baths, a powder room, separate living and dining rooms, a galley kitchen, bay window breakfast area and large utility room make up the 2,053 sq. ft. of living area in this compact colonial.

Total living area: 2,053 sq. ft.
(Not counting basement or garage)

Specify basement, crawlspace or slab foundation.

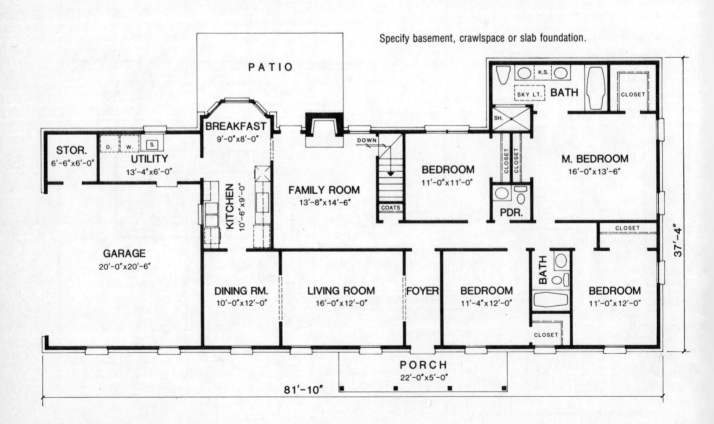

Blueprint Price Code C
Plan C-8635

A Modern Charmer

- This attractive plan combines the charm of an Early American exterior with a modern interior floor plan.
- The master suite, isolated for privacy, boasts a magnificent bath with garden tub, separate shower, double vanities and two walk-in closets.
- The large living room adjoins the kitchen via a convenient snack bar, and also features a corner fireplace.
- A roomy foyer offers easy access to the formal dining room, the living room, or a study which is ideally situated for a home office.
- A sunny eating nook protrudes onto the rear porch.
- The two secondary bedrooms share a second full bath.

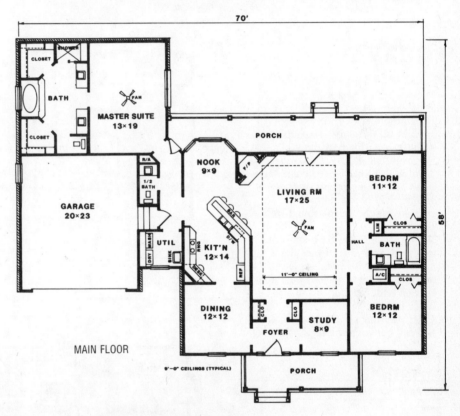

MAIN FLOOR

Plan VL-2069	
Bedrooms: 3	**Baths:** 2 ½
Space:	
Main floor	2,069 sq. ft.
Total Living Area	**2,069 sq. ft.**
Garage	460 sq. ft.
Exterior Wall Framing	2x4

Foundation options:
Crawlspace
Slab
(Foundation & framing conversion diagram available—see order form.)

Blueprint Price Code	C

Plan VL-2069

Today's Tradition

- The traditional two-story design is brought up to today's standards with this exciting new design.
- The front half of the main floor is devoted to formal entertaining. The living and dining rooms offer symmetrical bay windows overlooking the wrap-around front porch.
- The informal living zone faces the rear deck and yard. It includes a family room with fireplace and beamed ceiling as well as a modern kitchen with cooktop island and snack bar.
- There are four large bedrooms and two full baths on the upper sleeping level.

Plan AGH-2143

Bedrooms: 4	Baths: 2½
Space:	
Upper floor:	1,047 sq. ft.
Main floor:	1,096 sq. ft.
Total living area:	**2,143 sq. ft.**
Daylight basement:	1,096 sq. ft.
Garage:	852 sq. ft.
Exterior Wall Framing:	2x4

Foundation options:
Daylight basement.
(Foundation & framing conversion diagram available — see order form.)

Blueprint Price Code:	C

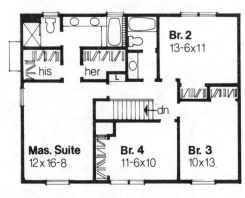

UPPER FLOOR

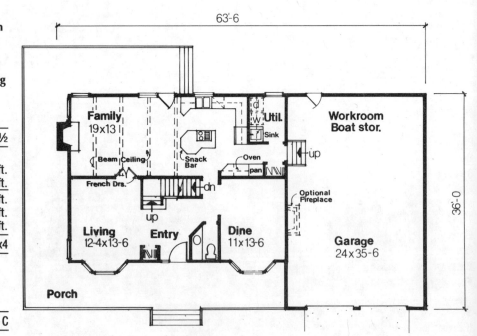

MAIN FLOOR

Plan AGH-2143

Colonial with a Contemporary Touch

- Open, flowing rooms highlighted by a two-story round-top window combine to give this colonial design a contemporary, today touch.
- To the left of the elegant, two-story foyer lies the living room, which flows into the rear-facing family room with fireplace.
- The centrally located kitchen serves both the formal dining room and the dinette, with a view of the family room beyond.
- All four bedrooms are located upstairs. The master suite includes a walk-in closet and private bath with double vanities, separate shower and whirlpool tub under skylights.

Plan AHP-9020

Bedrooms: 4	Baths: 2 ½
Space:	
Upper floor	1,021 sq. ft.
Main floor	1,125 sq. ft.
Total Living Area	**2,146 sq. ft.**
Basement	1,032 sq. ft.
Garage	480 sq. ft.
Exterior Wall Framing	**2x6**

Foundation options:
Standard Basement
Slab
(Foundation & framing conversion diagram available—see order form.)

Blueprint Price Code	**C**

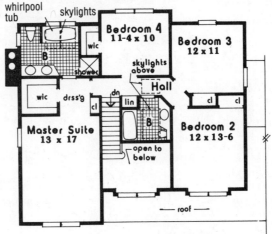

UPPER FLOOR

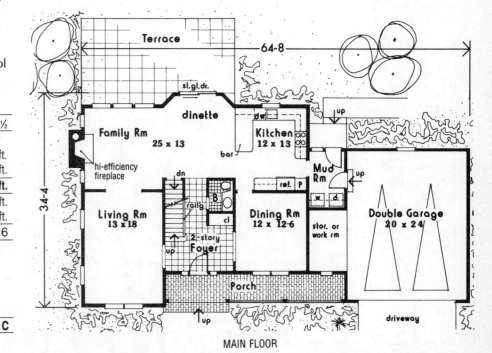

MAIN FLOOR

Plan AHP-9020

An Impressive Floor Plan

- This transitional two-story will complement any neighborhood.
- The covered porch opens to a vaulted foyer that offers a view to the formal living room and back to the roomy kitchen at the rear of the home. The living room adjoins the dining room for uninterrupted formal activities.
- The kitchen offers a pantry and a view of the attached deck; a counter bar divides it from the adjoining bayed dinette.

- A handy utility area with laundry facilities and a half-bath are near the garage access.
- A large family room has a nice fireplace and a rear window wall.
- The spectacular master bedroom on the upper level has a tray ceiling and a private bath with double vanity, dressing area and large walk-in closet.
- Three other generous-sized bedrooms complete this level.

Plan A-2270-DS	
Bedrooms: 4	**Baths:** 2 ½
Space:	
Upper floor	1,004 sq. ft.
Main floor	1,145 sq. ft.
Total Living Area	**2,149 sq. ft.**
Basement	1,145 sq. ft.
Garage	440 sq. ft.
Exterior Wall Framing	2x6

Foundation options:
Standard Basement
(Foundation & framing conversion diagram available—see order form.)

Blueprint Price Code	C

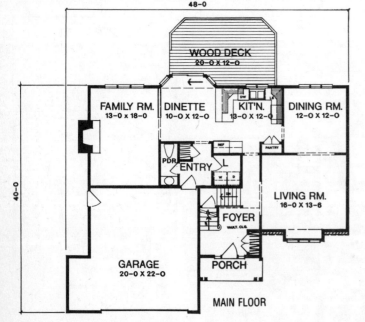

MAIN FLOOR

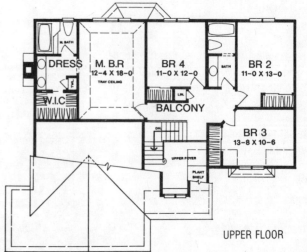

UPPER FLOOR

Plan A-2270-DS

A Colonial for Today

- Designed for a growing family, this handsome traditional home offers four bedrooms plus a den and three complete baths. The Colonial exterior is updated by a covered front entry porch topped off with a fanlight window above.
- The dramatic tiled foyer is two stories high and provides direct access to all the home's living areas. The spacious living room has an inviting brick fireplace and sliding pocket doors to the adjoining dining room.
- Overlooking the backyard, the huge combination kitchen/family room is the home's hidden charm. The family room has a window wall with sliding glass doors that open to an enticing terrace. The kitchen features a peninsula breakfast bar with seating for six. A built-in entertainment center and bookshelves line one wall of the family room.
- The adjacent mudroom is just off the garage entrance and includes a pantry closet. A full bath and a large den complete the first floor.
- The second floor is highlighted by a beautiful balcony that is open to the foyer below. The luxurious master suite is brightened by a skylight and boasts two closets, including an oversized walk-in closet. The master bath has a whirlpool tub and dual-sink vanity.
- The three remaining bedrooms are generously sized and have plenty of storage space. Another full bath serves these bedrooms.

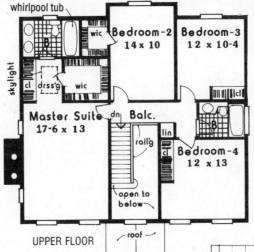

whirlpool tub

Bedroom-2 14 x 10
Bedroom-3 12 x 10-4

skylight

Master Suite 17-6 x 13   dn Balc.

wic wic cl drss'g

rail'g lin cl

Bedroom-4 12 x 13

open to below

UPPER FLOOR

roof

Plan AHP-7050

Bedrooms: 4-5	Baths: 3
Space:	
Upper floor	998 sq. ft.
Main floor	1,153 sq. ft.
Total Living Area	**2,151 sq. ft.**
Basement	1,067 sq. ft.
Garage & Storage	439 sq. ft.
Exterior Wall Framing	2x6

Foundation options:
Standard Basement
Slab
(Foundation & framing conversion diagram available—see order form.)

Blueprint Price Code	C

57-8

Terrace

up

sl.gl.dr.

up

Dining Rm 12 x 13   Kitchen   Family Rm 14 x 23

dw   t.v.

ref.   bar

shelf

32-10

Mud Rm

Living Rm 17-6 x 13

dn   p w d

Double Garage 20 x 20

fireplace

Den or Bedroom-5 12 x 13

stor.

2 story Foyer

driveway

Porch

up

MAIN FLOOR

Plan AHP-7050

Angular Accents

- A large round-top window accented with brick trim, a brick gable and a covered porch give this economical home stylish curb appeal.
- The angled entry opens to a dining room with arched openings and an adjoining, sunken living room, both with vaulted ceilings.
- A den or fourth bedroom is entered through double doors opposite.
- The spacious kitchen and nook offer an island work area, a desk and nearby laundry facilities.
- The kitchen shares a vaulted ceiling and a view of the brick fireplace with the merging family room; both rooms offer views to a covered patio.
- A coved ceiling and French doors add a romantic touch to the secluded master bedroom. Two secondary bedrooms share a second full bath.

Plan I-2174-A

Bedrooms: 3-4	Baths: 2
Space:	
Main floor	2,174 sq. ft.
Total Living Area	**2,174 sq. ft.**
Garage	398 sq. ft.
Exterior Wall Framing	2x6
Foundation options:	
Crawlspace	
(Foundation & framing conversion diagram available—see order form.)	
Blueprint Price Code	C

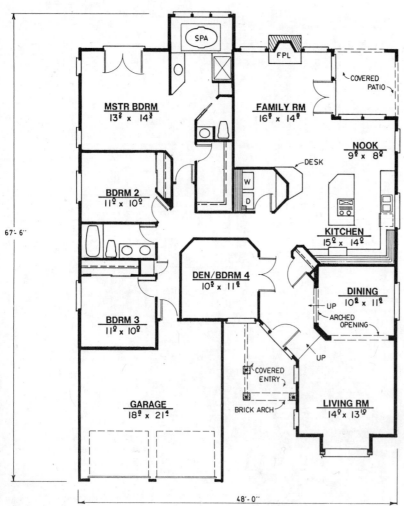

MSTR BDRM 13⁹ x 14³

FAMILY RM 16⁹ x 14⁹

COVERED PATIO

FPL

SPA

NOOK 9⁹ x 8⁹

DESK

BDRM 2 11⁹ x 10⁹

KITCHEN 15⁹ x 14⁹

DEN/BDRM 4 10⁹ x 11⁹

DINING 10⁹ x 11⁹

UP

ARCHED OPENING

BDRM 3 11⁹ x 10⁹

UP

COVERED ENTRY

GARAGE 18⁹ x 21⁴

BRICK ARCH

LIVING RM 14⁹ x 13¹⁰

67'- 6"

48'- 0"

Plan I-2174-A

Modernized Traditional

- Multi-paned window treatments give a traditional look to this Northwestern Contemporary design.
- The vaulted entry hall leads to a spacious dining/living room combination, which provides a large space for entertaining.
- To the left of the entry, you'll find a striking family room with a fireplace and an abundance of windows toward the rear.
- The efficient kitchen adjoins a handy breakfast nook which offers easy access to the patio. A pantry is provided under the stairway.
- The second floor features a luxurious master suite, with a deluxe bath, large walk-in closet and a sitting area.
- Two secondary bedrooms share another full bath, and a second-floor study offers a great place for a quiet retreat.

Plan R-2127

Bedrooms: 3	Baths: 2½
Space:	
Upper floor	1,165 sq. ft.
Main floor	1,020 sq. ft.
Total Living Area	**2,185 sq. ft.**
Garage	418 sq. ft.
Exterior Wall Framing	2x4
Foundation options:	
Crawlspace (Foundation & framing conversion diagram available—see order form.)	
Blueprint Price Code	**C**

UPPER FLOOR

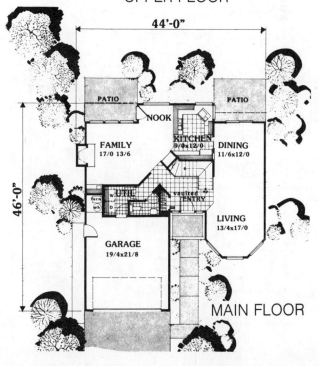

MAIN FLOOR

Plan R-2127

Great, Now & Later

- This exciting, efficient plan, with a main-floor master suite and adjacent den/guest/sitting room, will serve its growing family now, and its empty-nesters later.
- The traditional exterior, with stone and lap siding, covered entry porch and transom windows, will allow this home to blend into a new suburban development or an established city neighborhood.

- The heart of the main floor is the Great Room, with fireplace, tray ceiling, wet bar, and rear patio access.
- The island kitchen lies in-between the breakfast eating area and the formal dining room with vaulted ceiling and rear patio. The kitchen is also just steps away from the garage through the main-floor laundry for handy grocery hauling.
- The master suite offers a vaulted ceiling highlighting transom windows, a

spacious walk-in closet and private bath with dual vanities and separate tub and shower.
- The den/guest room has a vaulted ceiling, a quaint window seat and built-in shelves, as well as an adjacent, full bath.
- Older kids will enjoy the privacy of the two upstairs bedrooms, with a shared, full bath and plenty of closet and storage space.

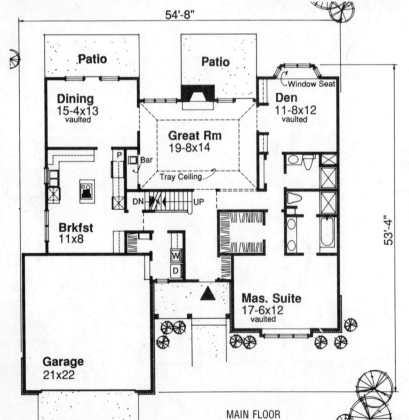

MAIN FLOOR

UPPER FLOOR

Plan B-89060	
Bedrooms: 3-4	**Baths:** 3
Space:	
Upper floor	502 sq. ft.
Main floor	1,698 sq. ft.
Total Living Area	**2,200 sq. ft.**
Basement	1,698 sq. ft.
Garage	462 sq. ft.
Exterior Wall Framing	2x4
Foundation options:	
Standard Basement	
(Foundation & framing conversion diagram available—see order form.)	
Blueprint Price Code	C

Plan B-89060

Dynamite Design

- A new twist for the move-up market's two-story executive family home is incorporated into this 2,205 sq. ft. plan with its dramatically vaulted Great Room and its secluded den. The dynamics are right where the family and friends will enjoy them every day.
- The kitchen features an island grill-range, a four-foot pantry and broom closet and a windowed breakfast area.
- The master suite, secluded upstairs, offers a luxurious bath treatment with glass divider partitions to the shower/toilet area and two walk-in closets.

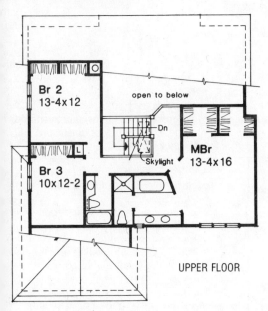

UPPER FLOOR

Plan B-123-8508

Bedrooms: 3-4	Baths: 3
Space:	
Upper floor:	963 sq. ft.
Main floor:	1,242 sq. ft.
Total living area:	**2,205 sq. ft.**
Basement:	1,242 sq. ft.
Garage:	505 sq. ft.
Exterior Wall Framing:	2x4
Foundation options:	
Standard basement. (Foundation & framing conversion diagram available — see order form.)	
Blueprint Price Code:	C

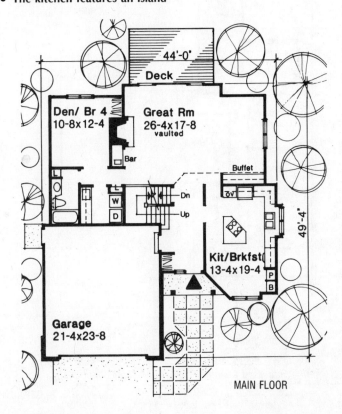

MAIN FLOOR

Plan B-123-8508

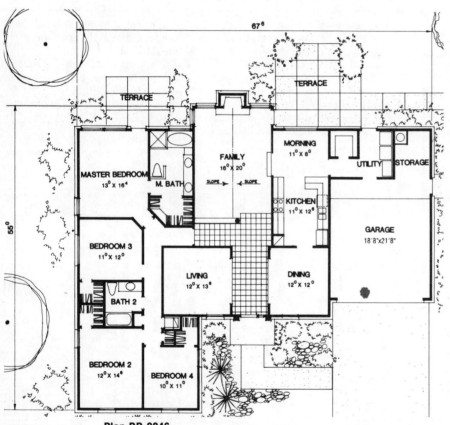

Elegant Excitement

- An elegant exterior envelopes an exciting interior, creating a home worth moving up to.
- The formal living and dining rooms flank the dramatic entry.
- The central, sunken family room features a cathedral ceiling and fireplace centered between double corner windows.
- The galley kitchen is well situated to serve the formal and informal eating rooms.
- This ranch plan includes four bedrooms. The master suite has a private terrace, walk-in closet, and open-feeling master bath.

Plan DD-2246

Bedrooms: 4	Baths: 2

Living Area:	
Main floor	2,212 sq. ft.

Total Living Area:	**2,212 sq. ft.**
Standard basement	2,212 sq. ft.
Garage:	404 sq. ft.

Exterior Wall Framing:	2x4

Foundation Options:
Standard basement
Crawlspace
Slab
(Typical foundation & framing conversion diagram available — see order form.)

BLUEPRINT PRICE CODE: C

Plan DD-2246

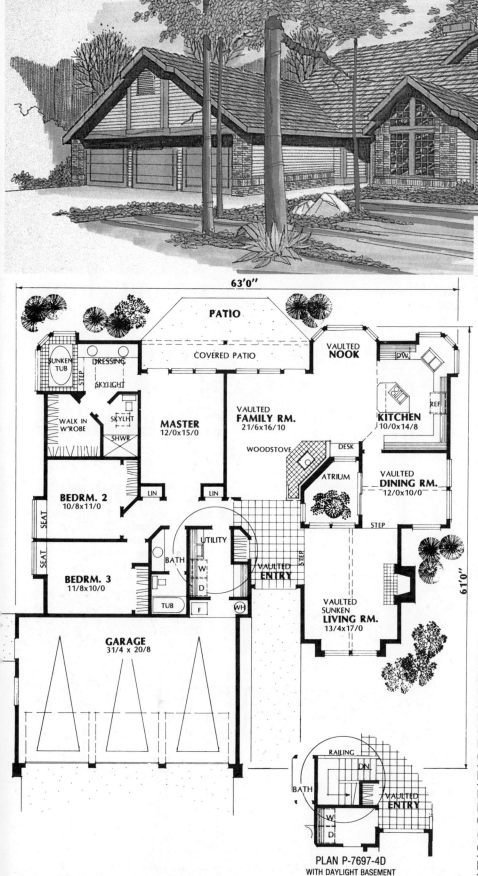

63'0"

PATIO

COVERED PATIO

VAULTED NOOK

DW

SUNKEN TUB | DRESSING | SKYLIGHT

WALK IN W'ROBE | SKYLHT | SHWR

MASTER
12/0x15/0

VAULTED FAMILY RM.
21/6x16/10

KITCHEN
10/0x14/8

REF

WOODSTOVE

DESK

ATRIUM

VAULTED DINING RM.
12/0x10/0

BEDRM. 2
10/8x11/0

LIN

LIN

STEP

SEAT

SEAT

UTILITY

BATH

W

D

F

VAULTED ENTRY

BEDRM. 3
11/8x10/0

TUB

WH

STEP

VAULTED SUNKEN LIVING RM.
13/4x17/0

GARAGE
31/4 x 20/8

61'0"

RAILING

DN

BATH

VAULTED ENTRY

W

D

PLAN P-7697-4D
WITH DAYLIGHT BASEMENT

Soaring Spaces under Vaulted Ceilings

- A dignified exterior and a gracious, spacious interior combine to make this an outstanding plan for today's families.
- The living, dining, family rooms and breakfast nook all feature soaring vaulted ceilings.
- An interior atrium provides an extra touch of elegance, with its sunny space for growing plants and sunbathing.
- The master suite is first class all the way, with a spacious sleeping area, opulent bath, large skylight and enormous walk-in closet.
- A gorgeous kitchen includes a large work/cooktop island, corner sink with large corner windows and plenty of counter space.

Plans P-7697-4A & -4D

Bedrooms: 3	Baths: 2

Space:

Main floor (crawlspace version):	2,003 sq. ft.
Main floor (basement version):	2,030 sq. ft.
Basement:	2,015 sq. ft.
Garage:	647 sq. ft.

Exterior Wall Framing:	2x4

Foundation options:
Daylight basement (Plan P-7697-4D).
Crawlspace (Plan P-7697-4A).
(Foundation & framing conversion diagram available — see order form.)

Blueprint Price Code:	C

Plans P-7697-4A & -4D

Photo by Mark Englund/HomeStyles

Plan E-2004

Bedrooms: 3		**Baths:** 2

Space:

Total living area:	2,023 sq. ft.
Garage:	484 sq. ft.
Storage & Porches:	423 sq. ft.

Exterior Wall Framing:	2x6

Foundation options:

Crawlspace.
Slab.
(Foundation & framing conversion diagram available — see order form.)

Blueprint Price Code:	C

Exciting Floor Plan In Traditional French Garden Home

- Creative, angular design permits an open floor plan.
- Living and dining rooms open to a huge covered porch.
- Kitchen, living and dining rooms feature impressive 12′ ceilings accented by extensive use of glass.
- Informal eating nook faces a delightful courtyard.
- Luxurious master bath offers a whirlpool tub, shower, and walk-in closet.
- Secondary bedrooms also offer walk-in closets.

**NOTE:
The above photographed home may have been modified by the homeowner. Please refer to floor plan and/or drawn elevation shown for actual blueprint details.

Floor Plan:

- GARAGE 22 ' x 22 '
- STOR
- PORCH
- STOR.
- DRY / WASH
- FREEZ
- UTIL
- SHELVES / PANT.
- COURTYARD
- DINING 12 ' x 12 ' (12′ CEILINGS)
- EATING 11 ' x 10 '
- SHELF
- OVENS
- BATH
- KITCHEN (12′ CEILINGS)
- SEAT
- PANTRY
- REF.
- LIVING 22 ' x 21 ' (12′ CEILINGS)
- BOOKS
- LINEN
- BATH
- BEDROOM 12 ' x 12 '
- HALL
- HEAT B.A.C.
- WET BAR
- MASTER SUITE 20 ' x 14 '
- PORCH
- BEDROOM 13 ' x 13 '
- BOOKS
- BOOKS

66 '

73 '

Plan E-2004

A Glorious Blend of New and Old

This three-bedroom, two and one-half-bath home is a glorious blend of contemporary and traditional lines. Inside, its 2,035 sq. ft. are wisely distributed among amply proportioned, practically appointed rooms. A vaulted entry gives way to a second reception area bordering on a broad, vaulted living room nearly 20' long.

With its walls of windows overlooking the back yard, this grand room's centerpiece is a massive woodstove, whose central location contributes extra energy efficiency to the home — upstairs as well as down. The dining room offers quiet separation from the living room, while still enjoying the warmth from its woodstove. Its sliding door accesses a large wraparound covered patio to create a cool, shady refuge.

For sun-seeking, another wraparound patio at the front is fenced but uncovered, and elegantly accessed by double doors from a well-lighted, vaulted nook.

Placed conveniently between the two dining areas is a kitchen with all the trimmings: pantry, large sink window, and an expansive breakfast bar.

A stylish upstairs landing overlooks the living room on one side and the entry on the other, and leads to a master suite that rambles over fully half of the second floor.

Adjacent to the huge bedroom area is a spacious dressing area bordered by an abundance of closet space and a double-sink bath area. Unusual extras include walk-in wardrobe in the third bedroom and the long double-sink counter in the second upstairs bath.

Note also the exceptional abundance of closet space on both floors, and the separate utility room that also serves as a clean-up room connecting with the garage.

Upper floor:	1,085 sq. ft.
Main floor:	950 sq. ft.
Total living area: (Not counting basement or garage)	2,035 sq. ft.

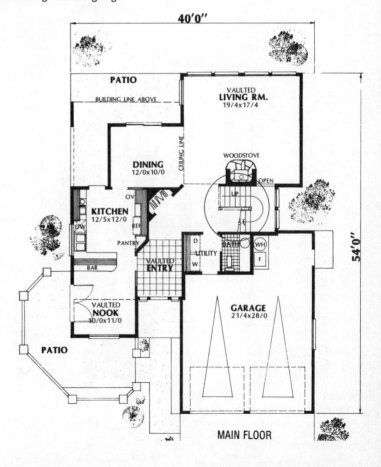

MASTER SUITE
17/8x15/8

OPEN TO LIVING BELOW

RAILING

DRESSING

SHWR

BATH

RAILING

OPEN TO ENTRY BELOW

DN

LIN

LIN

LIN

BATH

TUB

UPPER FLOOR

BEDRM. 3
10/6x12/8

BEDRM. 2
10/6x13/2

LIVING RM.

UP

DN

PLAN P-6597-2A
WITHOUT BASEMENT
(CRAWLSPACE FOUNDATION)

PLAN P-6597-2D
(WITH DAYLIGHT BASEMENT)

40'0"

PATIO

BUILDING LINE ABOVE

VAULTED LIVING RM.
19/4x17/4

CEILING LINE

DINING
12/0x10/0

WOODSTOVE

OPEN

UP

KITCHEN
12/5x12/0

OV

REF

DW

PANTRY

D

UTILITY

W

BATH

WH

F

BAR

VAULTED ENTRY

54'0"

VAULTED NOOK
10/0x11/0

GARAGE
21/4x28/0

PATIO

MAIN FLOOR

Spacious Narrow-Lot Design

PLAN R-2052
WITHOUT BASEMENT
(CRAWLSPACE FOUNDATION)

Soaring vaults and a creative room and window arrangement fill this narrow-lot plan with plenty of wide-open space. The heightened entry opens to the large, vaulted living/dining area for an expanded feeling of roominess.

A delightful bay window nook and coveted corner sink add sparkle to the kitchen's abundance of natural light.

Upstairs, the master bedroom includes a tasteful bay window sitting area, generous walk-in wardrobe and twin vanities. Another sensible feature you'll find in this popular floor plan is a convenient connecting bathroom, which opens to both the second and third bedrooms. Also note that both these bedrooms include their own walk-in closets.

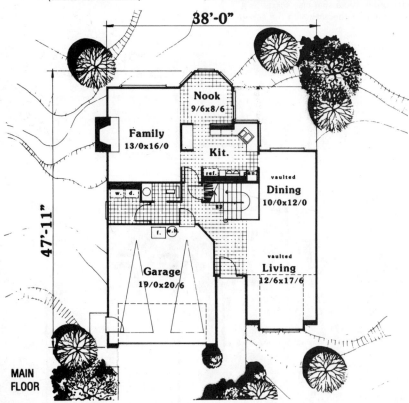

MAIN FLOOR

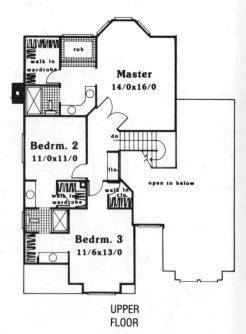

UPPER FLOOR

First floor:	1,078 sq. ft.
Second floor:	974 sq. ft.
Total living area:	2,052 sq. ft.
(Not counting garage)	

Blueprint Price Code C

Plan R-2052

Loaded with Features

- Great Room has fireplace and long windows to add to its elegance. Also has a nice view of open stair.
- Galley-type kitchen between formal dining room and secluded breakfast nook.
- Downstairs bedroom with full bath is perfect for guests or mother-in-law.
- Master bedroom is large and has trey ceiling. TV-stereo center allows for more useable floor space.
- Master bath has corner tub, shower, and window seat. Vaulted ceiling gives bath a spacious feeling.
- Optional bonus room can be used as a playroom, office or bedroom.

Plan C-8910

Bedrooms: 4	Baths: 3

Finished space:

Upper floor	1,025 sq. ft.
Main floor	1,033 sq. ft.
Bonus area:	284 sq. ft.
Total living area	**2,342 sq. ft.**
Garage:	484 sq. ft.

Features:
Great Room
Large breakfast nook
Guest bedroom
Deluxe master bedroom suite

Exterior Wall Framing	2x4

Foundation options:
Daylight basement.
Standard basement.
Crawlspace.
Slab.

Blueprint Price Code	C

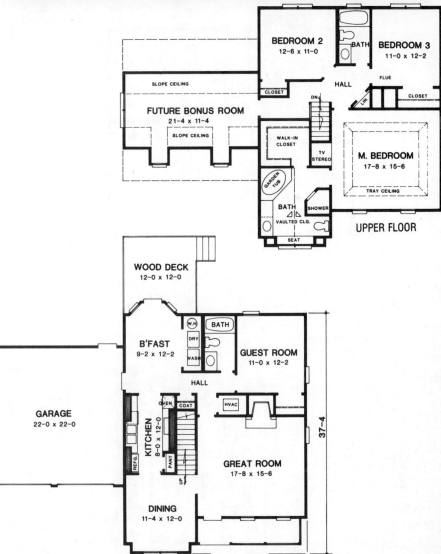

UPPER FLOOR

MAIN FLOOR

Plan C-8910

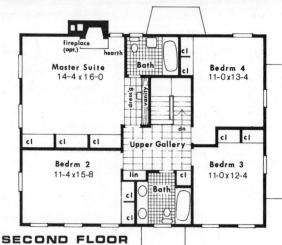

SECOND FLOOR

Master Suite
14-4 x 16-0

Bath

Bedrm 4
11-0 x 13-4

fireplace (opt.)
hearth
dress'g
vanity
dn

Bedrm 2
11-4 x 15-8

Upper Gallery

Bedrm 3
11-0 x 12-4

lin
Bath
cl

Energy-Conscious Early American

Many energy-saving details have been incorporated into this traditional home. Window treatment, horizontal siding and a dignified entryway give an impressive Colonial look. A central gallery provides direct access to all areas of the house. The family room, complete with brick fireplace and sliding glass doors to the back terrace and side porch, is designed for times of privacy, or to join with dinette-kitchen and/or living room by use of folding doors.

Upstairs are four bedrooms with a master suite featuring a private bath, dressing area, and optional wood-burning fireplace. First floor is 998 sq. ft.; second floor is 1,108 sq. ft., for a total of 2,106. Optional basement is 998; garage, etc., is 568.

First floor:	998 sq. ft.
Second floor:	1,108 sq. ft.
Total living area:	2,106 sq. ft.
Garage, etc.:	568 sq. ft.
Basement (opt.):	998 sq. ft.

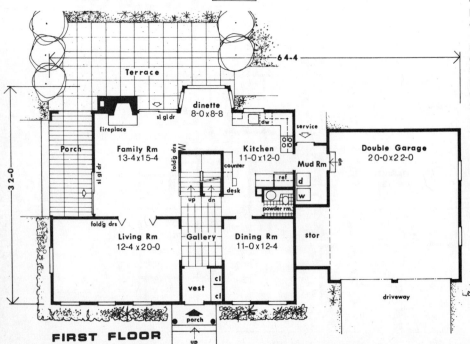

FIRST FLOOR

64-4

Terrace

32-0

Porch

fireplace
sl gl dr

Family Rm
13-4 x 15-4

fold'g drs

dinette
8-0 x 8-8
sl gl dr
dw

Kitchen
11-0 x 12-0

service

Double Garage
20-0 x 22-0

counter
desk
up dn

ref
Mud Rm
d
w
powder rm.

fold'g drs

Living Rm
12-4 x 20-0

Gallery

Dining Rm
11-0 x 12-4

stor

driveway

vest
cl

porch
up

Blueprint Price Code C

Plan K-168-S

Traditional Comfort

- With its wrap-around veranda and elegant traditional design, this home is sure to attract attention in any neighborhood.
- An enormous living room boasts beamed ceilings, an impressive fireplace and easy access to the rear porch.
- An efficient kitchen is flanked on one side by a gorgeous formal dining room, and on the other by a large casual eating area. Also note the large utility room and pantry.
- Upstairs, a majestic master suite is graced by an enticing sitting area and features a deluxe bath and two large closets.
- Two secondary bedrooms share a full bath and the front bedroom includes a pleasant window seat.
- Blueprints for this plan include a separate two-car garage which includes a 12' x 6' shop area and an equal-sized storage area.

Plan E-2104

Bedrooms: 3	Baths: 2½
Space:	
Upper floor	1,031 sq. ft.
Main floor	1,082 sq. ft.
Total Living Area	**2,113 sq. ft.**
Basement	1,081 sq. ft.
Porches & storage	576 sq. ft.
Garage (detached)	528 sq. ft.
Storage (in garage)	72 sq. ft.
Shop (in garage)	72 sq. ft.
Exterior Wall Framing	2x6
Foundation options:	

Standard basement
Crawlspace
Slab
(Foundation & framing conversion diagram available—see order form.)

Blueprint Price Code	C

UPPER FLOOR

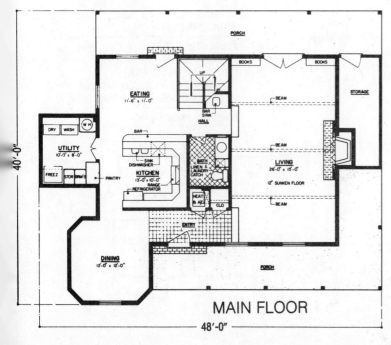

MAIN FLOOR

Plan E-2104

135

Early American Includes Solar Elements

- Classic Colonial styling creates a warm, inviting home with plenty of space for a busy family.
- The construction, however, is anything but Colonial, with energy-efficient features throughout.
- This plan also includes optional solar heating features, with provisions for solar heat collectors on a rear shed roof to supplement a conventional heating system.

- The main floor includes a spacious dining/living area, large family room, efficient kitchen and optional bedroom which could also serve as an office, den or study room.
- Upstairs, a roomy master suite includes a private bath and closets.
- Two secondary bedrooms share another full bath.
- Also note the downstairs bath and convenient laundry area.

Plans H-3704-1 & -1A

Bedrooms: 3-4	Baths: 3
Space:	
Upper floor:	943 sq. ft.
Main floor:	1,200 sq. ft.
Total living area:	2,143 sq. ft.
Basement:	1,200 sq. ft.
Garage:	461 sq. ft.
Exterior Wall Framing:	2x6

Foundation options:
Standard basement (H-3704-1).
Crawlspace (H-3704-1A).
(Foundation & framing conversion diagram available — see order form.)

Blueprint Price Code:	C

MAIN FLOOR

UPPER FLOOR

TO ORDER THIS BLUEPRINT,
CALL TOLL-FREE 1-800-547-5570
(prices and details on pp. 12-15.)

Plans H-3704-1 & -1A

Country Comfort

- An inviting three-sided veranda wraps around the living room in this wonderful country design.
- The interior is open and airy, with the living room flowing into a spacious hallway by the kitchen.
- In the front of the home, a large room is provided for formal dining or for a parlor, depending on your preference.
- A sunny eating area is provided to the right, with large windows and easy access to a private courtyard or garden.
- The master bedroom provides a deluxe bath and large walk-in closet, and is isolated for privacy.
- Upstairs, two more bedrooms share a second full bath and a large game or study room with a balcony over the living room.
- Blueprints include plans for a detached two-car garage.

Plan E-2103

Bedrooms: 3	Baths: 2½
Space:	
Upper floor	736 sq. ft.
Main floor	1,431 sq. ft.
Total Living Area	**2,167 sq. ft.**
Basement	1,431 sq. ft.
Porch	477 sq. ft.
Garage (detached)	484 sq. ft.
Storage (in garage)	56 sq. ft.
Exterior Wall Framing	**2x6**

Foundation options:

Standard basement

Crawlspace

Slab

(Foundation & framing conversion diagram available—see order form.)

Blueprint Price Code	**C**

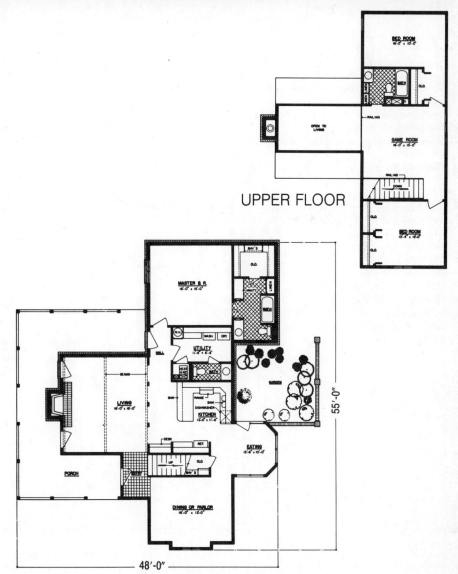

UPPER FLOOR

MAIN FLOOR

Plan E-2103

Southern Country

- This home is distinctly Southern Country in style, from its wide front porch to its multi-paned and shuttered windows.
- The living room boasts a 12' cathedral ceiling, a fireplace and French doors to the rear patio.
- The dining room is open, but defined by three massive columns with overhead beams.
- The delightful kitchen/nook area is spacious and well-planned for both efficiency and pleasant kitchen working conditions.
- A handy utility room and half-bath are on either side of a short hallway leading to the carport.
- The master suite offers his and hers walk-in closets and an incredible bath which incorporates a plant shelf above the garden tub.

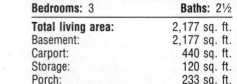

Plan J-86140	
Bedrooms: 3	**Baths:** 2½

Total living area:	2,177 sq. ft.
Basement:	2,177 sq. ft.
Carport:	440 sq. ft.
Storage:	120 sq. ft.
Porch:	233 sq. ft.

Exterior Wall Framing:	2x4
Ceiling Heights:	9'

Foundation options:
Standard basement.
Crawlspace.
Slab.
(Foundation & framing conversion diagram available — see order form.)

Blueprint Price Code:	C

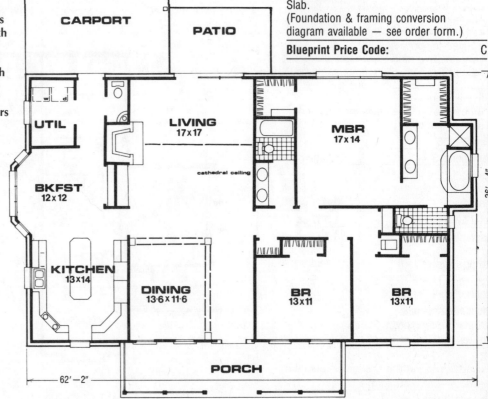

Plan J-86140

"Adult Retreat"
in Master Bedroom Suite

- Exciting living room is virtually open on three sides.
- Wet bar lies between living area and large kitchen, which offers an eating bar and island cooktop.

- Elegant master suite features sitting area and attached bath with romantic angled tub covered with skylight and flanked by his 'n hers vanities.

Plan E-2106

Bedrooms: 3	Baths: 2

Space:

Total living area:	2,177 sq. ft.
Basement:	approx. 2,177 sq. ft.
Garage and storage:	570 sq. ft.
Porches:	211 sq. ft.

Exterior Wall Framing:	2x4

Foundation options:
Standard basement.
Crawlspace.
Slab.
(Foundation & framing conversion diagram available — see order form.)

Blueprint Price Code:	C

**NOTE:
The above photographed home may have been modified by the homeowner. Please refer to floor plan and/or drawn elevation shown for actual blueprint details.

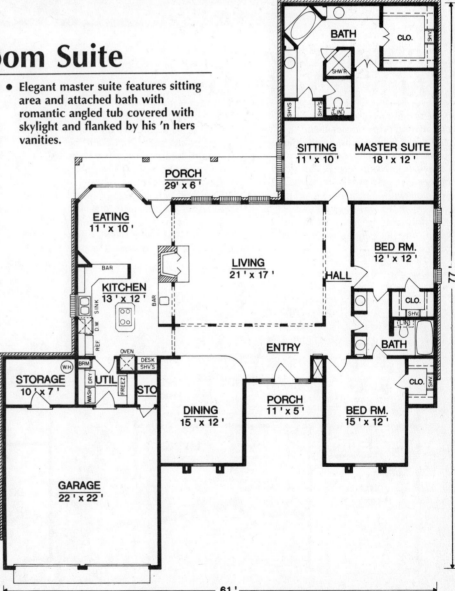

Plan E-2106

Contemporary Return to Yesterday

- Bold rooflines complemented by crisply angled windows blend the traditional with the new, a theme that is increasingly popular with today's home builders. Rough-sawn corner trim and the use of brick coupled with vertical cedar siding give this home an unusual look.
- The floor plan is based on an owner-proven concept with many pluses.

- Note the balcony library situated above the vaulted entry and the garage bonus space that could be the fourth bedroom or a rec room. A separate utility room with clothes-sorting counter is close to the kitchen and activity area.
- The master bath features double vanities, a raised tub platform in a three-cornered window extension and a separate shower.

Plan LRD-2180-A & -B

Bedrooms: 3-5	Baths: 2½
Living Area:	
Upper floor	1,051 sq. ft.
Main floor	1,184 sq. ft.
Bonus room	232 sq. ft.
Total Living Area:	**2,467 sq. ft.**
Standard basement	1,184 sq. ft.
Garage	374 sq. ft.
Exterior Wall Framing:	2x6
Foundation Options:	**Plan #**
Standard basement	LRD-2180-B
Crawlspace	LRD-2180-A
(Typical foundation & framing conversion diagram available—see order form.)	
BLUEPRINT PRICE CODE:	C

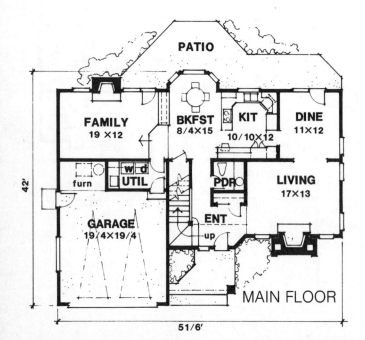

MAIN FLOOR

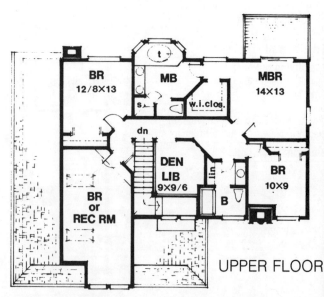

UPPER FLOOR

Plan LRD-2180-A & -B

Country Kitchen and Deluxe Master Bath

- Front porch, dormers and shutters give this home a decidedly country look on the outside, which is complemented by an informal modern interior.
- The roomy country kitchen connects with a sunny breakfast nook and utility area on one hand and a formal dining room on the other.
- The central portion of the home consists of a large family room with a fireplace and easy access to a rear deck.
- The downstairs master suite is particularly impressive for a home of this size, and features a majestic master bath with two walk-in closets and double vanities.
- Upstairs, you will find two more ample-sized bedrooms, a double bath and a large storage area.

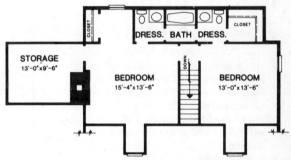

UPPER FLOOR

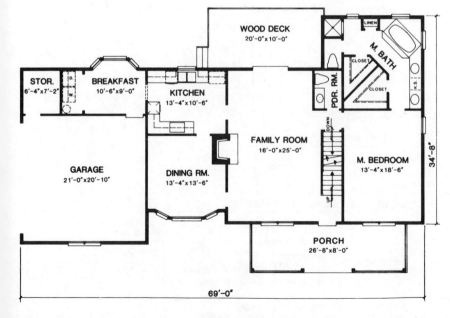

MAIN FLOOR

Plan C-8645

Bedrooms: 3	Baths: 2½

Space:	
Upper floor:	704 sq.ft.
Main floor:	1,477 sq.ft.

Total living area:	2,181 sq.ft.
Basement:	Approx. 1,400 sq.ft.
Garage:	438 sq.ft.
Storage:	123 sq.ft.

Exterior Wall Framing:	2x4

Foundation options:
Standard basement.
Crawlspace.
Slab.
(Foundation & framing conversion diagram available — see order form.)

Blueprint Price Code:	C

Plan C-8645

Contemporary Elegance

- This contemporary design includes elegant traditional overtones, and is finished in vertical cedar siding.
- An expansive space is devoted to the vaulted living room and adjoining family/dining room and kitchen.
- A convenient utility area is located between the kitchen and the garage, and includes a clothes sorting counter, deep sink and ironing space.
- The master suite is spacious for a home of this size, and includes a sumptuous master bath and large walk-in closet.
- A loft area can be used for an additional bedroom, playroom, exercise area or hobby space.
- An optional sunroom can be added to the rear at any time.

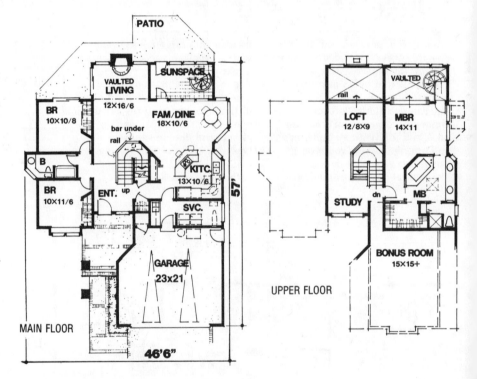

PATIO

SUNSPACE

VAULTED LIVING 12×16/6

FAM/DINE 18×10/6

bar under rail

BR 10×10/8

B

BR 10×11/6

KITC. 13×10/6

ENT. up

SVC.

GARAGE 23x21

57'

46'6"

MAIN FLOOR

LOFT 12/8×9

VAULTED

MBR 14×11

rail

STUDY

dn

MB

BONUS ROOM 15×15+

UPPER FLOOR

Plan LRD-1971

Bedrooms: 3-4	Baths: 2

Space:

Upper floor:	723 sq. ft.
Main floor:	1,248 sq. ft.
Bonus area:	225 sq. ft.
Total living area:	**2,196 sq. ft.**
Basement:	approx. 1,248 sq. ft.
Garage:	483 sq. ft.

Exterior Wall Framing:	2x6

Foundation options:
Standard basement.
Crawlspace.
(Foundation & framing conversion diagram available — see order form.)

Blueprint Price Code:	C

Plan LRD-1971

Fantastic Floor Plan!

- This is the famous house shown on the PBS "Hometime" television series.
- Impressive floor plan includes a deluxe master suite with a private courtyard, magnificent bath and large closet.
- The large island kitchen/nook combination includes a corner pantry and easy access to a rear deck.
- The spacious family room includes a fireplace and vaulted ceiling.
- The two upstairs bedrooms share a bath with double sinks.
- Note the convenient laundry room in the garage entry area.

Plan B-88015

Bedrooms: 3	Baths: 2½
Space:	
Upper floor:	534 sq. ft.
Main floor:	1,689 sq. ft.
Total living area:	2,223 sq. ft.
Basement:	approx. 1,689 sq. ft.
Garage:	455 sq. ft.
Exterior Wall Framing:	2x4
Foundation options:	
Standard basement only.	
Foundation & framing conversion	
diagram available — see order form.)	
Blueprint Price Code:	C

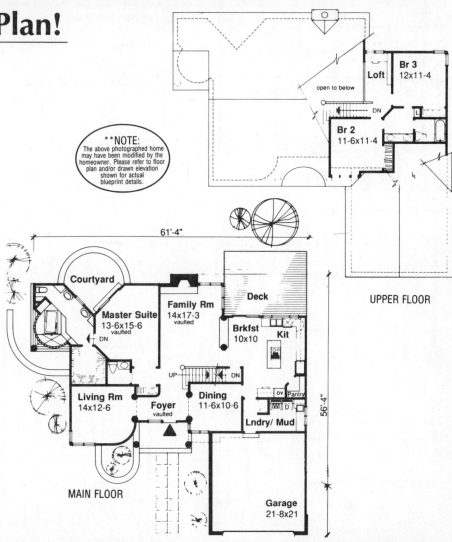

**NOTE: The above photographed home may have been modified by the homeowner. Please refer to floor plan and/or drawn elevation shown for actual blueprint details.

UPPER FLOOR

MAIN FLOOR

Plan B-88015

TO ORDER THIS BLUEPRINT, CALL TOLL-FREE 1-800-547-5570
(prices and details on pp. 12-15.) **143**

Modern Traditional-Style Home

- Covered porch and decorative double doors offer an invitation into this three or four bedroom home.
- Main floor bedroom may be used as a den, home office, or guest room, with convenient bath facilities.
- Adjoining dining room makes living room seem even more spacious; breakfast nook enlarges the look of the attached kitchen.
- Brick-size concrete block veneer and masonry tile roof give the exterior a look of durability.

UPPER FLOOR

PLAN H-1351-M1A
WITHOUT BASEMENT
(CRAWLSPACE FOUNDATION)

Plans H-1351-M1 & -M1A

Bedrooms: 3-4	Baths: 3
Space:	
Upper floor:	862 sq. ft.
Main floor:	1,383 sq. ft.
Total living area:	2,245 sq. ft.
Basement:	1,383 sq. ft.
Garage:	413 sq. ft
Exterior Wall Framing:	2x6

Foundation options:
Standard basement (Plan H-1351-M1).
Crawlspace (Plan H-1351-M1A).
(Foundation & framing conversion diagram available — see order form.)

Blueprint Price Code:

MAIN FLOOR

Plans H-1351-M1 & -M1A

Dramatic Entry to Exciting Home

This contemporary home shows traditional overtones in exterior window treatment, wise use of corner trim, and built-up entry columns. The exterior is finished with horizontal lap siding and wood shake roofing. The garage is illustrated 24" below the main level of the home, but may be raised without compromising the design. A large entry overhang grants good protection from the elements. Large, arched windows lend dramatic accent to the two-story-high Great Room with overlooking balcony.

The super master suite features a walk-in closet, a tiled platform tub, twin vanity, shower and a separate water closet compartment. The lower-level bedroom may be used as a guest bedroom or an added hobby room.

The gourmet kitchen will please the fussiest cook. The large, open bar adjacent to the dining area features a wine serving bar and overhead cabinets for visual privacy in the kitchen area.

Square footage totals 2,224. Width of the home is only 50' with depth at 60'-6". Exterior walls are of 2x6 construction for energy efficiency.

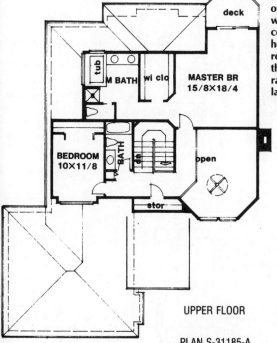

UPPER FLOOR

PLAN S-31185-A
WITHOUT BASEMENT
(CRAWLSPACE FOUNDATION)

PLAN S-31185-B
WITH BASEMENT

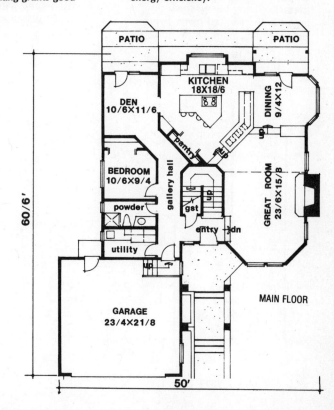

MAIN FLOOR

Main floor:	1,392 sq. ft.
Upper floor:	832 sq. ft.
Total living area: (Not counting basement or garage)	2,224 sq. ft.

Blueprint Price Code C

Plans S-31185-A & -B

Hillcrest Home

- The side-sloping hill is the perfect site for this side-to-side split-level design, which blends beautifully into its setting with multiple hip rooflines and a stylish chimney.
- Guests will walk up a few steps to the main living floor, which includes the vaulted foyer, living room, dining room, study, and island kitchen/breakfast room.
- The kitchen overlooks the family room a half-flight down, which is on the garage level.
- The sleeping quarters are a half-flight up, including a spacious master suite with double-doors, walk-in closet and skylit private bath.

Plan CDG-4003

Bedrooms: 3-4	Baths: 2½

Space:

Upper floor:	843 sq. ft.
Main floor:	1,385 sq. ft.
Total living area:	**2,228 sq. ft.**
Garage:	approx. 475 sq. ft.
	+ approx. 225 sq. ft. tandem third-car garage/storage area

Exterior Wall Framing:	2x4

Foundation options:
Crawlspace only.
(Foundation & framing conversion diagram available — see order form.)

Blueprint Price Code:	B

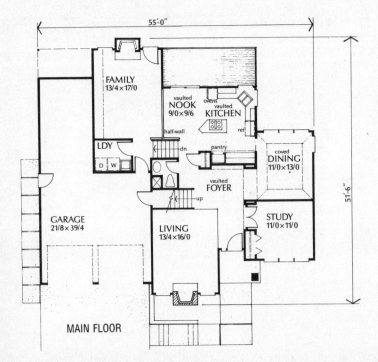

MAIN FLOOR

UPPER FLOOR

Plan CDG-4003

Big Space for Small Lot

- Simplicity and construction economy are benefits of this classic design.
- From the impressive foyer to the spacious master bedroom, this home gives the impression of being much larger than it actually is.
- The master bath features a step-up tub and separate shower.
- Note the second-floor laundry area and convenient entry to second bath from both secondary bedrooms.
- A downstairs guest bedroom with bath would also serve nicely as a home office.
- Kitchen and breakfast nook combine for a 'country kitchen' effect.
- Large Great Room includes a fireplace.

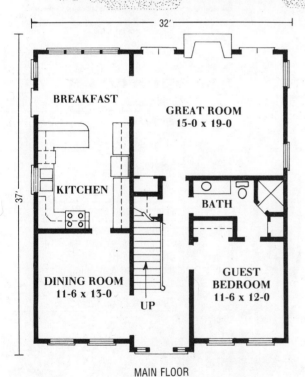

MAIN FLOOR

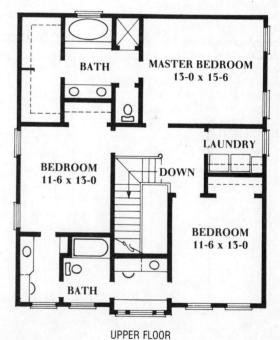

UPPER FLOOR

Plan V-2240-C

Bedrooms: 3-4	Baths: 3

Space:

Upper floor:	1,080 sq. ft.
Main floor:	1,160 sq. ft.
Total living area:	**2,240 sq. ft.**

Exterior Wall Framing:	2x6

Ceiling Heights:

Upper floor:	8'
Main floor:	9'

Foundation options:
Crawlspace only.
(Foundation & framing conversion diagram available — see order form.)

Blueprint Price Code:	C

Plan V-2240-C

Wrap-Around Veranda Lends Homey, Welcoming Look

Photo courtesy of HomeStyles Publishing and Marketing, Inc.

- Traditional farmhouse designs such as this never seem to lose their popularity.
- The large, welcoming veranda conjures up images of sipping lemonade with family and friends on mild summer evenings.
- A big living room includes a fireplace and three large windows.
- The breakfast nook is flooded with natural light from the bay window, and adjoins the family room.
- A convenient utility room and half-bath are located in the garage entry area.
- The luxurious master suite includes a sunny bay window, private bath and large walk-in closet.
- Bedrooms two and three also offer roomy closets and share a large, compartmentalized bath.

NOTE:
The above photographed home may have been modified by the homeowner. Please refer to floor plan and/or drawn elevation shown for actual blueprint details.

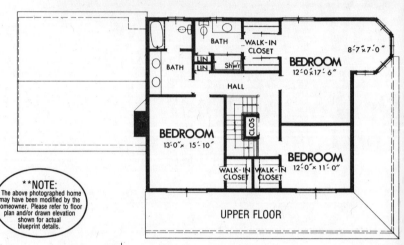

UPPER FLOOR

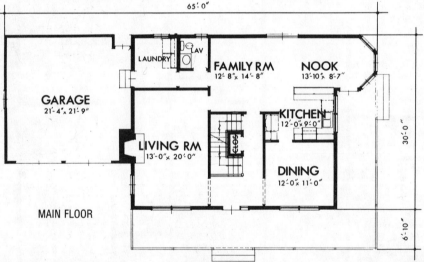

MAIN FLOOR

Plans H-1414-1 & -1A	
Bedrooms: 3	**Baths:** 2½
Space:	
Upper floor:	1,103 sq. ft
Main floor:	1,138 sq. ft
Total living area:	2,241 sq. ft
Basement:	1,138 sq. ft
Garage:	464 sq. ft
Exterior Wall Framing:	2x6

Foundation options:
Standard basement (H-1414-1).
Crawlspace (H-1414-1A).
(Foundation & framing conversion diagram available — see order form.)

Blueprint Price Code:

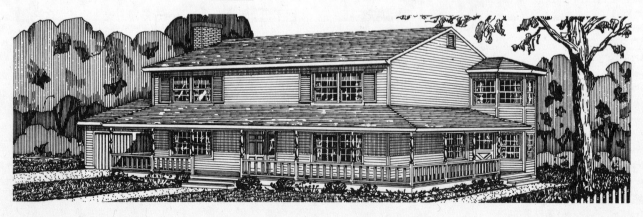

Plans H-1414-1 & -1A

Simple Plan Lets You Enjoy the View

- This straightforward plan would be at home on any lot, but is especially attractive if you have a nice scenic view to the rear. Almost every room features abundant window area to the back of the house.
- The dining and living rooms together make a large space for gatherings of any kind, and the sunken living room features a fireplace and vaulted ceiling.
- The kitchen, nook and family room flow together for a wide range of family activities, and a convenient utility area offers handy access to the garage.
- The upper floor hosts four bedrooms, with the master suite including a private bath and large walk-in closet.
- An optional daylight basement adds another 1,200 square feet of living space.

Plans P-7492-2A & -2D

Bedrooms: 4	Baths: 2½
Space:	
Upper floor	1,048 sq. ft.
Main floor	1,200 sq. ft.
Total Living Area	**2,248 sq. ft.**
Basement	1,200 sq. ft.
Garage	532 sq. ft.
Exterior Wall Framing	2x4
Foundation options:	**Plan #**
Daylight Basement	P-7492-2D
Crawlspace	P-7492-2A
(Foundation & framing conversion diagram available—see order form.)	
Blueprint Price Code	**C**

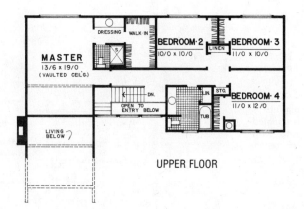

UPPER FLOOR

PLAN P-7492-2D
WITH DAYLIGHT BASEMENT

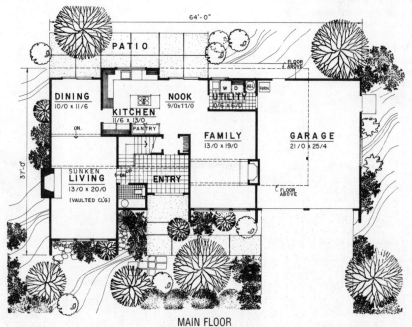

MAIN FLOOR
PLAN P-7492-2A
WITHOUT BASEMENT

Plans P-7492-2A & -2D

TO ORDER THIS BLUEPRINT,
CALL TOLL-FREE 1-800-547-5570
(prices and details on pp. 12-15.)

Stately Traditional with "Charisma"

Stately lines and charisma are built into this highly livable and thoroughly updated traditional home. Space is celebrated with vaulted living and dining room ceilings and an abundance of windows, including the impressive two-story arched window which highlights the dining and living room area.

The spacious bonus room upstairs (actually a third living area in addition to the living and family rooms) is indeed a rare surprise. Whether a child's playroom or an adult's gym or retreat, it is thoughtfully isolated from the rest of the house.

Note such other special touches as the kitchen's unique walk-in pantry and the balcony overlooking the entry and living and dining rooms below. It all adds up to a spectacular home.

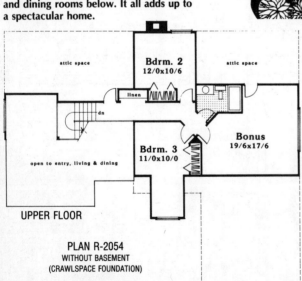

PLAN R-2054
WITHOUT BASEMENT
(CRAWLSPACE FOUNDATION)

Main floor:	1,744 sq. ft.
Upper floor:	506 sq. ft.
Total living area: (Not counting garage)	2,250 sq. ft.
Bonus area:	297 sq. ft.

Blueprint Price Code C

Plan R-2054

FRONT VIEW

REAR VIEW

Something Old, Something New

"Something old, something new" aptly describes the flavor and sentiment of this replica of earlier times.

Beveled oval plate glass with heavy oak surrounds and appropriate hand-carved wreaths and borders make entering the home the delightful experience it was meant to be. Inside one finds the huge central entry hall with the magnificent open staircase with turned balusters and shapely handrails.

With all bedrooms being on the second floor, the main level is entirely devoted to daily living in a generous atmosphere. The 14' x 23' living room and 14' x 13' dining room give one an idea of the spaciousness of this home.

Notice the 80 cubic foot pantry closet and the adjacent storage closet with an equal amount of space. A two-thirds bath and well equipped laundry room complete the mechanical area of the home.

Certainly the most provocative room on the main floor is the beautiful glass-enclosed morning or breakfast room. Huge skylight panels augment the bank of windows and sliding doors to create a delightful passive solar room suitable for many uses while contributing greatly to the heating efficiency of the entire building.

Upstairs two good-sized bedrooms with adjoining bathroom serve the junior members of the family while the parents enjoy the spacious master suite with walk-in wardrobes and private bath.

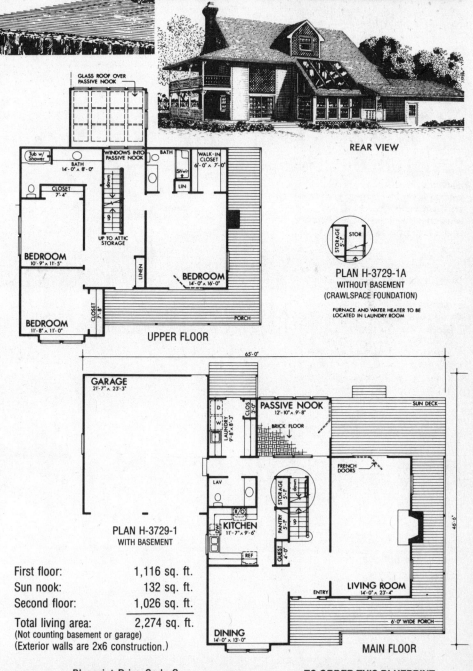

PLAN H-3729-1A
WITHOUT BASEMENT
(CRAWLSPACE FOUNDATION)

FURNACE AND WATER HEATER TO BE
LOCATED IN LAUNDRY ROOM

UPPER FLOOR

PLAN H-3729-1
WITH BASEMENT

First floor: 1,116 sq. ft.
Sun nook: 132 sq. ft.
Second floor: 1,026 sq. ft.
Total living area: 2,274 sq. ft.
(Not counting basement or garage)
(Exterior walls are 2x6 construction.)

MAIN FLOOR

Blueprint Price Code C

Plans H-3729-1 & H-3729-1A

**TO ORDER THIS BLUEPRINT,
CALL TOLL-FREE 1-800-547-5570**
(prices and details on pp. 12-15.) **151**

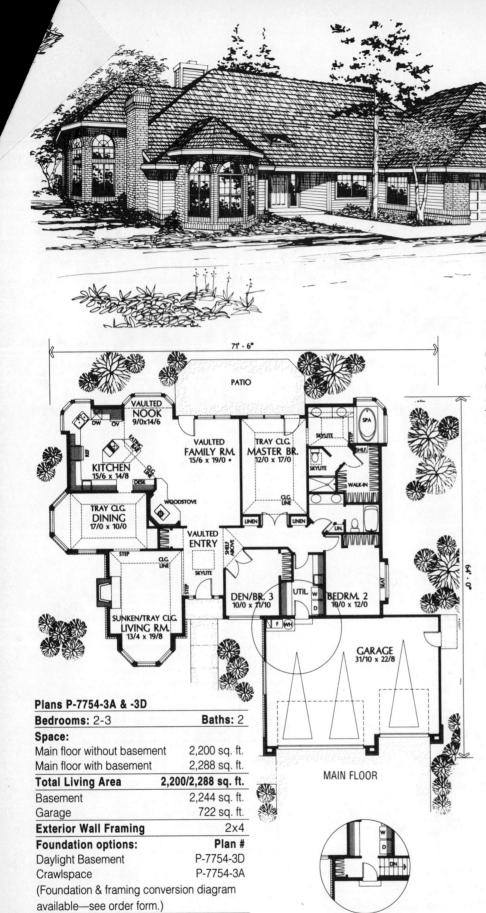

Stunning One-Story Design

- The recessed front entry opens to a vaulted, skylighted foyer.
- The sunken living room has a tray ceiling, a fireplace and a turret-like bay with high arched windows.
- The dining room, one step up, also features a tray ceiling and a large bay window.
- The unusual kitchen includes a built-in desk, a corner sink surrounded by lots of counter space and windows, and a cooktop island with eating bar.
- The adjacent nook and family room boast vaulted ceilings and an abundance of windows facing the rear patio. A woodstove tucked into one corner of the family room radiates heat.
- Double doors topped by an overhead plant shelf provide an elegant introduction to the den or third bedroom.
- The master bedroom is also entered through double doors. A tray ceiling and a rear window wall add light and height to the sleeping area. Note the private access to the patio.
- The magnificent master bath includes a step-up garden spa tub, a large dressing area with double-sink vanity, a separate shower and a large walk-in closet. Two skylights shower the bath with light.
- Another full bath, a bedroom with a window seat and a walk-through utility room complete this stunning one-story design.

Plans P-7754-3A & -3D

Bedrooms: 2-3	Baths: 2
Space:	
Main floor without basement	2,200 sq. ft.
Main floor with basement	2,288 sq. ft.
Total Living Area	**2,200/2,288 sq. ft.**
Basement	2,244 sq. ft.
Garage	722 sq. ft.
Exterior Wall Framing	**2x4**
Foundation options:	**Plan #**
Daylight Basement	P-7754-3D
Crawlspace	P-7754-3A
(Foundation & framing conversion diagram available—see order form.)	
Blueprint Price Code	**C**

MAIN FLOOR

BASEMENT

Plans P-7754-3A & -3D

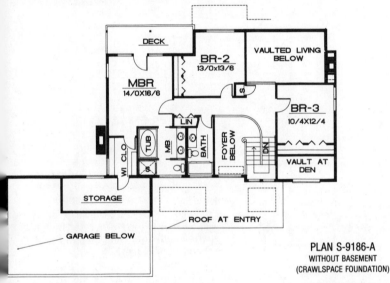

PLAN S-9186-A
WITHOUT BASEMENT
(CRAWLSPACE FOUNDATION)

PLAN S-9186-B
WITH BASEMENT

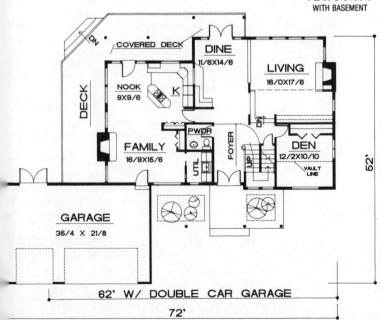

A Warm, Welcoming Family Home

A warm home with the welcoming look of wood, this 3-bedroom design is just 2,484 sq. ft. The vaulted entry contains an open stairwell which leads to an upper level balcony.

The den, which can double as a guest bedroom, has a vaulted ceiling and a large window section that makes it an ideal study.

The kitchen/nook/family room combination creates an active informal zone for everyday living. A large covered deck area extends this living space to the outdoors.

The partially vaulted living room contains a large window wall. Note the built-in cabinet wall system for storing books and entertainment equipment. In the adjacent dining room, a couple of labor-saving features are the built-in bar and a pass-through to the kitchen.

The windowed staircase leads to the second floor sleeping areas. The balcony views down to the living room and foyer below. The vaulted master suite opens onto a private deck. The master bath is segregated by a pocket door for double use. Note the large 7'x19' storage area behind the walk-in closet, an ideal place for those seasonal clothes.

This contemporary home measures 72' wide by 52' deep with the three-car garage. However, for more restrictive land parcels, width can be reduced to 62' by dropping the third garage bay.

First floor:	1,267 sq. ft.
Second floor:	1,025 sq. ft.
Total living area:	2,292 sq. ft.

(Not counting basement or garage)

Blueprint Price Code C

Plans S-9186-A & S-9186-B

TO ORDER THIS BLUEPRINT, CALL TOLL-FREE 1-800-547-5570
(prices and details on pp. 12-15.) **153**

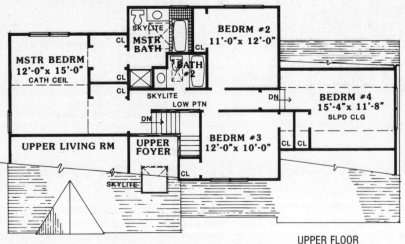

CER TILE LEDGE

MSTR BEDRM
12'-0"x 15'-0"
CATH CEIL

SKYLITE
MSTR
BATH
CL

BEDRM #2
11'-0"x 12'-0"

BATH
#2
CL

SKYLITE

LOW PTN

DN

BEDRM #4
15'-4"x 11'-8"
SLPD CLG

DN

UPPER LIVING RM

UPPER
FOYER

BEDRM #3
12'-0"x 10'-0"

CL CL

SKYLITE

CL

UPPER FLOOR

Distinctive Two-Story

- A playful and distinctive exterior invites you into a functional, contemporary interior.
- The sunken living room features a soaring cathedral ceiling open to the second floor balcony.
- The adjoining step-down family room is connected to allow for overflow and easy circulation of traffic.
- A luxurious master suite and room for three additional bedrooms are found on the second floor, with a dramatic balcony and a view of the foyer and the living room.

Plan AX-8922-A

Bedrooms: 3-4	Baths: 2½
Living Area:	
Upper floor	840 sq. ft.
Main floor	1,213 sq. ft.
Optional fourth bedroom	240 sq. ft.
Total Living Area:	**2,293 sq. ft.**
Standard basement	1,138 sq. ft.
Garage	470 sq. ft.
Exterior Wall Framing:	2x4

Foundation Options:
Standard basement
Slab
(Typical foundation & framing conversion diagram available—see order form.)

BLUEPRINT PRICE CODE: C

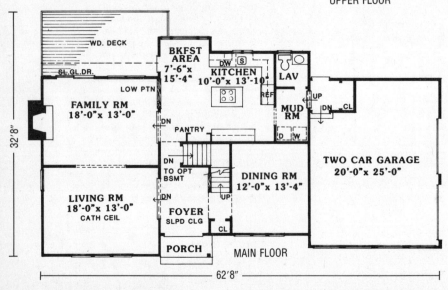

WD. DECK

GL.GL.DR.

LOW PTN

BKFST
AREA
7'-6"x
15'-4"

KITCHEN
10'-0"x 13'-10"

DW S

LAV

REF

MUD
RM

UP

DN CL

FAMILY RM
18'-0"x 13'-0"

PANTRY

32'8"

DN

DN
TO OPT
BSMT

DINING RM
12'-0"x 13'-4"

TWO CAR GARAGE
20'-0"x 25'-0"

DN

UP

LIVING RM
18'-0"x 13'-0"
CATH CEIL

FOYER
SLPD CLG

CL

PORCH

MAIN FLOOR

62'8"

Plan AX-8922-A

Spanish Hacienda

- This stylish home combines visual impact and easy living with construction economies.
- Its one-story layout, relatively simple roofline and basic rectangular shapes, plus a slab foundation and use of pre-manufactured trusses are major factors that make this home cost-effective.
- The interior boasts a large sunken living room, formal dining room and a spacious kitchen/nook area.
- The master bedroom is isolated on one side, and boasts a private bath and large walk-in closet.
- Two secondary bedrooms are on the opposite side and share a walk-through bath.
- The study off the foyer could serve as a guest bedroom or convenient home office.

Plan Q-2298-1A

Bedrooms: 3-4	Baths: 2½
Total living area:	2,298 sq. ft.
Garage:	433 sq. ft.
Exterior Wall Framing:	2x4

Foundation options:
Slab.
(Foundation & framing conversion diagram available — see order form.)

Blueprint Price Code: C

Plan Q-2298-1A

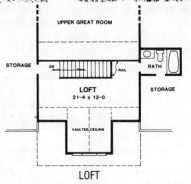

UPPER GREAT ROOM

STORAGE

DN RAIL BATH

LOFT
21-4 x 12-0

STORAGE

VAULTED CEILING

LOFT

Gracious Traditional

- Traditional style ranch is perfect for a corner building lot. Long windows and dormers add distinctive elegance.
- Floor plan has popular "split-bedroom" design. Master bedroom is secluded away from other bedrooms.
- Large Great Room has vaulted ceiling and stairs leading up to a loft.

- Upstairs loft is perfect for recreation area, and also has a full bath.
- Master bedroom bath has large corner tub and his-n-her vanities. Large walk-in closet provides plenty of storage.
- Two other bedrooms have large walk-in closets, desks, and share a full bath.
- Kitchen and private breakfast nook are located conveniently near the utility/garage area.

Plan C-8920

Bedrooms: 3	Baths: 3

Space:

Upper floor:	305 sq. ft.
Main floor:	1,996 sq. ft.

Total living area:	**2,301 sq. ft.**
Basement:	1,996 sq. ft.
Garage:	469 sq. ft.

Exterior Wall Framing:	2x4

Foundation options:
Daylight basement.
Standard basement.
Crawlspace.
(Foundation & framing conversion diagram available — see order form.)

Blueprint Price Code:	C

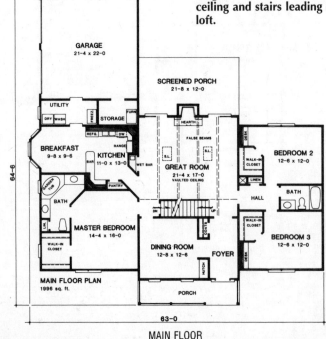

GARAGE
21-4 x 22-0

SCREENED PORCH
21-8 x 12-0

UTILITY

DRY WASH   STORAGE   FURN

FREEZ

HEARTH

REFG.   DW   FALSE BEAMS

BREAKFAST
9-8 x 9-6   KITCHEN
11-0 x 13-0   RANGE

BAR   WET BAR

GARDEN TUB   PANTRY   GREAT ROOM
21-4 x 17-0
VAULTED CEILING

BATH

S.L.   S.L.

WALK-IN
CLOSET   BEDROOM 2
12-6 x 12-0

LINEN

HALL   BATH

WALK-IN
CLOSET

MASTER BEDROOM
14-4 x 16-0

WALK-IN
CLOSET

DN   CLOSET

DINING ROOM
12-8 x 12-6   FOYER   BEDROOM 3
12-6 x 12-0

MAIN FLOOR PLAN
1996 sq. ft.

PORCH

64-6

63-0

MAIN FLOOR

Plan C-8920

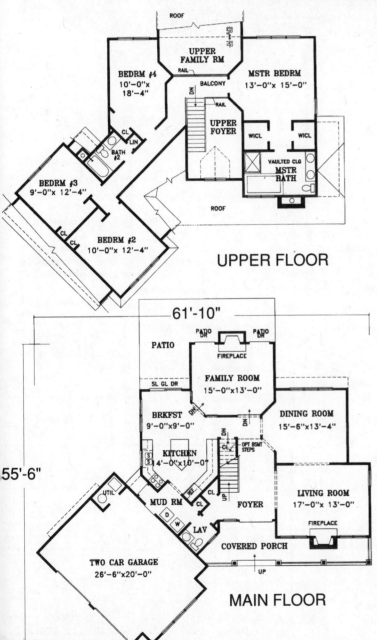

UPPER FLOOR

MAIN FLOOR

Angled Four-Bedroom

- A covered front porch, half-round windows and an angled garage with attractive window treatment give this two-story an inviting look.
- Inside, the spacious foyer offers a view of the formal living room with fireplace and view of the front porch and yard.
- Between the formal dining room and the island kitchen and breakfast area is the generous-sized sunken family room; a second fireplace is flanked by patio doors that overlook a rear patio.
- Between the upper-level master bedroom and three secondary bedrooms is a balcony open to the family room below.
- In the vaulted master bath you'll find dual vanities, a large tub and separate shower.

Plan AX-90309

Bedrooms: 4	Baths: 2 ½
Space:	
Upper floor	1,148 sq. ft.
Main floor	1,190 sq. ft.
Total Living Area	**2,338 sq. ft.**
Basement	1,082 sq. ft.
Garage	545 sq. ft.
Exterior Wall Framing	2x4

Foundation options:
Standard Basement
Slab
(Foundation & framing conversion diagram available—see order form.)

Blueprint Price Code	C

Plan AX-90309

You Asked For It!

- Our most popular plan in recent years, E-3000, has now been downsized for affordability, without sacrificing character or excitement.
- Exterior appeal is created with a covered front porch with decorative columns, triple dormers and rail-topped bay windows.
- The floor plan has combined the separate living and family rooms available in E-3000 into one spacious family room with corner fireplace, which flows into the dining room through a columned gallery.
- The kitchen serves the breakfast eating room over an angled snack bar, and features a huge walk-in pantry.
- The stunning main-floor master suite offers a private sitting area, a walk-in closet and a dramatic, angled master bath.
- There are two large bedrooms upstairs accessible via a curved staircase with bridge balcony.

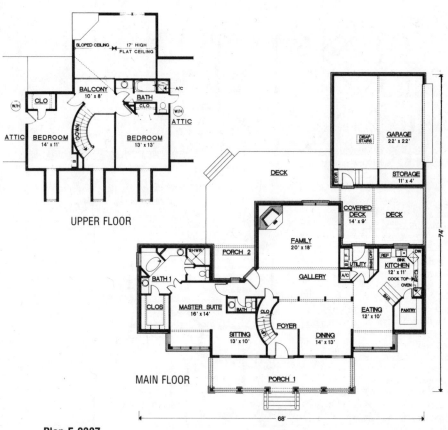

UPPER FLOOR

MAIN FLOOR

Plan E-2307

Bedrooms: 3		Baths: 2½
Space:		
Upper floor:		595 sq. ft.
Main floor:		1,765 sq. ft.
Total living area:		**2,360 sq. ft.**
Basement:		1,765 sq. ft.
Garage:		484 sq. ft.
Storage area:		44 sq. ft.

Exterior Wall Framing: 2x6

Foundation options:
Standard basement.
Crawlspace.
Slab.
(Foundation & framing conversion diagram available — see order form.)

Blueprint Price Code: C

Plan E-2307

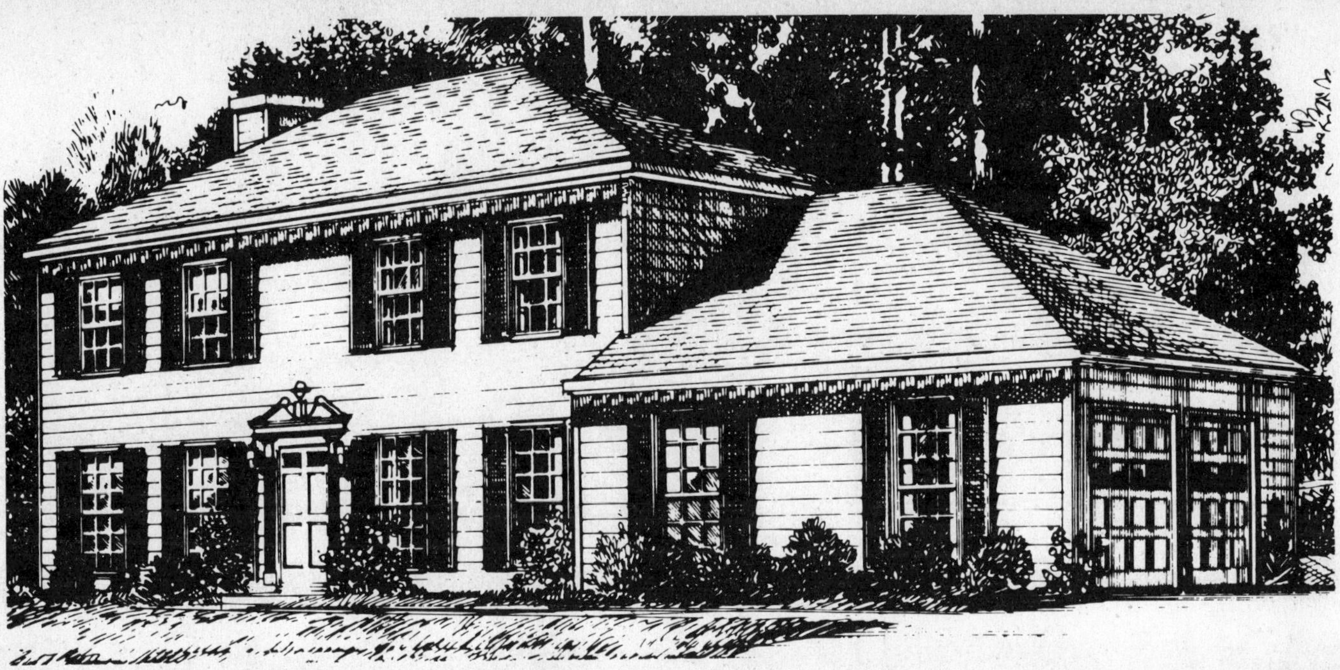

Time-Tested Traditional Includes Deluxe Master Suite

This 2,360 square foot traditional design features a master suite with a walk-in closet as well as a deluxe compartmentalized bath with another walk-in closet, linen closet, double vanity, vaulted ceiling, large glass area, garden tub and separate shower stall. Two additional bedrooms with ample closets and a second full bath and linen closet are included on the 1,146 square foot upper floor.

The formal foyer is flanked by a dining room on one side and a study on the other. Behind the dining room is a U-shaped kitchen with breakfast bay. Double doors onto the rear patio, a raised-hearth fireplace, a half bath and a coat closet are included in the living room. The large utility room behind the garage completes the 1,214 square foot mainfloor.

Multi-paned windows, shutters, lap siding and a formal entrance combine for a traditional exterior.

First floor:	1,214 sq. ft.
Second floor:	1,146 sq. ft.
Total living area: (Not counting basement or garage)	2,360 sq. ft.

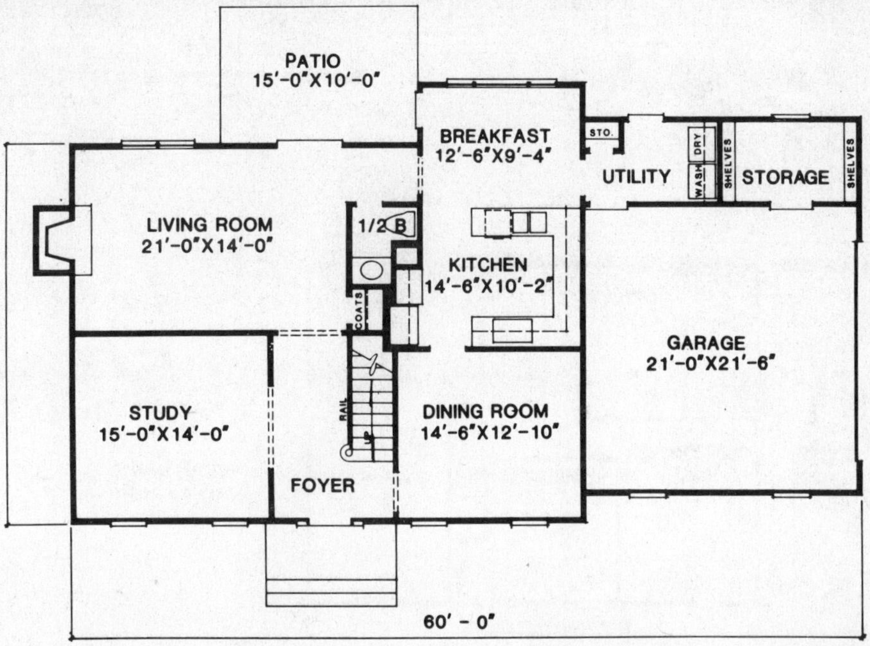

FIRST FLOOR

Specify basement or crawlspace foundation.

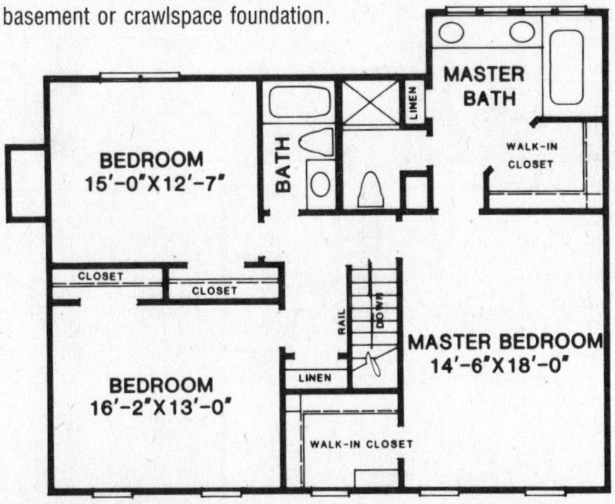

SECOND FLOOR

Blueprint Price Code C

Plan C-8350

TO ORDER THIS BLUEPRINT, CALL TOLL-FREE 1-800-547-5570

(prices and details on pp. 12-15.)

Classic Styling for Exceptional Plan

An appealing exterior is accented by the second floor overhang and gabled windows. Inside, a snack counter divides the U-shaped kitchen and breakfast area. Note the step down into the sunken family room with its brick fireplace.

A powder room and mud room in the entry from the garage allows for clean-up before entering main living area.

The master suite is enhanced by a large walk-in closet and deluxe bath with corner deck, tub and double vanity.

Three additional bedrooms, two with walk-in closets, complete this exceptional layout.

First floor: 1,212 sq. ft.

Second floor: 1,160 sq. ft.

Total living area: 2,372 sq. ft.
(Not counting basement or garage)

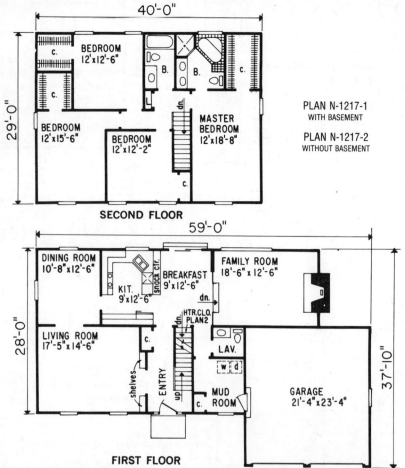

PLAN N-1217-1
WITH BASEMENT

PLAN N-1217-2
WITHOUT BASEMENT

Blueprint Price Code C

Plans N-1217-1 & -2

A Horizontal Emphasis

- A metal roof with 4' overhangs offer this unique home energy savings and distinction; a horizontal emphasis is created with the use of blocks.
- The foyer opens to a spacious living and dining room arrangement with see-thru fireplace.
- The family room, on the other side, has vaulted ceiling and rear window wall overlooking the patio.
- The island kitchen is open to the family room and breakfast nook, which offers a second fireplace.
- The main-floor master suite features his 'n her walk-in closets, access to the adjoining patio and a luxury bath.
- Two additional bedrooms share the upper level.

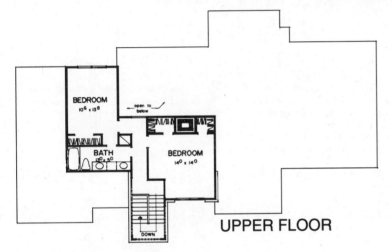

UPPER FLOOR

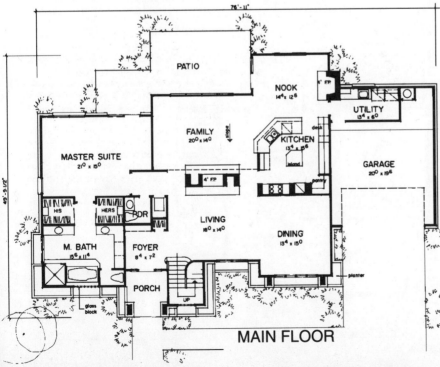

MAIN FLOOR

Plan DW-2394

Plan DW-2394	
Bedrooms: 3	**Baths:** 2 ½
Space:	
Upper floor	501 sq. ft.
Main floor	1,893 sq. ft.
Total Living Area	**2,394 sq. ft.**
Basement	1,893 sq. ft.
Garage	390 sq. ft.
Exterior Wall Framing	2x4
Foundation options:	
Standard Basement	
Crawlspace	
Slab	
(Foundation & framing conversion diagram available—see order form.)	
Blueprint Price Code	C

Master Suite Features Luxurious Bath

This lovely French Provincial design features a master suite with a deluxe compartmentalized bath which includes a vaulted ceiling with sky lights, garden tub, shower, linen closet and a separate dressing room with double vanity and large walk-in closet. Two additional bedrooms with ample closet space share a second compartmentalized bath.

Living and dining rooms are located to the side of the formal foyer. The family room features a raised hearth fireplace and double doors leading onto a screened-in back porch. A U-shaped kitchen with an island counter opens to the breakfast bay allowing more casual living. Fixed stairs in the family room provide access to attic storage above.

Also included in the 2,400 sq. ft. of heated living area is a utility room with half bath.

Total living area: 2,400 sq. ft.
(Not counting basement or garage)

Specify crawlspace, basement or slab foundation when ordering.

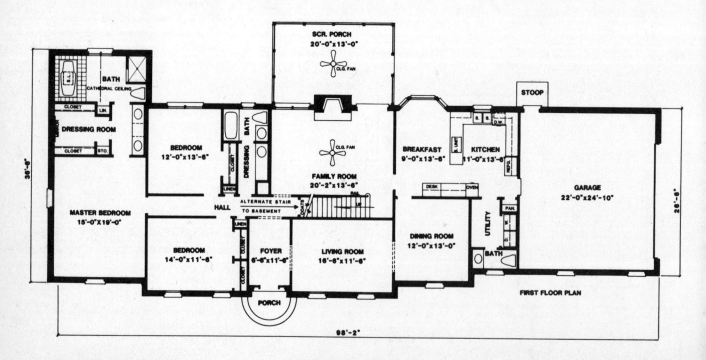

Blueprint Price Code C
Plan C-8363

UPPER FLOOR

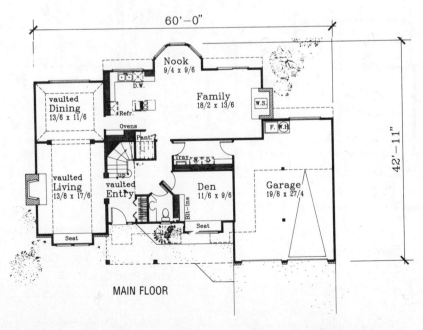

MAIN FLOOR

Old-Fashioned Charm

- A trio of dormers add old-fashioned charm to this modern design.
- Living and dining rooms both offer vaulted ceilings and flow together for feeling of spaciousness.
- The open kitchen/nook/family room arrangement features a sunny alcove, walk-in pantry and a wood stove.
- Master suite includes walk-in closet and deluxe bath with spa tub and shower.

Plan CDG-2004

Bedrooms: 3	Baths: 2½
Space:	
Upper floor:	928 sq. ft.
Main floor:	1,317 sq. ft.
Bonus area:	192 sq. ft.
Total living area:	2,437 sq. ft.
Basement:	780 sq. ft.
Garage:	537 sq. ft.
Exterior Wall Framing:	2x6

Foundation options:
Partial daylight basement
Crawlspace
(Foundation & framing conversion diagram available — see order form.)

Blueprint Price Code:	C

Plan CDG-2004

Panoramic Porch

- A gracious, ornate rounded front porch and a two-story turreted bay lend a Victorian charm to this home.
- A two-story foyer with round-top transom windows and plant ledge above greets guests at the entry.
- The living room enjoys a panoramic view overlooking the front porch and yard.
- The formal dining room and den each feature a bay window for added style.
- The kitchen/breakfast room incorporates an angled island cooktop, from which the sunken family room with corner fireplace can be enjoyed.
- The three bedrooms and two full baths upstairs are highlighted by a stunning master suite. The master bath offers a quaint octagonal sitting area within the turret bay.

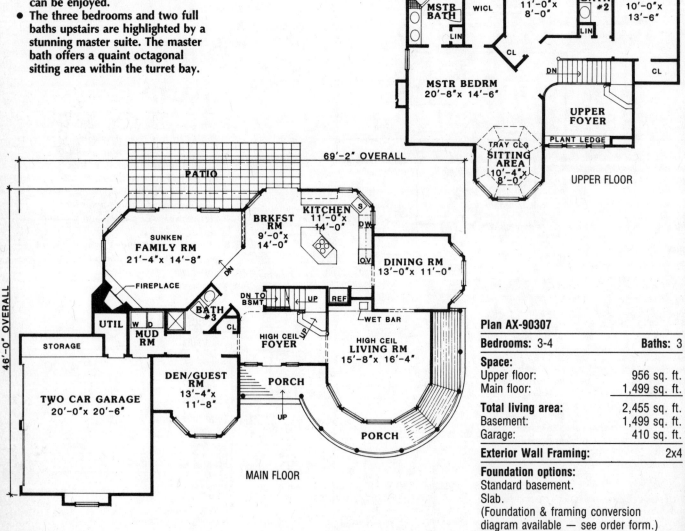

UPPER FLOOR

MAIN FLOOR

Plan AX-90307

Bedrooms: 3-4	Baths: 3
Space:	
Upper floor:	956 sq. ft.
Main floor:	1,499 sq. ft.
Total living area:	**2,455 sq. ft.**
Basement:	1,499 sq. ft.
Garage:	410 sq. ft.
Exterior Wall Framing:	2x4

Foundation options:
Standard basement.
Slab.
(Foundation & framing conversion diagram available — see order form.)

Blueprint Price Code:	C

Plan AX-90307

Elegantly Different

Arched brickwork and windows lend a uniqueness and elegance that is immediately noticeable in this three-bedroom home.

A covered entry leads to a vaulted foyer opening to the formal living and dining room area. Here you'll find large windows and a vaulted ceiling that add a light airiness to the room, balanced by the coziness of a warm fireplace.

With skylights and a windowed nook opening onto the back deck, the kitchen is bright and sunny — perfect for those who enjoy cooking and entertaining. An angled island with convenient eating bar highlight the kitchen, along with a handy pantry and a centrally located desk that is ideal for household planning. A generous family room with a practical wood stove off the kitchen is certain to make this part of your home the center of family activity.

A hallway from the garage passes a utility room designed with the emphasis on "utility." The counter space lends itself to many projects, and a built-in ironing board provides convenience and saves space.

The secluded study on the lower level provides a place for work or quiet leisure activities.

Upstairs, the two children's bedrooms show their individuality — one with a window seat and the other with a bay window. The master bedroom is a treat, with an octagonal sitting area to capture the view, a large walk-in closet, and a bath area with a step-up spa tub and double vanity.

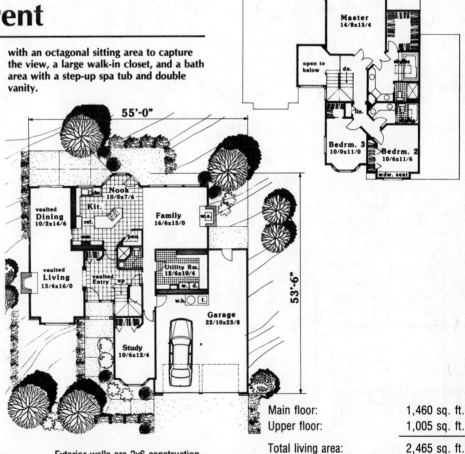

Exterior walls are 2x6 construction.

Please specify basement or crawlspace foundation when ordering.

Main floor:	1,460 sq. ft.
Upper floor:	1,005 sq. ft.
Total living area: (Not counting garage)	2,465 sq. ft.

Blueprint Price Code C

Plan R-2117

A Pillar of Success

- A stunning two-story entry porch with heavy support pillars creates a look of success for this exciting new design.
- Once inside the entry, there is a wide-open view ahead into the vaulted Great Room, with dramatic angled, two-story window-walls. The Great Room also features a fireplace and TV niche.
- The galley kitchen has a cooktop island with snack counter and overlooks the dining bay and view deck beyond ample windows.
- The main-floor master suite has a trayed ceiling, angled windows, private deck access, dressing area, and a private bath with separate tub and shower.
- A main-floor den/guest room has a vaulted ceiling, private deck access, and is just steps away from a full bath. Two more bedrooms, a full bath, and a hobby area are upstairs.

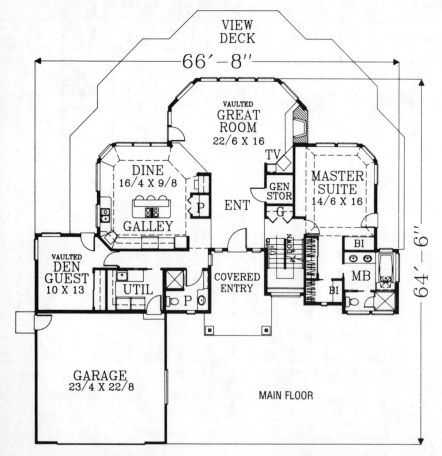

MAIN FLOOR

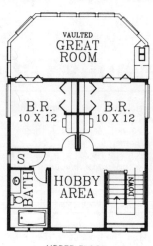

UPPER FLOOR

Plan S-32190

Bedrooms: 3-4	Baths: 3
Space:	
Upper floor	606 sq. ft.
Main floor	1,865 sq. ft.
Total Living Area	**2,471 sq. ft.**
Basement	1,865 sq. ft.
Garage	529 sq. ft.
Exterior Wall Framing	2x6

Foundation options:
Standard Basement
Crawlspace
(Foundation & framing conversion diagram available—see order form.)

Blueprint Price Code	C

Plan S-32190

For A Strong First Impression

This home is designed for those who like to make a strong first impression. The front entryway soars, with skylights providing the first glimpse of even more open, light-filled space to come.

This home has a convenient lower level master bedroom with its own private bath and large walk-in closet. A centrally located family room has a bar counter and fireplace. Also downstairs is a sizable kitchen and dining room with French doors and a double-bow window enhancing its charm. A spacious utility room connected to the garage is a necessary convenience.

A second floor with dramatic views of the downstairs on almost every step of the upstairs passage bridge will delight you. Also upstairs is something every modern family should have — its own computer room complete with built-in desk. One bedroom has a deck off the side and both have more than enough storage space.

This two-story contemporary has 2,508 sq. ft. of living area, and an optional side- or front-entry double-car garage. Exterior walls feature 2x6 construction for energy efficiency.

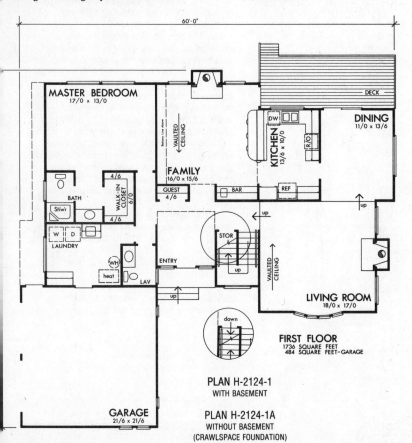

FIRST FLOOR
1736 SQUARE FEET
484 SQUARE FEET-GARAGE

PLAN H-2124-1
WITH BASEMENT

PLAN H-2124-1A
WITHOUT BASEMENT
(CRAWLSPACE FOUNDATION)

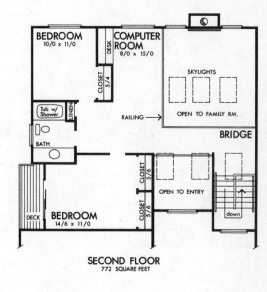

SECOND FLOOR
772 SQUARE FEET

First floor:	1,736 sq. ft.
Second floor:	772 sq. ft.
Total living area:	2,508 sq. ft.
(Not counting basement or garage)	

Blueprint Price Code D

Plans H-2124-1 & -1A

TO ORDER THIS BLUEPRINT, CALL TOLL-FREE 1-800-547-5570
(prices and details on pp. 12-15.)

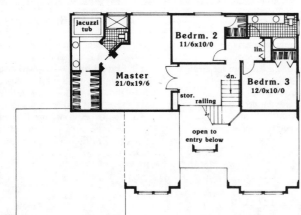

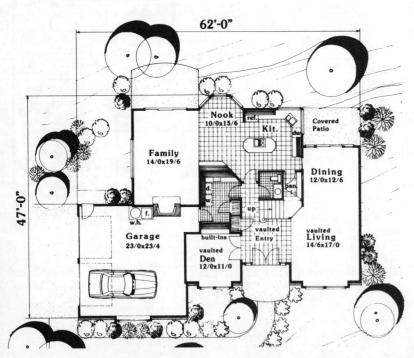

Exterior walls are 2x6 construction.

Timeless Beauty

You can look, but it will be hard to find a home that presents itself in as grand a manner as this home does, all in slightly over 2,500 sq. ft.

From the brick facade to the peaked windows reflecting the vaulted ceilings of both den and living room, this home bespeaks class!

Double doors enhance the volume of both entry and den, lending an additional touch of elegance in the process.

The head chef will find little to complain about in the layout of the kitchen, which lies conveniently between the dining room and nook. With features including a walk-in pantry and cooking island, this space will be a joy to use for years to come.

To highlight the upper floor, an open landing has been incorporated at the top of the stairs, which provides an interesting perspective of the entry below, and also serves as a foyer to the generous master suite.

Entering through double doors, we find among the master suite's many amenities a sitting alcove with view, walk-in closet, compartmentalized bathroom with double vanity, and a splendid spa for a relaxing soak at the end of a hard day.

With all these features it would be hard to understand how someone could resist the timeless beauty of this magnificent home.

PLAN R-2095
WITHOUT BASEMENT
(CRAWLSPACE FOUNDATION)

Main floor:	1,510 sq. ft.
Upper floor:	1,000 sq. ft.
Total living area: (Not counting garage)	2,510 sq. ft.

Blueprint Price Code D
Plan R-2095

Simple, Efficient, Spacious

First floor:	1,702 sq. ft.
Second floor:	816 sq. ft.
Total living area: (Not counting basement or garage)	2,518 sq. ft.

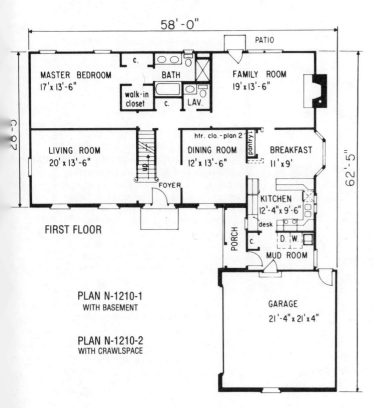

58'-0"

PATIO

MASTER BEDROOM
17' x 13'-6"

c.

BATH

walk-in closet

c.   LAV.

FAMILY ROOM
19' x 13'-6"

LIVING ROOM
20' x 13'-6"

DINING ROOM
12' x 13'-6"

htr. clo. - plan 2

pantry

BREAKFAST
11' x 9'

FOYER

62'-5"

KITCHEN
12'-4" x 9'-6"

desk

D   W.

PORCH

c.

MUD ROOM

FIRST FLOOR

PLAN N-1210-1
WITH BASEMENT

PLAN N-1210-2
WITH CRAWLSPACE

GARAGE
21'-4" x 21'-4"

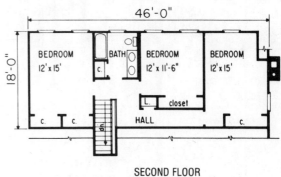

46'-0"

18'-0"

BEDROOM
12' x 15'

BATH

c.

BEDROOM
12' x 11'-6"

BEDROOM
12' x 15'

closet

HALL

c.   c.

dn.

c.

SECOND FLOOR

TO ORDER THIS BLUEPRINT,
CALL TOLL-FREE 1-800-547-5570
(prices and details on pp. 12-15.) **169**

Mediterranean Dream Home

- Brilliant columns and spectacular window treatments give a stately look to this impressive Mediterranean.
- The foyer, dining and living rooms share a 14' ceiling.
- The large, central family room ahead offers an entertainment center, fireplace and sliders to the rear patio.
- The generous kitchen and breakfast area also share a grand rear view.
- Three bedrooms are found on one wing with convenient laundry facilities and two baths, one also accessible from the patio.
- The master bedroom has private patio access, a huge walk-in closet and a luxury bath with step-up, corner tub and a separate walk-in shower.

Plan HDS-90-809

Bedrooms: 4	Baths: 3
Space:	
Main floor	2,553 sq. ft.
Total Living Area	**2,553 sq. ft.**
Garage	476 sq. ft.
Exterior Wall Framing	2x4
Foundation options:	
Slab	
(Foundation & framing conversion diagram available—see order form.)	
Blueprint Price Code	D

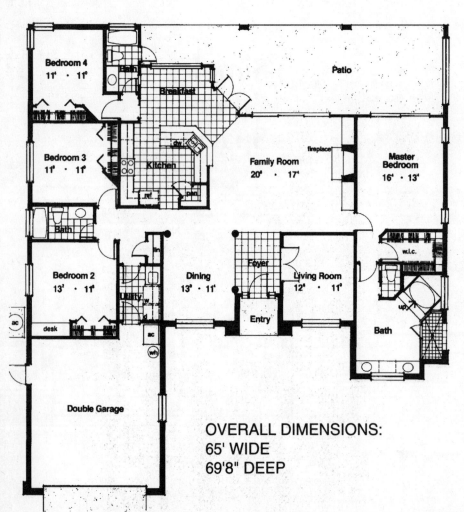

Bedroom 4
11⁴ · 11⁰

Bath

Breakfast

Patio

Bedroom 3
11⁴ · 11⁰

Kitchen

dw

ref

pan

Family Room
20⁴ · 17⁴

fireplace

Master Bedroom
16⁴ · 13⁴

Bath

Bedroom 2
13² · 11⁴

desk

UTILITY

w

d

ln

Dining
13⁰ · 11⁴

Foyer

Entry

Living Room
12⁸ · 11⁰

w.i.c.

up

Bath

ac

sc

wh

Double Garage

OVERALL DIMENSIONS:
65' WIDE
69'8" DEEP

Plan HDS-90-809

Traditional Design for Sloping Lot

- A striking traditional design, this residence offers 2,899 square feet of gracious living space. The high arched windows and the elaborately glassed front door give this home an exceptional curb appeal for any high-income neighborhood.
- The high vaulted entry lends further traditional atmosphere to the interior of the home, with double curved stairs leading to the upper level. Passing through the foyer, you enter the formal living and dining areas. These rooms are view-oriented to the rear of the home.
- A special family area is located to the right of the dining room. The family room, nook and kitchen can be completely closed off from the more formal part of the home or opened up for easy guest circulation when

entertaining. A den off the living room provides privacy when needed for the older family members. The vaulted arch window gives this room a special touch of elegance.
- The upstairs includes two secondary bedrooms, a bonus room and a luxurious master suite. Even the second bath has special features, such as double vanities and a specialty tub.
- Plentiful storage and large closets are available in all of the bedrooms. The bonus area may be utilized for additional storage space, or as a studio, hobby room or fourth bedroom.

Plan SD-8815

Bedrooms: 4	Baths: 2
Living Area:	
Upper floor	1,140 sq. ft.
Main floor	1,356 sq. ft.
Bonus room	403 sq. ft.
Total Living Area:	**2,899 sq. ft.**
Standard basement	1,356 sq. ft.
Garage	575 sq. ft.
Exterior Wall Framing:	2x6

Foundation Options:

Standard basement
Crawlspace
(Typical foundation & framing conversion diagram available—see order form.)

BLUEPRINT PRICE CODE:	D

UPPER FLOOR

- DECK
- BEDRM-3 12/0 X11/0
- BEDRM-2 12/0X 11/0
- MASTER SUITE 16/6 X16/0
- UTIL.
- DN.
- DN.
- OPEN
- BONUS ROOM

MAIN FLOOR

59'-0

46'-0

- PATIO
- PATIO
- LIVING 17/0 X15/0
- DINING 12/0 X15/6
- FAM. RM. 18/6 X14/6
- BAR
- DN.
- KITCHEN 15/6 X9/0
- OPTIONAL STAIRS
- ENTRY 17/0 X11/6
- UP
- LIBRARY BEDRM-4 11/0X12/0
- DN.
- 3-BAY GARAGE 29/6 X19/6
- DN.

Plan SD-8815

TO ORDER THIS BLUEPRINT,
CALL TOLL-FREE 1-800-547-5570
(prices and details on pp. 12-15.) **171**

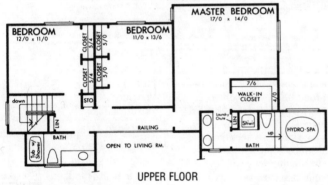

UPPER FLOOR

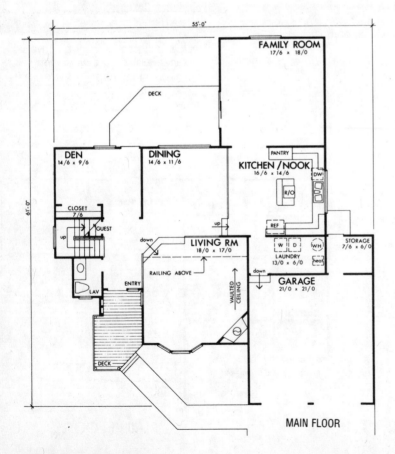

MAIN FLOOR

Grace and Prestige

- Dormer and bay windows and a hipped roof give this home a modern, yet traditional look.
- Tri-level room arrangement features a sunken living room, step-up U-shaped kitchen with island work center, and a second floor sleeping section with hallway balcony overlooking the living room.
- Living room boasts an entrance bordered by 3-ft. railings, corner fireplace, and vaulted ceilings.
- Master suite includes a convenient laundry chute, double-sink vanity, and a relaxing hydro-spa.

Plan H-2123-1A

Bedrooms: 3	Baths: 2½
Space:	
Upper floor:	989 sq. ft.
Main floor:	1,597 sq. ft.
Total living area:	2,586 sq. ft.
Garage:	441 sq. ft.
Storage:	45 sq. ft.
Exterior Wall Framing:	2x6

Foundation options:
Crawlspace only.
(Foundation & framing conversion diagram available — see order form.)

Blueprint Price Code:	D

Plan H-2123-1A

Spectacular Rear Views

- Dramatic rear living areas include a combination living and dining room with a fireplace and columns; a sun room separates the dining room from the attached rear deck.
- The peninsula kitchen, the bayed morning area and the family room offer a casual atmosphere with a fireplace

and window walls.
- The master bedroom also has a rear window wall and a private bath with a garden tub and a separate shower.
- A second main-floor bedroom has a nearby bath; the two remaining bedrooms are located on the upper level.

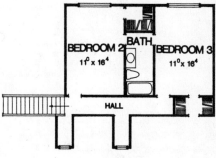

UPPER FLOOR

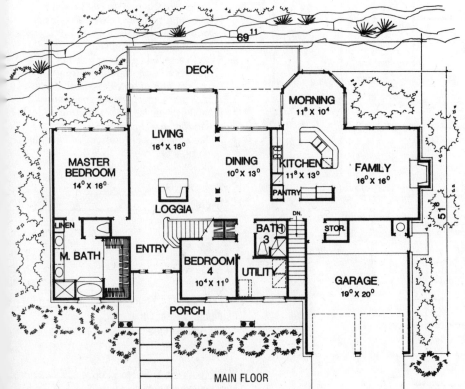

MAIN FLOOR

Plan DD-2541

Plan DD-2541	
Bedrooms: 4	**Baths:** 3
Space:	
Upper floor	588 sq. ft.
Main floor	2,011 sq. ft.
Total Living Area	**2,599 sq. ft.**
Basement	2,011 sq. ft.
Garage	380 sq. ft.
Exterior Wall Framing	2x4
Foundation options:	
Standard Basement	
Crawlspace	
Slab	
(Foundation & framing conversion diagram available—see order form.)	
Blueprint Price Code	D

A Ranch with Distinction

- A covered front porch supported by pillars gives a formal appearance to this distinguished one-story.
- Flanking the foyer is a study or fourth bedroom and formal living and dining rooms.
- The big family room at the rear shares views of a covered porch with the adjoining breakfast room; the family room also has a sloped ceiling centered over a warming fireplace.
- A modern, island kitchen sits between the morning room and the dining room for convenient service to both. A half-bath and laundry room are nearby.
- A 10-foot-high gambrel ceiling and rear window wall highlight the generous-sized master bedroom. Its private bath features his 'n her vanities, walk-in closets and a garden tub.

Plan DD-2606

Bedrooms: 3-4	Baths: 2½
Space:	
Main floor	2,606 sq. ft.
Total Living Area	**2,606 sq. ft.**
Basement	2,606 sq. ft.
Garage	393 sq. ft
Exterior Wall Framing	2x4

Foundation options:
Standard Basement
Crawlspace
Slab
(Foundation & framing conversion diagram available—see order form.)

Blueprint Price Code

Floor Plan

83³

COVERED PORCH

FAMILY 18⁴ X 22⁰

BEDROOM 2 14⁶ X 14⁰

MASTER BEDROOM 13⁸ X 21⁶

STORAGE

1/2 BATH

UTILITY

MORNING 10⁰ X 14⁰

BATH 2

49³

ISLAND KITCHEN 12⁴ X 13⁴

GARAGE

LIVING 14⁰ X 18⁴

FOYER

M. BATH

PANTRY

DINING 12⁸ X 13⁵

STUDY / BEDROOM 4 11⁰ X 14⁰

BEDROOM 3 13⁶ X 11⁶

PORCH

Plan DD-2606

Raised Living for Heightened Views

- Picture your new home nestled into an upsloping lot with an entire living room window wall looking back to your panoramic view.
- The raised main level gives a better view of the surroundings, without being blocked by a road, cars, or low trees. The resulting larger windows and walk-out on the lower level avoid a basement feeling in the rec room.
- The sunken living room, at the top of a half-flight of stairs, has a dramatic cathedral ceiling highlighted by angled transom windows.
- A see-through fireplace separates the living room from the formal dining room, also with a cathedral ceiling.
- The kitchen incorporates a spacious breakfast bay overlooking the rear deck.
- The main floor also houses three bedrooms and two full baths.

Plan AX-8486-A

Bedrooms: 3	Baths: 2

Space:	
Main floor:	1,630 sq. ft.
Basement & rec room:	978 sq. ft.

Total living area:	2,608 sq. ft.
Garage:	400 sq. ft.
Storage area:	110 sq. ft.

Exterior Wall Framing:	2x4

Foundation options:
Daylight basement.
(Foundation & framing conversion diagram available — see order form.)

Blueprint Price Code:	D

Plan AX-8486-A

TO ORDER THIS BLUEPRINT, CALL TOLL-FREE 1-800-547-5570
(prices and details on pp. 12-15.)

Well-Planned Walkout

- A dramatic double-back stair atrium descending from the Great Room to the bonus family room below ties the main floor design to the walkout lower level.
- A traditional exterior leads into a dramatic, open-feeling interior.
- The vaulted Great Room and dining room are separated by stylish columns.
- A see-thru fireplace is shared by the Great Room and the exciting kitchen with octagonal breakfast bay.
- A double-doored den/guest room opens off the Great Room.
- The spacious main floor master suite includes a huge walk-in closet and lavish master bath.

Plan AG-9105

Bedrooms: 3-4	Baths: 2½

Space:

Main floor:	1,838 sq. ft.
Daylight basement:	800 sq. ft.
Total living area:	2,638 sq. ft.
Unfinished basement area:	1,038 sq. ft.
Garage:	462 sq. ft.

Exterior Wall Framing:	2x6

Foundation options:
Daylight basement.
(Foundation & framing conversion diagram available — see order form.)

Blueprint Price Code:	D

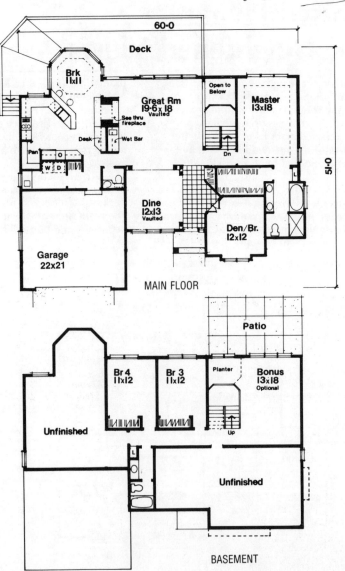

MAIN FLOOR

BASEMENT

TO ORDER THIS BLUEPRINT,
CALL TOLL-FREE 1-800-547-5570
176 (prices and details on pp. 12-15.)

Plan AG-9105

UPPER FLOOR

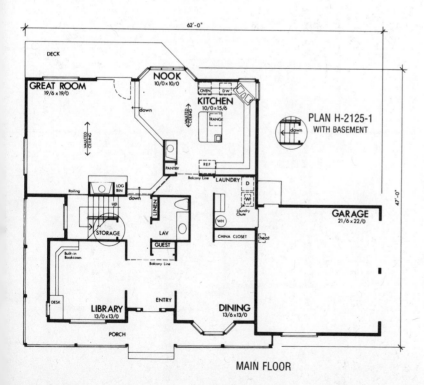

MAIN FLOOR

Delightful Blend of Old and New

- A contemporary floor plan is hidden in a traditional farmhouse exterior.
- Vaulted entrance is open to the upper level; adjacent open stairwell is lit by a semi-circular window.
- French doors open into a library with built-in bookcase and deck.
- Sunken Great Room features a fireplace, vaulted ceiling open to the upstairs balcony, and French doors leading to a backyard deck.
- Roomy kitchen has center cooking island, eating bar, and attached nook with corner fireplace.
- Upper level has reading area and exciting master suite with hydro-spa.

Plans H-2125-1 & -1A

Bedrooms: 3	Baths: 2½

Space:

Upper floor:	1,105 sq. ft.
Main floor:	1,554 sq. ft.

Total living area:	**2,659 sq. ft.**
Basement:	approx. 1,554 sq. ft.
Garage:	475 sq. ft.

Exterior Wall Framing:	2x6

Foundation options:
Standard basement (Plan H-2125-1).
Crawlspace (Plan H-2125-1A).
(Foundation & framing conversion diagram available — see order form.)

Blueprint Price Code:	D

Plans H-2125-1 & -1A

Bordered in Brick

- Decorative brick borders, front columns and arched windows give a classy look to this two-story palace.
- The entry is flanked by formal dining and living rooms, both with dramatic front windows.
- A fireplace warms the massive family room that stretches to the morning room and the kitchen at the rear of the home. The bayed morning room offers access to an attached deck; the kitchen has an island worktop.
- A unique sun room also overlooks the deck.
- Windows also surround the master bedroom, which has a large bath.
- Three nice-sized bedrooms share a second full bath on the upper level.

Plan DD-2689

Bedrooms: 4	Baths: 2 ½
Space:	
Upper floor	755 sq. ft.
Main floor	1,934 sq. ft.
Total Living Area	**2,689 sq. ft.**
Basement	1,934 sq. ft.
Garage	436 sq. ft.
Exterior Wall Framing	2x4

Foundation options:

Standard Basement

Crawlspace

Slab

(Foundation & framing conversion diagram available—see order form.)

Blueprint Price Code	D

UPPER FLOOR

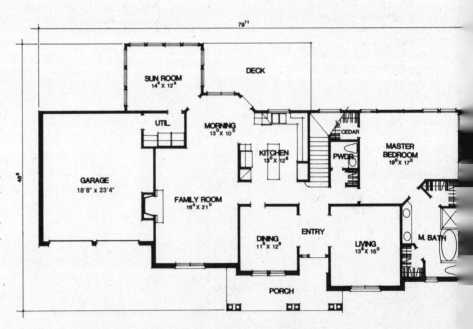

MAIN FLOOR

Plan DD-2689

Classic Cape Cod

- An isolated downstairs master suite with three bedrooms up is just one of the keynotes of this sophisticated design.
- Attention-getting dormer windows and a charming front porch distinguish the exterior.
- The spacious first floor offers formal living and dining rooms as well as a spacious family living area.
- The skylighted, vaulted family room has a fireplace flanked by windows and French doors. A half-bath is close by.
- The sunny breakfast room has a rear window wall, and the kitchen has an angled counter to keep the cook in touch with family activities. A laundry is accessible from both the kitchen and the garage.
- The deluxe master bedroom suite has a vaulted ceiling, two walk-in closets, a shower and a separate commode area, not to mention a skylighted spa tub and dual-sink vanity.
- The three bedrooms upstairs share another full bath and a view to the family room below.

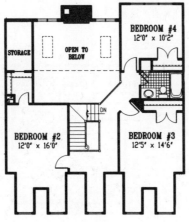

UPPER FLOOR

Plan CH-445-A	
Bedrooms: 4	Baths: 2 ½
Space:	
Upper floor	988 sq. ft.
Main floor	1,707 sq. ft.
Total Living Area	**2,695 sq. ft.**
Basement	1,118 sq. ft.
Garage	802 sq. ft.
Exterior Wall Framing	2x4
Foundation options:	
Daylight Basement	
Standard Basement	
(Foundation & framing conversion diagram	
available—see order form.)	
Blueprint Price Code	D

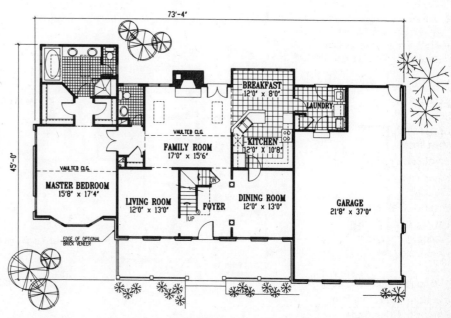

MAIN FLOOR

Plan CH-445-A

Tudor Style Blends Wood, Brick & Stone

- A warm combination of textures and finishes lends this exterior extra appeal.
- The interior offers plenty of space for a big, busy family.
- The large living room includes an impressive fireplace, and joins the dining room to create a super space for entertaining.
- The spacious family room also includes a fireplace, and is a step down from the dinette/kitchen area.
- A library off the impressive foyer would be great for a home office.
- The master suite, upstairs, provides a large sleeping area plus a luxurious private bath and large walk-in closet.

Plan A-130

Bedrooms: 4	Baths: 2½

Space:	
Upper floor:	1,305 sq. ft.
Main floor:	1,502 sq. ft.

Total living area:	2,807 sq. ft.
Basement:	1,502 sq. ft.
Garage:	576 sq. ft

Exterior Wall Framing:	2x

Foundation options:
Standard basement only.
(Foundation & framing conversion diagram available — see order form.)

Blueprint Price Code:	

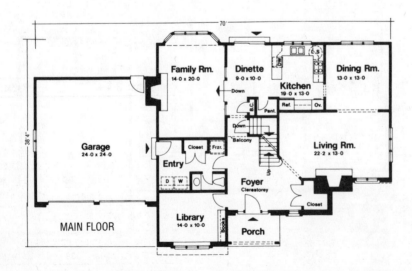

UPPER FLOOR

MAIN FLOOR

TO ORDER THIS BLUEPRINT,
CALL TOLL-FREE 1-800-547-5570
180 (prices and details on pp. 12-15.)

Plan A-130

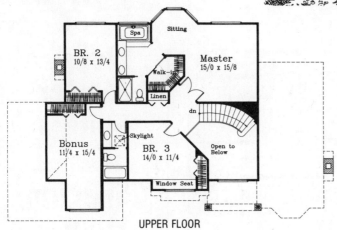

UPPER FLOOR

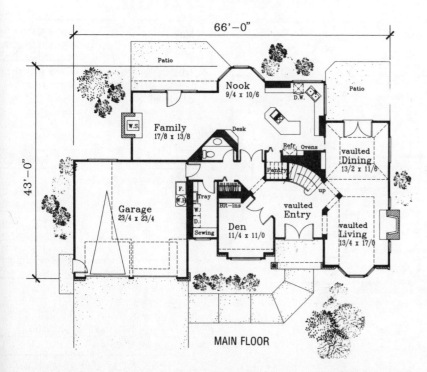

MAIN FLOOR

Impressive and Distinguished

- An impressive vaulted entrance with double doors and an eye-catching transom window greets visitors.
- Inside, the vaulted living room is highlighted by a cheerful bay window and fireplace flanked by side windows.
- In the 10' high vaulted dining room, you'll find built-in cabinetry and French doors which lead out to the patio.
- The kitchen features an angled island for added efficiency and counter space, plus corner windows which illuminate the sink area.
- Take special note of the large master bedroom with its alcove sitting area and relaxing spa tub.

Plan CDG-2007

Bedrooms: 3-4 +	Baths: 2½
Space:	
Upper floor:	1,036 sq. ft.
Main floor:	1,563 sq. ft.
Bonus area:	225 sq. ft.
Total living area:	2,824 sq. ft.
Garage:	841 sq. ft.
Exterior Wall Framing:	2x6

Foundation options:
Crawlspace.
(Foundation & framing conversion diagram available — see order form.)

Blueprint Price Code:	D

Plan CDG-2007

Deluxe Master Suite in Spacious Home

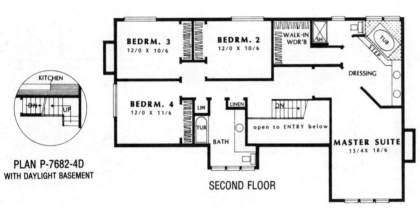

BEDRM. 3
12/0 X 10/6

BEDRM. 2
12/0 X 10/6

WALK-IN WDR'B

SH

TUB
STEP

DRESSING

BEDRM. 4
12/0 X 11/6

LIN

LINEN

DN

TUB

BATH

open to ENTRY below

MASTER SUITE
13/4 X 18/6

KITCHEN

DN   UP

PLAN P-7682-4D
WITH DAYLIGHT BASEMENT

SECOND FLOOR

Main floor:	1,526 sq. ft
Second floor:	1,314 sq. ft
Total living area: (Not counting basement or garage)	2,840 sq. ft
Basement level:	1,526 sq. ft

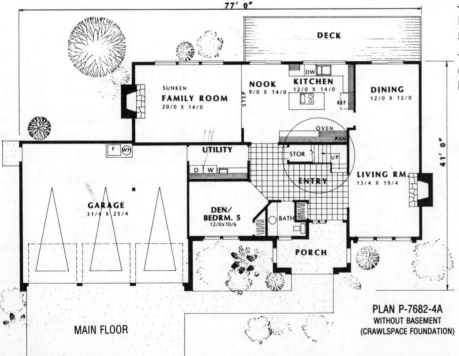

77' 0"

41' 0"

DECK

SUNKEN
FAMILY ROOM
20/0 X 14/0

NOOK
9/0 X 14/0

DW

KITCHEN
12/0 X 14/0

REF

DINING
12/0 X 12/0

STEP

F   WH

UTILITY

OVEN

PAN

STOR

UP

D   W

GARAGE
31/4 X 25/4

**DEN/
BEDRM. 5**
12/0x10/6

ENTRY

BATH

LIVING RM.
13/4 X 19/4

PORCH

MAIN FLOOR

PLAN P-7682-4A
WITHOUT BASEMENT
(CRAWLSPACE FOUNDATION)

Blueprint Price Code D
Plans P-7682-4A & -4D

A Distinguished Look

- Towering columns flank the entrance of this distinguished brick two-story.
- Inside, the two-story entry with angled stairway offers a view to the living room with fireplace and arched opening and the family room on the other side with second fireplace and built-in entertainment center.
- The spacious island kitchen boasts a pantry and work area and an adjoining nook with sliders to the rear patio. A half-bath and handy laundry room is nestled between the kitchen and garage.
- A coffered ceiling hovers above the elegant master suite with private den, fireplace and master bath with walk-in closet and spa tub.
- Two secondary bedrooms share a bath built for two.

Plan U-90-204	
Bedrooms: 3	**Baths:** 2 ½
Space:	
Upper floor	1,536 sq. ft.
Main floor	1,314 sq. ft.
Total Living Area	**2,850 sq. ft.**
Basement	1,314 sq. ft.
Garage	505 sq. ft.
Exterior Wall Framing	2x6
Foundation options:	**Plan #**
Crawlspace	U-90-204-A
Standard Basement	U-90-204-B
Slab	U-90-204-C
(Foundation & framing conversion diagram available—see order form.)	
Blueprint Price Code	**D**

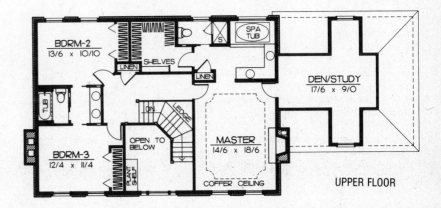

UPPER FLOOR

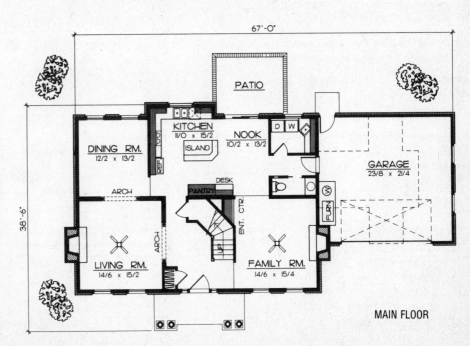

MAIN FLOOR

Plan U-90-204

Two-Story Great Room

- A large two-story Great Room, with a fireplace and sliding glass doors to a backyard deck, is the highlight of this distinguished brick home.
- The front dining room and study both feature bay windows; the study can be used as an extra bedroom or guest room.
- A second stairway off the breakfast room accesses a home office or bonus space; an optional bath could also be built in.
- The main-floor master suite offers his and hers walk-in closets, a splashy master bath, and private access to the rear deck.
- Three secondary bedrooms are located off the second-floor balcony that overlooks the Great Room and the foyer.

Plan C-9010

Bedrooms: 4-5	Baths: 2½-3½
Living Area:	
Upper floor	761 sq. ft.
Main floor	1,637 sq. ft.
Bonus room	347 sq. ft.
Optional bath and closet	106 sq. ft.
Total Living Area:	**2,851 sq. ft.**
Standard basement	1,637 sq. ft.
Garage	572 sq. ft.
Exterior Wall Framing:	2x4

Foundation Options:

Standard basement
Crawlspace
(Typical foundation & framing conversion diagram available—see order form.)

BLUEPRINT PRICE CODE: **D**

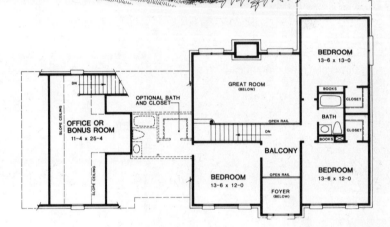

UPPER FLOOR

MAIN FLOOR

TO ORDER THIS BLUEPRINT,
CALL TOLL-FREE 1-800-547-5570
184 (prices and details on pp. 12-15.)

Plan C-9010

Grand Traditional

- Grace and grandeur sum up this four-bedroom home. The symmetrical design is set off by the center gable that draws attention to the beautiful Palladian window above the front door.
- Inside, the floor plan offers the customary formal living and dining rooms, plus a great family area overlooking the backyard.
- The family room hosts a central fireplace framed by windows. The breakfast nook has a bay window, with a French door that opens to the patio. A large picture window above the sink fills the island kitchen with light. Note the centrally located powder room and pantry closet.
- The second floor is highlighted by the super master suite, which features a tray ceiling in the sleeping area and a wonderful bath with a garden tub, dual vanities and tons of closet space.
- Three roomy bedrooms and a two more full baths put the finishing touches on this grand home.

DOUBLE GARAGE
23⁴ x 20⁴

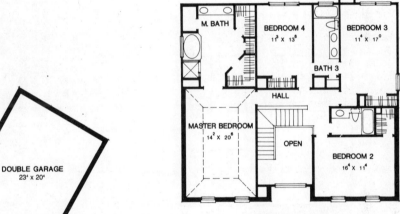

UPPER FLOOR

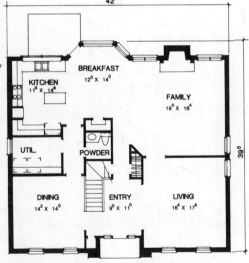

MAIN FLOOR

Plan DD-2928-A

Bedrooms: 4	**Baths:** 3½

Living Area:	
Upper floor	1,381 sq. ft.
Main floor	1,518 sq. ft.
Total Living Area:	**2,899 sq. ft.**
Standard basement	1,518 sq. ft.
Garage	474 sq. ft.
Exterior Wall Framing:	2x4

Foundation Options:
Standard basement
Crawlspace
Slab
(Typical foundation & framing conversion diagram available—see order form.)

BLUEPRINT PRICE CODE:	D

Plan DD-2928-A

TO ORDER THIS BLUEPRINT,
CALL TOLL-FREE 1-800-547-5570
(prices and details on pp. 12-15.)

Early American with Four Bedrooms

- Time-tested traditional shows the symmetry of design that keeps this style always popular.
- Basically rectangular two-story with simple, straight roofline offers big space for economical costs.
- Main floor presents spacious family room and living room.
- Large island kitchen adjoins a bright, bay-windowed dinette area.
- Formal dining room is large enough for a good-sized dinner party.
- A study behind the garage is available for an exercise or hobby room, or perhaps a home office or work room.
- Upstairs, the spacious master suite includes a deluxe bath and large walk-in closet.

Plan A-118-DS

Bedrooms: 4	Baths: 2½

Space:

Upper floor:	1,344 sq. ft.
Main floor:	1,556 sq. ft.

Total living area:	**2,900 sq. ft.**
Basement:	approx. 1,556 sq. ft.
Garage:	576 sq. ft.

Exterior Wall Framing:	2x4

Foundation options:
Standard basement only.
(Foundation & framing conversion diagram available — see order form.)

Blueprint Price Code:	D

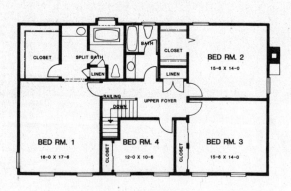

UPPER FLOOR

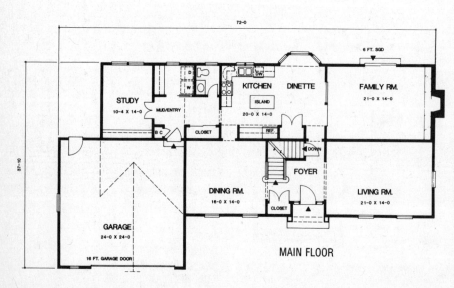

MAIN FLOOR

Plan A-118-DS

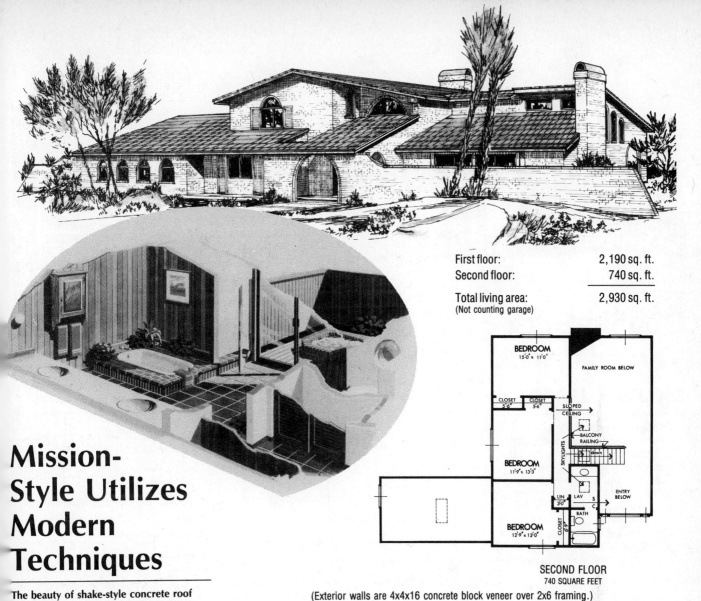

Mission-Style Utilizes Modern Techniques

The beauty of shake-style concrete roof tile is never more apparent than on a hacienda such as this where Old World heritage and charm are married to modern building methods and concepts. Concrete block veneer in the distinctive "slump block" style simulating ancient adobe bricks is the perfect companion for this beautiful roof.

Once past the garden walls and flower festooned patios, one becomes aware of modern living concepts unimagined by the conquistadors or their successors: Living and dining areas whose vaulted ceilings are softly lighted through clerestory windows high overhead; U-shaped kitchen; a marvel of electronic equipment unimagined in the days of Pancho Villa; a master bedroom suite suitable for the grandest senor or senora with 1,600 cubic feet of wardrobe space; a Roman-style walk-up bath; enclosed shower and toilet rooms; separate lavatories; and perhaps most luxurious of all, a private hydro-spa in a private corner of a private patio.

Many more areas of interest will become evident as one studies the nearly 3,000 sq. ft. of living space enclosed in this modern hacienda.

First floor: 2,190 sq. ft.
Second floor: 740 sq. ft.

Total living area: 2,930 sq. ft.
(Not counting garage)

SECOND FLOOR
740 SQUARE FEET

(Exterior walls are 4x4x16 concrete block veneer over 2x6 framing.)

(SLAB-ON-GRADE CONSTRUCTION)

MAIN FLOOR
2190 SQUARE FEET

Blueprint Price Code D
Plan H-3714-M3A

Double-Deck Veranda Adds Extra Charm

- Two levels of porches, wood columns and dormers with shutters make for an eye-catching facade.
- Inside you'll find an equally attractive and functional room arrangement.
- A central living room has fireplace and rear porch.
- The secluded master suite offers a private study through double doors and a large bath with luxury tub.

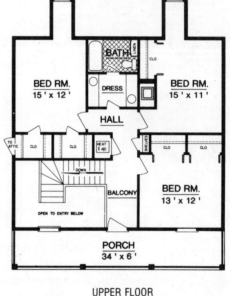

UPPER FLOOR

Plan E-2900	
Bedrooms: 4	**Baths:** 2 full, 2 half
Space:	
Upper floor:	903 sq. ft.
Main floor:	2,029 sq. ft.
Total living area:	2,932 sq. ft.
Garage and storage:	470 sq. ft.
Exterior Wall Framing:	2x6

Foundation options:
Standard basement.
Crawlspace.
Slab.
(Foundation & framing conversion diagram available — see order form.)

Blueprint Price Code:	D

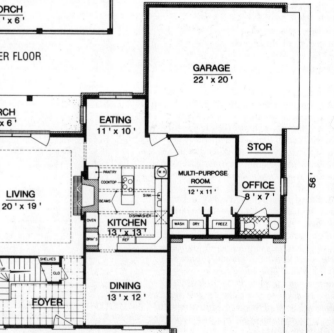

MAIN FLOOR

TO ORDER THIS BLUEPRINT, CALL TOLL-FREE 1-800-547-5570

Plan E-2900

Upper floor plan labels:

BEDROOM 15'-0" x 11'-0"
FAMILY ROOM BELOW
CLOSET 5'-6"
CLOSET 5'-6"
SLOPED CEILING
BALCONY RAILING
SKYLIGHTS
down
BEDROOM 11'-9" x 13'-3"
LIN 3'-0"
LAV
ENTRY BELOW
BATH
CLOSET 6'-0"
BEDROOM 12'-9" x 12'-0"
UPPER FLOOR

Pure Luxury in a Choice of Styles

- Southwestern colonial or Western contemporary exteriors are available when deciding if this spacious design is for you.
- Elaborate master suite features attached screened spa room, regular and walk-in closets, and luxurious bath with skylight.

- Study, large family and living room with sloped ceilings and rear patio are other points of interest.
- Three additional bedrooms make up the second level.
- The Spanish version (M2A) offers a stucco exterior and slab foundation.

Plans H-3714-1/1A/1B/M2A

Bedrooms: 4	Baths: 3

Space:	
Upper floor:	740 sq. ft.
Main floor:	2,190 sq. ft.

Total living area:	2,930 sq. ft.
Basement:	1,153 sq. ft.
Garage:	576 sq. ft.

Exterior Wall Framing:	2x6

Foundation options:
Daylight basement (Plan H-3714-1B).
Standard basement (Plan H-3714-1).
Crawlspace (Plan H-3714-1A).
Slab (Plan H-3714-M2A).
(Foundation & framing conversion diagram available — see order form.)

Blueprint Price Code:	D

Main floor plan labels:

6" HIGH SCREEN WALL
78'-0"
HYDRO SPA
BEDROOM 13'-0" x 19'-0"
FAMILY ROOM 15'-6" x 20'-6"
PATIO
SLOPED CEILING
Sh'w'r
BATH
CLOSET 5'-0"
HYDRO-SPA EQUIPMENT
UTILITY 7'-0" x 13'-6"
TUB
WH
SKYLIGHT
HEAT
GARAGE 23'-6" x 24'-6"
PULL DOWN LADDER FOR STORAGE ABOVE
W D
LAUNDRY
7'-0" LINEN
BATH
Sh'w'r
STUDY 15'-6" x 10'-0"
PLANTER
WALK-IN CLOSET 5'-6" x 7'-0"
CLOSET 8'-6"
down
up
STOR
CLOSET 4'-9"
ENTRY
KITCHEN 11'-9" x 11'-0"
DW
DINING 12'-0" x 11'-6"
REF
R/O
SLOPED CEILING
LIVING ROOM 23'-6" x 15'-0"
STOR 5'-3"
up
STORAGE
CLOSET 4'-3"
52'-0"
MAIN FLOOR

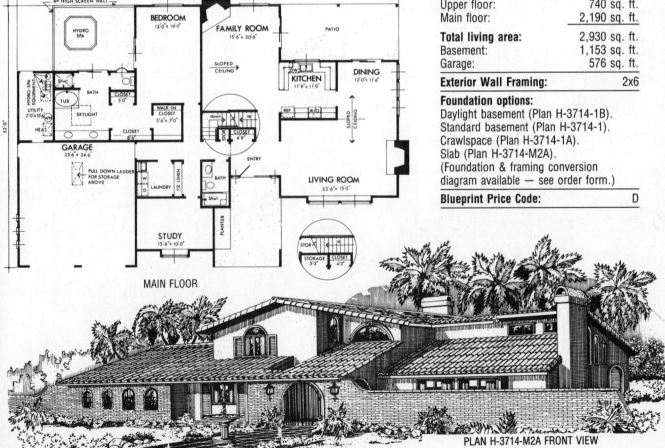

PLAN H-3714-M2A FRONT VIEW

Plans H-3714-1/1A/1B/M2A

 TO ORDER THIS BLUEPRINT, CALL TOLL-FREE 1-800-547-5570
(prices and details on pp. 12-15.) **189**

First floor: 1,756 sq. ft.
Second floor: 1,200 sq. ft.

Total living area: 2,956 sq. ft.
(Not counting basement or garage)

Country-Estate Home Designed For Indoor and Outdoor Living

- Dramatic entry portico, front door detailing and diamond-lite windows make this home unique and appealing.
- Open entry foyer with its imposing curved stairway is truly dramatic.
- Wide opening from formal dining room to spacious sunken family room with its brick fireplace allows for a view of outdoor activities.
- Wood deck off of living room.
- Angled kitchen is enhanced by the breakfast area bay window.
- Master bedroom with dramatic curved wall, deluxe bath and private balcony.

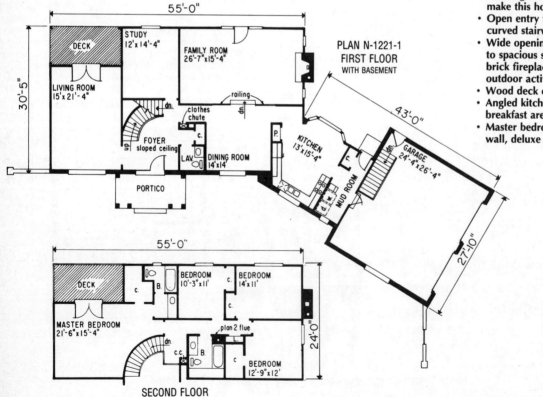

PLAN N-1221-1
FIRST FLOOR
WITH BASEMENT

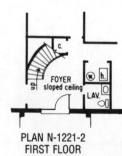

PLAN N-1221-2
FIRST FLOOR
WITH CRAWLSPACE

Blueprint Price Code D
Plans N-1221-1 & -2

Roomy Four-Bedroom French Provincial

This French Provincial design features a master suite with a spacious deluxe bath that includes a garden tub, shower, linen closet, double vanity and large walk-in closets. Three additional bedrooms share a compartmentalized bath.

The living and dining rooms are located to the side of the formal foyer. The family room and kitchen allow for more casual living. The family room features a fireplace bordered by built-in bookshelves and double doors opening to a screened-in back porch. The U-shaped kitchen hosts an island counter facing the cozy breakfast bay. Stairs off the family room lead to attic storage space above, a full basement below.

Also included in the 2,968 sq. ft. of living space is a large utility room with a half-bath. Please specify crawlspace, basement or slab foundation when ordering.

Total living area: 2,968 sq. ft.
(Not counting basement or garage)

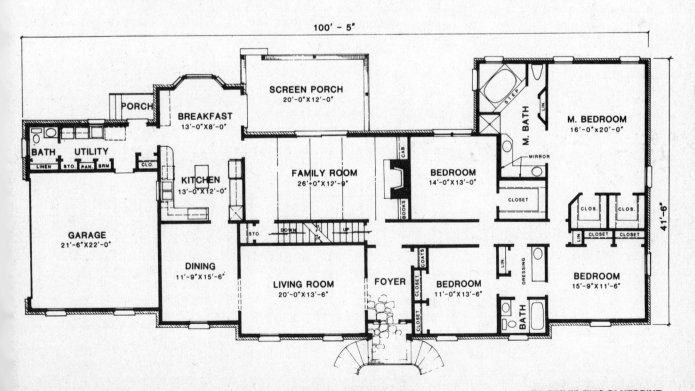

Blueprint Price Code D

Plan C-8615

Stately Elegance

- This four-bedroom, three-and-one-half-bath home incorporates many luxurious features for a home that has such a basic structure. The Georgian/Palladian design provides a very formal appearance.
- Downstairs there are two living areas, a formal colonnaded dining area, a secluded study, a powder room, an open kitchen with breakfast area, and a utility room. The family room is conveniently located for entertaining and features a fireplace and a wet bar.
- Upstairs there are four bedrooms and three full baths. The master suite includes a sumptuously large bedroom and an elegant bath. Large glass expanses on the rear of the home provide an even larger feel to the home while taking advantage of the view.

UPPER FLOOR

MAIN FLOOR

Plan DD-2968

Bedrooms: 4+	**Baths:** 3½
Space:	
Upper floor	1,382 sq. ft.
Main floor	1,586 sq. ft.
Total Living Area	**2,968 sq. ft.**
Basement	1,586 sq. ft.
Garage	521 sq. ft.
Exterior Wall Framing	2x4
Ceiling Heights	
Upper floor	9'
Main floor	9'
Foundation options:	
Standard Basement	
Crawlspace	
Slab	
(Foundation & framing conversion diagram available—see order form.)	
Blueprint Price Code	D

TO ORDER THIS BLUEPRINT,
CALL TOLL-FREE 1-800-547-5570
192 (prices and details on pp. 12-15.)

Plan DD-2968

Balanced Beauty

- Symmetry and balance are the beauty of this design. The columned and gabled wings of the home set off the center portion, which features an arched transom window, a Palladian window and a half-round window.

- Ten-foot ceilings are the rule for the first floor, with the exception of the 12-ft. ceiling in the gigantic Great Room. This dazzling room is further expanded by a rear wall lined with French doors and topped by half-round windows.

- The stairway divides the Great Room from the sunny breakfast nook and the island kitchen. The formal dining room is convenient to both the kitchen and the Great Room.

- The first-floor master bedroom is a treat, with its corner garden tub and opposite shower, double vanity and walk-in closets. A bank of French doors and windows overlooks the backyard.

- The guest bedroom has its own bath. Another bath and two bedrooms are on the upper floor, which has 9-ft. ceilings.

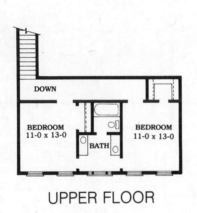

UPPER FLOOR

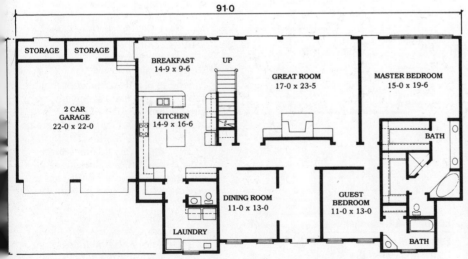

MAIN FLOOR

Plan V-2985	
Bedrooms: 4	**Baths:** 3½
Space:	
Upper floor	591 sq. ft.
Main floor	2,394 sq. ft.
Total Living Area	**2,985 sq. ft.**
Garage	484 sq. ft.
Exterior Wall Framing	2x6
Foundation options:	
Crawlspace (Foundation & framing conversion diagram available—see order form.)	
Blueprint Price Code	D

Plan V-2985

Luxurious Contemporary Ranch

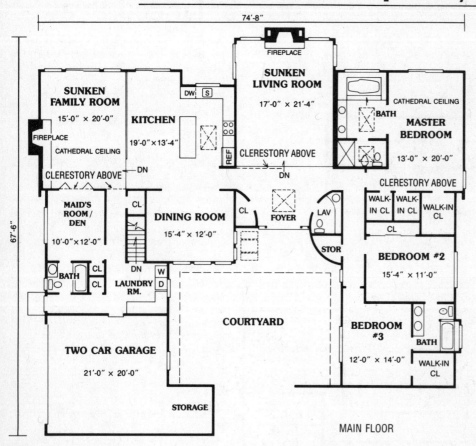

MAIN FLOOR

Plan AX-3002

Bedrooms: 3-4		Baths: 3½
Space:		
Total living area:		3,002 sq. ft.
Basement:		approx. 3,002 sq. ft.
Garage:		420 sq. ft.
Storage area:		80 sq. ft.

Exterior Wall Framing:	2x4
Foundation options:	
Standard basement.	
(Foundation & framing conversion diagram available — see order form.)	
Blueprint Price Code:	E

- This fabulous contemporary ranch home exudes luxury, from the private atrium courtyard to the spacious rooms within.
- Entry into the skylit foyer provides an open vista of the magnificent sunken living room with its vaulted ceiling, clerestory window, and fireplace.
- The exciting country kitchen off the hall, to the left, features a center island serving bar, plus a beamed vaulted skydome ceiling, and a spacious adjoining breakfast area.
- Large expanses of glass bathe the formal dining room in light, and its openness to the kitchen creates another large, open vista.
- A glass-walled, sunken family room, located adjacent to the breakfast area, features a beamed vaulted ceiling, enhanced by clerestory windows, a fireplace, and wood bin.
- Adjoining is a flexible room that can serve as a maid's, sewing, or guest room, plus a full bath, laundry, and spacious service area.
- The bedroom wing, located to the right of the foyer, includes three large bedrooms, an abundance of closet space, two full baths and a powder room located just off the foyer.
- The dramatic, vaulted-ceilinged master bedroom is also enhanced by a clerestory and includes three walk-in closets and a sumptuous private bath with a raised tub plus a separate shower.

Plan AX-3002

Angles Add Spark to Floor Plan

- Here's a one-story plan that provides plenty of space for active family living as well as business or personal entertaining.
- A majestic entry leads into a splendid sunken living room with fireplace, vaulted ceiling and built-in planter.
- A uniquely angled dining area is bathed in light from multiple windows and overlooks the living room.

- A stunning multi-sided kitchen includes a convenient island and adjoins a large pantry, breakfast nook and utility area.
- An incredible master suite boasts a magnificent bath, two huge walk-in closets and a striking bow window.
- A second bedroom also includes a large closet, and shares a walk-through bath with the parlor which could easily be a third bedroom, guest room or office.

Plan Q-3009-1A	
Bedrooms: 2-3	Baths: 2½
Space:	
Total living area:	3,009 sq. ft.
Garage:	632 sq. ft.
Exterior Wall Framing:	2x4
Foundation options: Slab only. (Foundation & framing conversion diagram available — see order form.)	
Blueprint Price Code:	E

91-0

47-0

covered patio

bath 1

Mast. B. R.
21-4 X 19-10

Dining
12-0 X15-6

GREENHOUSE

dn.

lin.

Kitchen
14-2 X 14-2
ISLAND

brkfst.
10-0 X9-8

clo.

Living
27-6 X 20-0

PLANTER

clo.

lin

clo.

SUNKEN
CATHEDRAL CLG.

pantry

utility

LINE OF
8' CLG.

dn.
Entry

bath

Garage
31-4 X 20-2

Bed Rm.
13-8 X15-4

clo.

bath 2

lin.

Parlor
16-6 X 15-8

OPT. BED RM.

COVERED
ENTRY

PLANTER

Plan Q-3009-1A

Suburban Serenity

- Spacious, open, bright rooms that let the outdoors in give this dazzling two-story plenty of appeal.
- A serene front porch welcomes guests inside to a stunning, two-story foyer with balcony bridge above and a view into the vaulted family room straight ahead.
- To the right of the foyer is a sunken living room with bay window and a view into the family room with fireplace.
- The formal dining room overlooks the front porch. It is just steps away from the island kitchen with breakfast room.
- The main floor also includes a mud room and optional maid's room or mother-in-law's apartment.
- Upstairs there are four bedrooms, including a lavish master suite with cathedral ceiling, huge walk-in closet and private bath with corner spa tub.

Plan AX-91308

Bedrooms: 4-5	Baths: 3 ½
Space:	
Upper floor	1,302 sq. ft.
Main floor	1,720 sq. ft.
Total Living Area	**3,022 sq. ft.**
Basement	1,650 sq. ft.
Garage	420 sq. ft.
Exterior Wall Framing	2x4

Foundation options:

Standard Basement

(Foundation & framing conversion diagram available—see order form.)

Blueprint Price Code	E

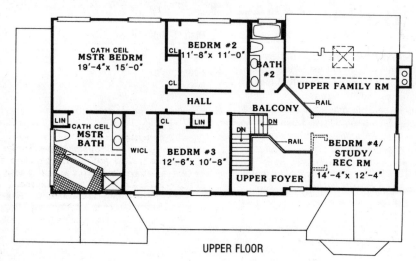

UPPER FLOOR

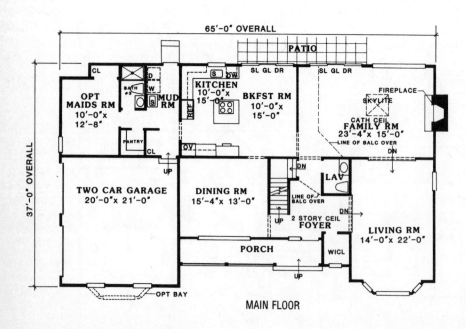

MAIN FLOOR

Plan AX-91308

UPPER FLOOR

BEDROOM
12'-0"x17'-6"

DRESS

BATH

CLOSET

28'-6"

BEDROOM
13'-0"x11'-10"

BEDROOM
12'-8"x11'-10"

CLOSET

CLOSET

SITTING
8'-0"x10'-8"

RAIL

DN

STORAGE
18'-0"x10'-4"

STOR

65'-6"

Bay Windows Enhance a Country Home

A large master bedroom suite includes a deluxe bath with separate shower, garden tub, twin vanities and two large walk-in closets. Kitchen has direct access to both the breakfast nook and the dining room, which features a large bay window. Three bedrooms, a sitting area and storage or bonus room combine to form the second level.

First floor:	2,005 sq. ft.
Second floor:	1,063 sq. ft.
Total living area:	3,068 sq. ft.

(Not counting basement or garage)

SCREENED PORCH
23'-10"x16'-0"

WOOD DECK
18'-0"x8'-0"

MASTER BATH

LINEN

CLOSET

BATH

FAMILY ROOM
23'-2"x14'-10"

BAR

BREAKFAST AREA
13'-6"x10'-6

PANTRY

WASH DRY

UTILITY
8'-4"x10'-0"

33'-0"

FOYER
10'-6"x12'-0"

COATS

LIVING ROOM
18'-6"x12'-0"

KITCHEN
13'-0"x9'-6"

UP

2 CAR GARAGE
21'-6"x21'-0"

MASTER BEDROOM
12'-10"x16'-10"

UP

DINING ROOM
13'-0"x11'-10"

MAIN FLOOR

PORCH
29'-6"x4'6"

78'-10"

Specify basement, crawlspace or slab foundation.

Impressive Home for Sloping Lot

PLAN Q-3080-1A
WITHOUT BASEMENT
(SLAB-ON-GRADE FOUNDATION)

First floor: 1,505 sq. ft.
Second floor: 1,575 sq. ft.

Total living area: 3,080 sq. ft.
(Not counting garage)

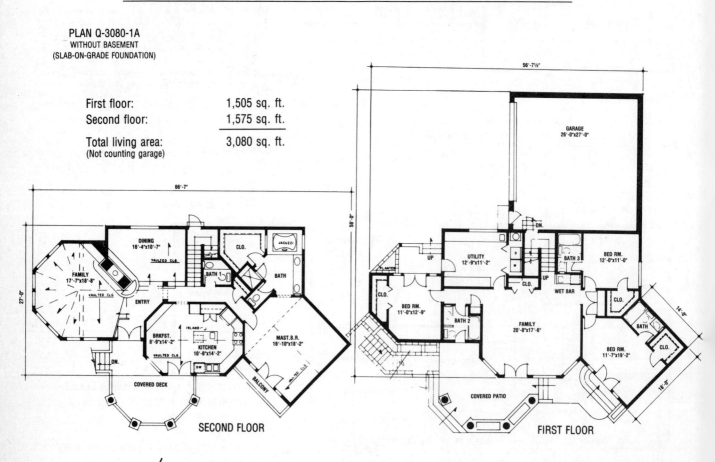

SECOND FLOOR

FIRST FLOOR

NOTE: This house was designed for a lot sloping down in the direction of the arrow.

Blueprint Price Code E

Plan Q-3080-1A

Spectacular View From Loft

- A soaring foyer and vaulted, step-down parlor with fireplace and decorative brick columns can be seen from an overhead loft in this distinguished two-story.
- Flanking the parlor are a vaulted library with built-in shelves along two walls and a formal dining room with brilliant 12' ceiling.
- Rich-looking brick borders the cooktop in the roomy island kitchen with a handy pantry; an adjoining bayed breakfast room offers a sunny patio.
- The exciting sunken family room off the kitchen features a unique gambrel ceiling, massive fireplace, corner windows and refreshing wet bar.
- Three steps up from the loft is the spacious master suite with private, bayed sitting area and lavish bath with separate vanities and walk-in closets, a garden tub and romantic deck.

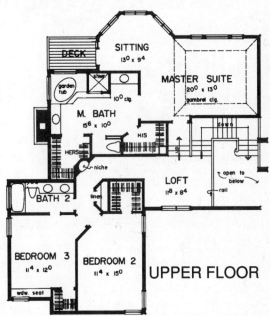

UPPER FLOOR

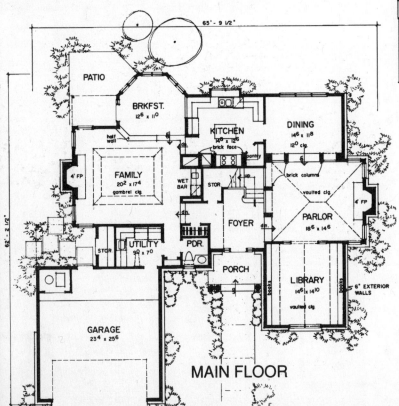

MAIN FLOOR

Plan DW-3108	
Bedrooms: 3	**Baths: 2 ½**
Space:	
Upper floor	1,324 sq. ft.
Main floor	1,784 sq. ft.
Total Living Area	**3,108 sq. ft.**
Basement	1,784 sq. ft.
Garage	595 sq. ft.
Exterior Wall Framing	2x6
Foundation options: (Please Specify)	
Standard Basement	
Crawlspace	
Slab	
(Framing conversion diagram available—see order form.)	
Blueprint Price Code	E

Traditional Elegance

- A stately traditional exterior is enhanced by brick with quoin corner details and a stunning two-story entry.
- The formal living and dining rooms flank the entry foyer at the front of the main floor.
- The informal living areas of the island kitchen, dinette bay, and sunken family room with fireplace face the rear yard.
- The main floor also includes a handy mud room with laundry and powder room accessible from a second entrance as well as a den/5th bedroom.
- The upper floor houses four spacious bedrooms and two full baths, including a lavish master bath with corner spa tub and separate shower.

Plan A-2230-DS

Bedrooms: 4-5	Baths: 2 ½
Space:	
Upper floor	1,455 sq. ft.
Main floor	1,692 sq. ft.
Total Living Area	**3,147 sq. ft.**
Basement	1,692 sq. ft.
Garage	484 sq. ft.
Exterior Wall Framing	2x6

Foundation options:

Standard Basement

(Foundation & framing conversion diagram available—see order form.)

Blueprint Price Code	E

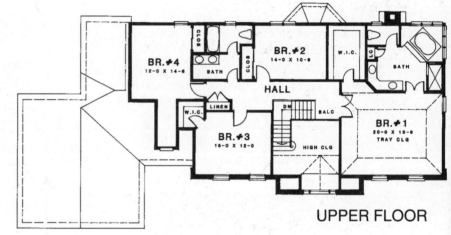

UPPER FLOOR

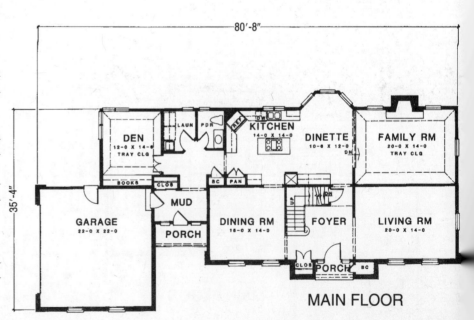

MAIN FLOOR

Plan A-2230-DS

Inviting Veranda Adds Look of Warm Welcome

- An exciting interior bridge overlooks the huge family room that stretches from the front of the home to the rear.
- Stairways in both the family room and foyer access the upper level.
- An open kitchen, breakfast room, and dining room stretch across the rear of the home.
- A luxurious master suite and a bonus room highlight the upper level.

Plan W-3219	
Bedrooms: 4-5	**Baths:** 3
Space:	
Upper floor	1,120 sq. ft.
Main floor	1,689 sq. ft.
Bonus room	429 sq. ft.
Total Living Area	**3,238 sq. ft.**
Basement	1,130 sq. ft.
Garage and storage	540 sq. ft.
Exterior Wall Framing	2x4
Foundation options:	
Partial Basement	
(Foundation & framing conversion diagram available—see order form.)	
Blueprint Price Code	E

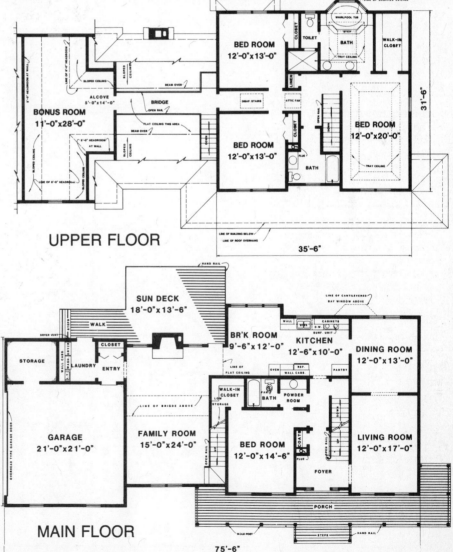

UPPER FLOOR

MAIN FLOOR

Plan W-3219

Design Excellence

- This stunning one-story offers dramatics and function.
- The brick exterior and exciting window treatments beautifully conceal an equally spectacular interior design.
- Twelve-foot ceilings throughout the formal areas and the family room, decorative niches and transom windows are some of its dramatic highlights.
- Other features include a three-way fireplace and a built-in entertainment center in the family room, an octagonal breakfast room with adjoining porch, a sunken living room with a second fireplace, and an amazing master suite with private sitting area and luxurious bath.

Plan KLF-922

Bedrooms: 3-4	Baths: 3 ½
Space:	
Main floor	3,450 sq. ft.
Total Living Area	**3,450 sq. ft.**
Garage and Workshop	698 sq. ft.
Exterior Wall Framing	2x4
Foundation options:	
Slab	
(Foundation & framing conversion diagram available—see order form.)	
Blueprint Price Code	E

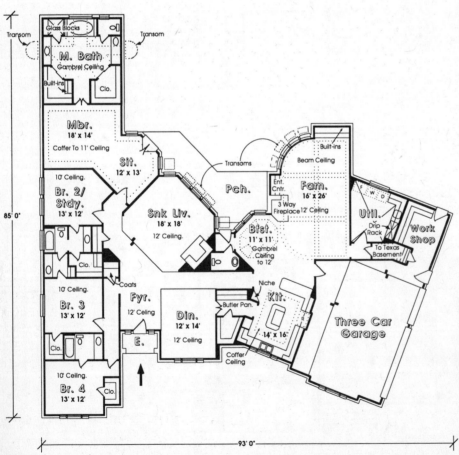

Plan KLF-922

A Natural Setting

- The large front porch of this traditionally styled home offers a warm accent to its durable stone exterior.

- The open and informal interior has a country feel.
- The spacious living and dining rooms allow for good traffic flow and large get-togethers. A fireplace, sloped ceilings open to the balcony above, and rear views to the large deck make this a perfect conversation area.
- A modern island kitchen and a sunny morning room are separated by a pantry and a counter bar.
- Privacy and relaxation are found in the master suite at one end of the home; the private sitting area has a cozy fireplace and a lovely corner window. The master bath offers a huge tub, a separate shower and twin vanities.
- A third bedroom and optional bonus space are found on the upper level.

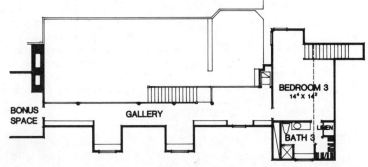

UPPER FLOOR

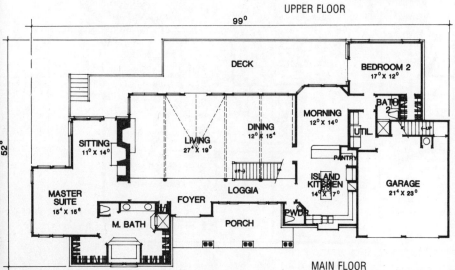

MAIN FLOOR

Plan DD-3467

Bedrooms: 3	**Baths:** 3½
Space:	
Upper floor	822 sq. ft.
Main floor	2,645 sq. ft.
Total Living Area	**3,467 sq. ft.**
Basement	2,645 sq. ft.
Garage	491 sq. ft.
Exterior Wall Framing	2x4

Foundation options:

Standard Basement

Crawlspace

Slab

(Foundation & framing conversion diagram available—see order form.)

Blueprint Price Code   E

Plan DD-3467

Splashy Master Bath

- Beautiful bay windows protruding from the living and dining rooms that flank the foyer add a classic touch to the facade of this stately home.
- Equally attractive is its interior, with an exciting sunken family room featuring a huge fireplace and wet bar.
- A large wood deck with octagonal conversation area is nestled between the family room and adjoining breakfast area set in a large bay window.
- The modern, roomy kitchen has an island worktop and extended counter bar.
- Three secondary bedrooms and a master suite with a spectacular private bath featuring a tray ceiling, separate vanities and an oversized luxury tub set in a bay window are found on the upper level.

Plan A-2255-DS

Bedrooms: 4	Baths: 3 ½
Space:	
Upper floor	1,880 sq. ft.
Main floor	1,643 sq. ft.
Total Living Area	**3,523 sq. ft.**
Basement	1,643 sq. ft.
Garage	962 sq. ft.
Exterior Wall Framing	2x6

Foundation options:

Standard Basement

(Foundation & framing conversion diagram available—see order form.)

Blueprint Price Code	F

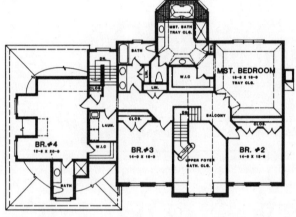

UPPER FLOOR

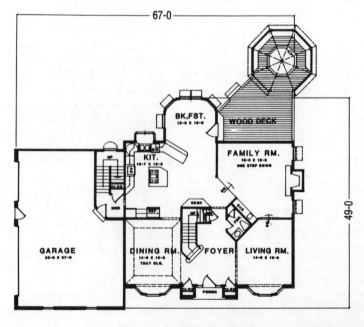

MAIN FLOOR

Plan A-2255-DS

Handsome Hill-Hugging Haven

- Multiple octagonal rooms allow this dramatic home to take full advantage of surrounding views.
- A dazzling two-story entry greets guests from the three-car garage motor courtyard.
- Once inside the front door, a soaring dome ceiling catches the eye past the octagonal stairway.
- A sunken living and dining room

with cathedral and domed ceiling face out to the rear deck and views.
- The octagonal island kitchen and breakfast nook are sure to please.
- The main floor den features a second fireplace and front-facing window seat.
- The entire second floor houses the master bedroom suite with a sensational master bath.

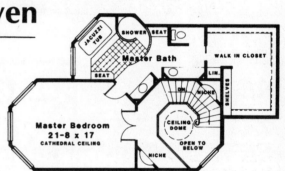

UPPER FLOOR

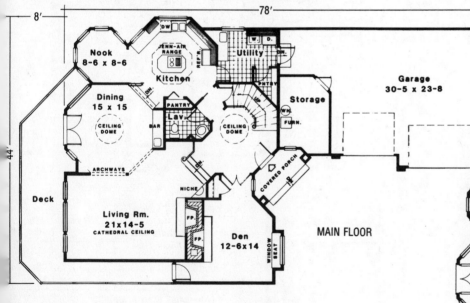

MAIN FLOOR

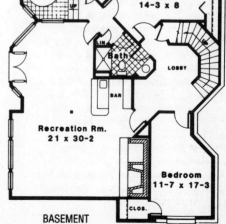

BASEMENT

Plan NW-229			
Bedrooms: 2-4		Baths: 2½	
Space:			
Upper floor:		815 sq. ft.	
Main floor:		1,446 sq. ft.	
Daylight basement:		1,330 sq. ft.	
Total living area:		**3,591 sq. ft.**	

Exterior Wall Framing:	2x6
Foundation options: Daylight basement. (Foundation & framing conversion diagram available — see order form.)	
Blueprint Price Code:	F

Plan NW-229

Spectacular Sun-Drenched Home

- Sweeping hip rooflines, stucco siding with interesting quoins and banding, and interesting arched transom windows give this exciting sunbelt design a special flair.
- From an important 1½ story covered entry leading into the foyer, guests are greeted with a stunning view. A bay-window-wall opens the living room, straight ahead, to the covered patio, rear yard, and possible pool. To the left is an open-feeling formal dining room with columns and spectacular receding tray ceiling.
- The island kitchen overlooks the large family room with corner fireplace and breakfast bay.
- The master wing, well separated from the secondary bedrooms, features a coffered ceiling, sitting area with patio access, massive walk-in closet, and sun-drenched garden bath.

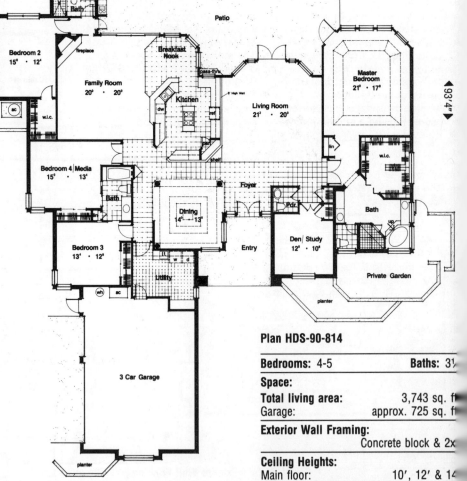

Plan HDS-90-814

Bedrooms: 4-5	Baths: 3½
Space:	
Total living area:	3,743 sq. ft
Garage:	approx. 725 sq. ft
Exterior Wall Framing:	
	Concrete block & 2x
Ceiling Heights:	
Main floor:	10', 12' & 14
Foundation options:	
Slab.	
(Foundation & framing conversion diagram available — see order form.)	
Blueprint Price Code:	

Plan HDS-90-814

A - TRADITIONAL

Sprawling Plan For A Growing Family

B - CONTEMPORARY

- Your choice of exterior is offered in this elegant and spacious floor plan, a hip-roofed traditional Georgian Style (AX-89314-A), or a highly attractive contemporary version (AX-89314-B).
- Both designs feature a two-story high foyer and a well-lit interior.
- An enormous living room/family room arrangement accommodates traffic overflow and entertaining needs.
- The roomy breakfast area adjoins the kitchen, which overlooks a rear greenhouse or porch.
- A curving staircase leads to a second floor balcony overlooking the foyer.
- The master suite has double doors, three walk-in closets, dressing room, and a bath with whirlpool tub.

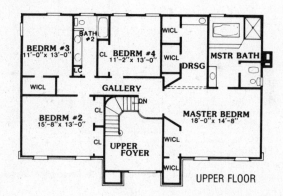

UPPER FLOOR

Plan AX-89314-A, B	
Bedrooms: 4-5	Baths: 3½
Space:	
Upper floor:	1,524 sq. ft.
Main floor:	2,265 sq. ft.
Total living area:	3,789 sq. ft.
Basement:	1,699 sq. ft.
Garage:	576 sq. ft.
Exterior Wall Framing:	2x4
Foundation options:	
Standard basement.	
(Foundation & framing conversion diagram available — see order form.)	
Blueprint Price Code:	E

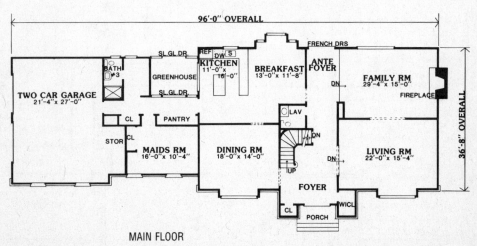

MAIN FLOOR

Plan AX-89314-A, B

TO ORDER THIS BLUEPRINT, CALL TOLL-FREE 1-800-547-5570
(prices and details on pp. 12-15.)

Plan DD-4300-B

Bedrooms: 4	Baths: 4½
Space:	
Upper floor	868 sq. ft.
Main floor	3,416 sq. ft.
Total Living Area	**4,284 sq. ft.**
Basement	3,416 sq. ft.
Garage	633 sq. ft.
Storage	approx. 50 sq. ft.
Exterior Wall Framing	2x4 or 2x6
Ceiling Heights:	
Upper floor	9'
Main floor	10'

Foundation options:
Standard Basement
Crawlspace
Slab
(Foundation & framing conversion diagram available—see order form.)

Blueprint Price Code	**G**

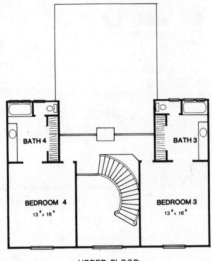

UPPER FLOOR

Colonial Recall

- The symmetry, massing, materials, and colonnaded entry porch all recall the best of colonial design on this estate home.
- The formal dining and parlor rooms, each with high glass windows, flank the entry's graceful curved staircase.
- The informal living spaces are oriented to the rear greenspaces. They include a two-story volumed family room with fireplace, transom windows and an adjoining library room, as well as a large island kitchen with breakfast eating area.
- The main-floor master suite presses all the right buttons with its fireplace wall, his and her walk-in closets, and private bath with platform tub, separate shower, compartmented tub and double vanities.
  - The three additional bedrooms each boast full private baths.

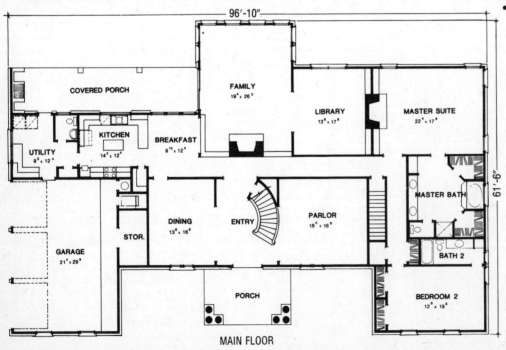

MAIN FLOOR

Plan DD-4300-B

PLANS H-3711-1 & H-3711-1A
(WITH GARAGE)

**NOTE:
The above photographed home may have been modified by the homeowner. Please refer to floor plan and/or drawn elevation shown for actual blueprint details.

All-American Country Home

- Romantic, old-fashioned and spacious living areas combine to create this modern home.
- Off the entryway is the generous living room with fireplace and French doors which open onto the traditional rear porch.
- Country kitchen features an island table for informal occasions, while the adjoining family room is ideal for family gatherings.
- Practically placed, a laundry/mud room lies off the garage for immediate disposal of soiled garments.
- This plan is available with garage (H-3711-1) or without garage (H-3711-2) and with or without basement.

UPPER FLOOR

WALK-IN CLOSET 7'-6" x 7'-6"

BATH

Shw'r

LINEN 6'-0"

BATH

STOR.

BEDROOM 13'-3" x 11'-0"

CLOSET 4'-9" CLOSET 4'-9"

UP TO ATTIC

CLOSET 4'-9"

BEDROOM 13'-0" x 19'-0"

BEDROOM 15'-0" x 10'-0"

BEDROOM 16'-0" x 13'-3"

Plans H-3711-1/1A & -2/2A	
Bedrooms: 4	**Baths:** 2½

Space:

Upper floor:	1,176 sq. ft.
Main floor:	1,288 sq. ft.
Total living area:	**2,464 sq. ft.**
Basement:	approx. 1,288 sq. ft.
Garage:	505 sq. ft.

Exterior Wall Framing:	2x6

Foundation options:
Standard basement (Plans H-3711-1 & -2).
Crawlspace (Plans H-3711-1A & -2A).
(Foundation & framing conversion diagram available — see order form.)

Blueprint Price Code:	C

MAIN FLOOR

74'-0"

FRENCH DRS.

DINING 11'-9" x 13'-3"

DW

LAUNDRY 13'-0" x 7'-6"

STORAGE 15'-8" x 13'-6"

REF.

PANTRY

ISLAND

COUNTRY KITCHEN 15'-0" x 27'-0"

W/H

GARAGE 23'-6" x 21'-6"

down

44'-0"

LIVING ROOM 13'-0" x 27'-0"

ENTRY

LAV.

FAMILY ROOM

CLOS. 3'-0"

8' WIDE COVERED PORCH

PLANS H-3711-2 & H-3711-2A
(WITHOUT GARAGE)

Plans H-3711-1/1A & -2/2A

Photo by Mark Englund

Vivacious Victorian

- A traditional Victorian exterior appeal is created with a cupola room, covered front porch with dainty detailing, and bay windows with leaded glass.
- Inside, however, the house functions like a modern 1990s family home, rather than an 1890s home of yesteryear. Bright, open-feeling rooms flow into each other to allow maximum family interaction.
- The front entry opens to an octagon-shaped parlor with adjacent stairwell. To the right of the entry is the formal dining room with quaint bay window.
- The island kitchen is conveniently situated between the formal dining room and the informal breakfast eating area. Just beyond is the great room with fireplace and rear deck access.
- There are three bedrooms and two full baths upstairs, including a lavish master bedroom suite with two walk-in closets, separate shower and tub under the commanding cupola.

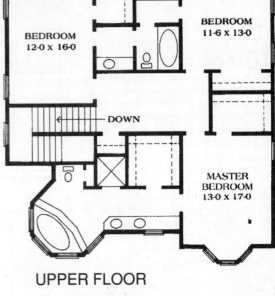

UPPER FLOOR

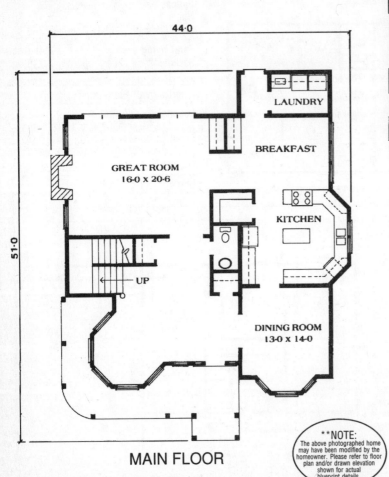

MAIN FLOOR

**NOTE:
The above photographed home may have been modified by the homeowner. Please refer to floor plan and/or drawn elevation shown for actual blueprint details.

Plan V-2440	
Bedrooms: 3	**Baths:** 2½
Space:	
Upper floor	1,266 sq. ft.
Main floor	1,482 sq. ft.
Total Living Area	**2,748 sq. ft.**
Exterior Wall Framing	2x6
Foundation options:	
Crawlspace (Foundation & framing conversion diagram available—see order form.)	
Blueprint Price Code	D

Plan V-2440

High Luxury in One-Story Plan

- 12' ceilings are featured in the entryway and living room.
- 400 sq. ft. living room boasts a massive fireplace and access to the rear porch.
- Corridor-style kitchen has angled eating bar and convenient nearby laundry facilities.
- Master suite incorporates unusual bath arrangement consisting of an angled whirlpool tub and separate shower.
- Secondary bedrooms are zoned for privacy and climate control.

Plan E-2302

Bedrooms: 4	Baths: 2

Space:

Total living area:	2,396 sq. ft.
Garage and storage:	590 sq. ft.
Porches:	216 sq. ft.
Exterior Wall Framing:	2x6

Foundation options:
Standard basement.
Crawlspace.
Slab.
(Foundation & framing conversion diagram available — see order form.)

Blueprint Price Code:	C

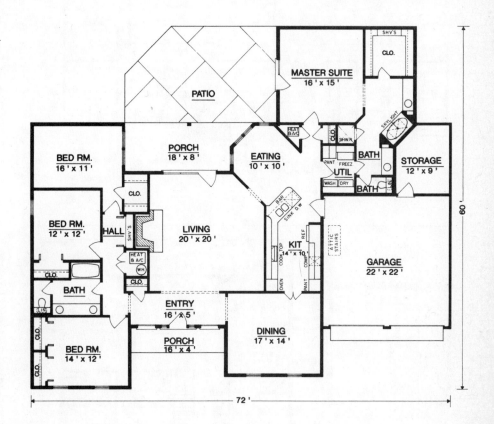

Plan E-2302

Photo by Mark Englund/HomeStyles

French Farmhouse

- An optional game room or fifth bedroom is offered in this classic French-styled farmhouse. The upper level also features a balcony that overlooks the Great Room.
- Bay windows are found throughout the main level, including the formal dining room, versatile studio, the nook and the secluded master suite and bath.
- At the center of the home, the Great Room has a vaulted ceiling, massive corner fireplace and access to the rear porch.
- A convenient utility room houses extra freezer, storage space and washer/dryer.

**NOTE: The above photographed home may have been modified by the homeowner. Please refer to floor plan and/or drawn elevation shown for actual blueprint details.

UPPER FLOOR

Plan VL-2716	
Bedrooms: 4-5	**Baths: 2 ½-3 ½**
Space:	
Upper floor	1,127 sq. ft.
Main floor	1,589 sq. ft.
Total Living Area	**2,716 sq. ft.**
Garage	469 sq. ft.
Exterior Wall Framing	2x4
Foundation options:	
Crawlspace	
Slab	
(Foundation & framing conversion diagram available—see order form.)	
Blueprint Price Code	D

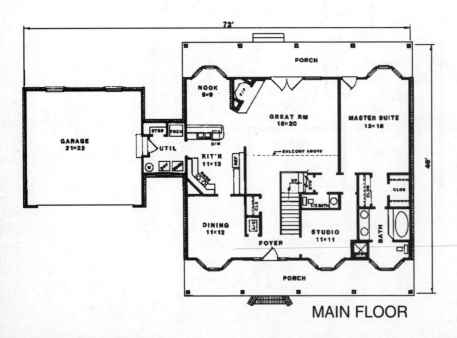

MAIN FLOOR

Plan VL-2716

Sprawling, Substantial Ranch

- Here's another design that proves it pays to keep it simple.
- Clean lines and a straightforward floor plan make for solid, economical construction and easy-living comfort.
- A welcoming porch with columns and planters opens to a functional, attractive entryway, leading ahead to a magnificent family room or to a formal living/dining area at the right.
- The huge family room features a vaulted, beamed ceiling, impressive fireplace and hearth with a built-in wood box, plus built-in bookshelves and desk.
- The large, beautiful kitchen is between the formal dining room and informal eating area, and next to a convenient and spacious utility area, half-bath and garage entry.
- The majestic master suite includes a sumptuous private bath and huge walk-in closet.
- Three secondary bedrooms likewise have large closets, and share a second full bath.

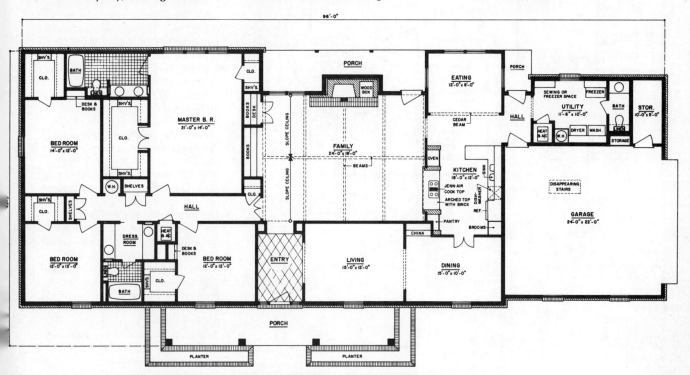

Plan E-2700

Bedrooms: 4		Baths: 2½

Space:

Total living area:	2,719 sq. ft.
Garage:	533 sq. ft.
Storage:	50 sq. ft.
Porches:	350 sq. ft.

Exterior Wall Framing: 2x6

Foundation options:
Crawlspace.
Slab.
(Foundation & framing conversion diagram available — see order form.)

Blueprint Price Code: D

Plan E-2700

Photo by Mark Englund/HomeStyles

NOTE:
The above photographed home may have been modified by the homeowner. Please refer to floor plan and/or drawn elevation shown for actual blueprint details.

Unique Inside and Out

- This plan gives new dimension to one-story living. The exterior features graceful arched windows and a sweeping roofline The interior is marked by unusual angles and curves.
- The living areas are clustered around a large "lanai," or covered porch. French doors in the master bedroom and the family room angle toward the porch.
- Extras include the two-way fireplace, warming both the family room and the living room. The home's expansiveness is enhanced by ceilings that slope up to 10 feet. Columns frame both the living room and the formal dining room, echoing the columns of the porches.
- The island kitchen and the morning room are open to the family room, which features a wet bar. The living room is highlighted by French doors and arched transom windows.
- The formal dining room and the study are stationed near the front of the home, away from the major activity areas.
- The master bedroom includes an irresistible bath with a spa tub, dual vanities, two walk-in closets and a separate shower.
- Two more good-sized bedrooms share another full bath.
- A large utility room and a half-bath are conveniently located between the kitchen and the garage.

Floor Plan (Plan DD-2802)

69¹¹

81⁵

- LANAI
- MASTER BEDROOM 14⁶ X 23⁰
- LIVING ROOM 18⁰ X 18⁰
- FAMILY ROOM 17⁴ X 18⁴
- M. BATH
- WET BAR
- MORNING 12⁰ X 12⁰
- FOYER
- BATH 2
- PANTRY
- STUDY 11⁴ X 12⁶
- DINING 12⁰ X 14⁰
- ISLAND KITCHEN 13⁶ X 14⁰
- BEDROOM 2 13⁶ X 12⁴
- BEDROOM 3 12⁴ X 14⁸
- PORCH
- UTILITY
- 1/2 BATH
- GARAGE 24⁰ X 23⁸

Plan DD-2802

Bedrooms: 3-4	Baths: 2½

Space:

Main floor	2,899 sq. ft.
Total Living Area	**2,899 sq. ft.**
Basement	2,899 sq. ft.
Garage	568 sq. ft.
Exterior Wall Framing	2x4

Foundation options:

Basement
Crawlspace
Slab
(Foundation & framing conversion diagram available—see order form.)

Blueprint Price Code	D

Plan DD-2802

Photo by Gil Ford

Spacious and Stately

- Covered porches front and rear.
- Downstairs master suite with spectacular bath.
- Family/living/dining areas combine for entertaining large groups.
- Classic Creole/plantation exterior.

Plan E-3000

Bedrooms: 4	Baths: 3½

Space:

Upper floor:	1,027 sq. ft.
Main floor:	2,008 sq. ft.
Total living area:	**3,035 sq. ft.**
Porches:	429 sq. ft.
Basement:	2,008 sq. ft.
Garage:	484 sq. ft.
Storage:	96 sq. ft.

Exterior Wall Framing:	2x6

Typical Ceiling Heights:

Upper floor:	8'
Main floor:	9'

Foundation options:
Standard basement.
Crawlspace.
Slab.
(Foundation & framing conversion diagram available — see order form.)

Blueprint Price Code:	E

**NOTE:
The above photographed home may have been modified by the homeowner. Please refer to floor plan and/or drawn elevation shown for actual blueprint details.

Plan E-3000

**TO ORDER THIS BLUEPRINT,
CALL TOLL-FREE 1-800-547-5570**
(prices and details on pp. 12-15.)

Photo by Wally Stein

Tudor-Inspired Hillside Design

- The vaulted entry opens to a stunning living room with a high ceiling and massive fireplace.
- The dining room, five steps higher, overlooks the living room for a dramatic effect.
- Double doors lead into the informal family area, which consists of a beautifully integrated kitchen, nook and family room.
- The magnificent master suite, isolated downstairs, includes a sumptuous bath, enormous wardrobe and double-door entry.
- The upstairs consists of three more bedrooms, a bath and balcony hallway open to the entry below.
- Three-car garage is tucked under the family room/dining room area.

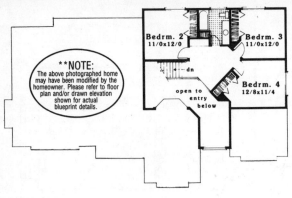

**NOTE:
The above photographed home may have been modified by the homeowner. Please refer to floor plan and/or drawn elevation shown for actual blueprint details.

Bedrm. 2
11/0x12/0

Bedrm. 3
11/0x12/0

Bedrm. 4
12/8x11/4

dn

open to entry below

UPPER FLOOR

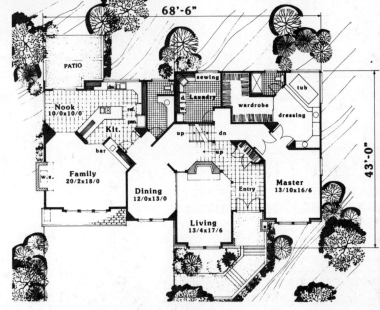

68'-6"

PATIO

sewing

Laundry

wardrobe

tub

dressing

Nook
10/0x10/0

Kit.

ref.

up

dn

up

43'-0"

bar

w.s.

Family
20/2x18/0

Dining
12/0x13/0

Entry

Master
13/10x16/6

Living
13/4x17/6

MAIN FLOOR

Plan R-4001

Bedrooms: 4	Baths: 2½

Space:

Upper floor:	709 sq. ft.
Main floor:	2,388 sq. ft.

Total living area:	3,097 sq. ft.
Garage:	906 sq. ft.

Exterior Wall Framing:	2x4

Foundation options:
Crawlspace only.
(Foundation & framing conversion diagram available — see order form)

Blueprint Price Code:	E

PLAN R-4001
WITHOUT BASEMENT
(CRAWLSPACE FOUNDATION)

f.

w.h.

up

Garage
32/0x28/4

Plan R-4001

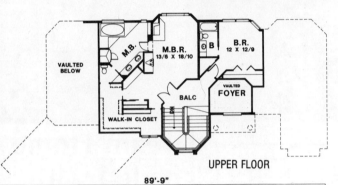

UPPER FLOOR

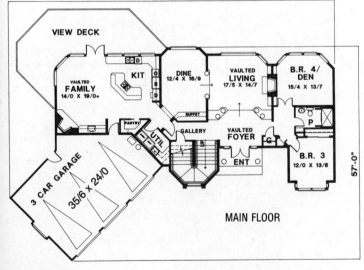

MAIN FLOOR

Designed with Elegance in Mind

- This expansive home boasts 3,220 sq. ft. of living space designed with elegance in mind.
- The front of the home is finished in stucco, with the rest in lap siding for economy.
- The vaulted foyer leads directly into an impressive sunken and vaulted living room guarded by columns that echo the exterior treatment.
- The formal dining room is visually joined to the living room to make an impressive space for entertaining.
- An unusually fine kitchen opens to a large family room, thereby avoiding the closed feeling found in many kitchens.
- In the front, the extra-wide staircase is a primary attraction, with its large feature window, which floats past the staircase landing.
- A terrific master suite includes a splendid master bath with double sinks and a huge walk-through closet.
- A second upstairs bedroom also includes a private bath.

Plan S-11388

Bedrooms: 3-4		Baths: 3

Space:	
Upper floor	1,095 sq. ft.
Main floor	2,125 sq. ft.
Total Living Area	**3,220 sq. ft.**
Basement	2,125 sq. ft.
Garage	802 sq. ft.

Exterior Wall Framing	2x6

Foundation options:
Standard Basement
Crawlspace
(Foundation & framing conversion diagram available—see order form.)

Blueprint Price Code	E

Plan S-11388

Dream Home Loaded with Amenities

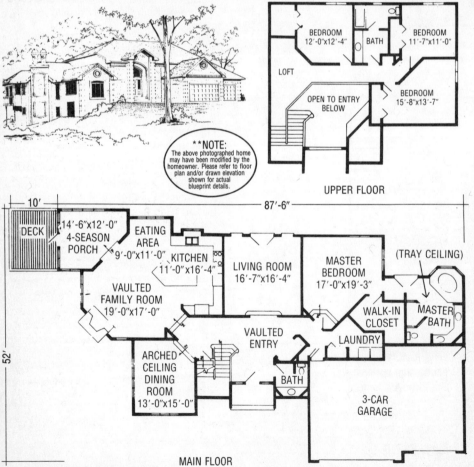

NOTE:
The above photographed home may have been modified by the homeowner. Please refer to floor plan and/or drawn elevation shown for actual blueprint details.

UPPER FLOOR

Upper floor plan labels:
- BEDROOM 12'-0"x12'-4"
- BATH
- BEDROOM 11'-7"x11'-0"
- LOFT
- OPEN TO ENTRY BELOW
- BEDROOM 15'-8"x13'-7"

- Unique family room with vaulted ceiling.
- Large vaulted entry.
- Luxurious master suite.
- Large island kitchen.
- Striking design inside and out.

Plan AH-3230

Bedrooms: 4	Baths: 2½

Space:

Upper floor:	890 sq. ft.
Main floor:	2,340 sq. ft.

Total living area:	3,230 sq. ft.
Basement:	2,214 sq. ft.
Garage:	693 sq. ft.

Exterior Wall Framing:	2x6

Ceiling Heights:

Upper floor:	8'
Main floor:	9'

Foundation options:
Basement only.
(Foundation & framing conversion diagram available — see order form.)

Blueprint Price Code:	E

Main floor plan labels:
- DECK
- 4-SEASON PORCH 14'-6"x12'-0"
- EATING AREA 9'-0"x11'-0"
- KITCHEN 11'-0"x16'-4"
- LIVING ROOM 16'-7"x16'-4"
- MASTER BEDROOM 17'-0"x19'-3" (TRAY CEILING)
- VAULTED FAMILY ROOM 19'-0"x17'-0"
- WALK-IN CLOSET
- MASTER BATH
- ARCHED CEILING DINING ROOM 13'-0"x15'-0"
- VAULTED ENTRY
- LAUNDRY
- BATH
- 3-CAR GARAGE
- 10'
- 87'-6"
- 52'

MAIN FLOOR

TO ORDER THIS BLUEPRINT, CALL TOLL-FREE 1-800-547-5570

Plan AH-3230

Graceful Elegance

This graceful French country home with ageless brick veneer, corner quoins, and interesting roofline typifies elegance.

Double front doors welcome visitors to a foyer accentuated by beautiful spiral stairs and case openings leading to the living area. The centrally located kitchen is especially well designed with modern appliances, triple sinks and handy garbage compactor. The kitchen flows together with the nook and dining room for easy traffic flow.

Everything is big in the family room: the windows, the raised hearth fireplace and the room itself. Bay windows flanking the main entry delightfully detail the study and the living room.

Four bedrooms are located on the second floor, allowing extra privacy from the rest of the living area. The master bedroom has excellent space usage with walk-in closet and a private bath. A double bowl vanity is included in the second bath for the three other bedrooms. Linen and closet space is plentiful.

The double garage has side entrance and immediate access to the laundry area, which also includes abundant cabinetry. Exterior walls, behind the brick facade, are framed with 2x6 studs for energy efficiency. Basement plan included.

First floor:	1,884 sq. ft.
Second floor:	1,348 sq. ft.
Total living area:	3,232 sq. ft.
(Not counting basement or garage)	

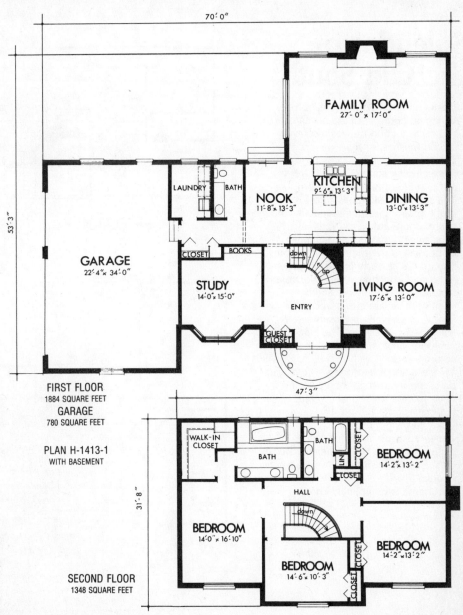

FIRST FLOOR
1884 SQUARE FEET
GARAGE
780 SQUARE FEET

PLAN H-1413-1
WITH BASEMENT

SECOND FLOOR
1348 SQUARE FEET

Blueprint Price Code E
Plan H-1413-1

TO ORDER THIS BLUEPRINT,
CALL TOLL-FREE 1-800-547-5570
(prices and details on pp. 12-15.)

Splendor of the Old South

- Designed after "Monteigne," an Italianate home from the Natchez area, this reproduction utilizes modern stucco finishes for the exterior.
- The formal foyer is accented by the large circular stairwell. The foyer is open to the upper-floor balcony.
- The sun room stretches across the rear of the main house and overlooks the center courtyard.
- A uniquely located entertainment center serves the main activity rooms.
- The master suite and bath are super-plush and contain every imaginable feature — including his and hers vanities, a separate mirrored make-up vanity, large walk-in closets and a glassed-in garden tub. The king-sized bedroom suite even utilizes the adjoining study.
- Two additional bedrooms with private baths are located on the upper level. They share a study and a veranda. On the main floor, a fourth bedroom serves as a guest room or nursery.
- The living room and study have 14' ceilings. Typical ceiling heights are 9' on the main floor and 8' on the upper floor.
- This home is completely energy-efficient.

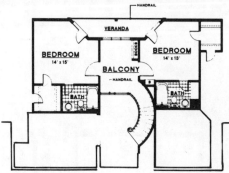

UPPER FLOOR

Plan E-3200	
Bedrooms: 4	**Baths:** 4
Living Area:	
Upper floor	629 sq. ft.
Main floor	2,655 sq. ft.
Total Living Area:	**3,284 sq. ft.**
Standard basement	2,655 sq. ft.
Garage and storage	667 sq. ft.
Exterior Wall Framing:	2x6
Foundation Options:	
Standard basement	
Crawlspace	
Slab	
(Typical foundation & framing conversion diagram available—see order form.)	
BLUEPRINT PRICE CODE	E

MAIN FLOOR

Plan E-3200

Spacious Elegance

Lower level:	1,944 sq. ft.
Upper level:	1,427 sq. ft.
Total living area:	3,371 sq. ft.
Garage, storage & exterior bar:	732 sq. ft.
Porches & balcony:	769 sq. ft.
Total under roof:	4,872 sq. ft.

Exterior walls are 2x6 construction.
Specify basement, crawlspace or slab foundation.

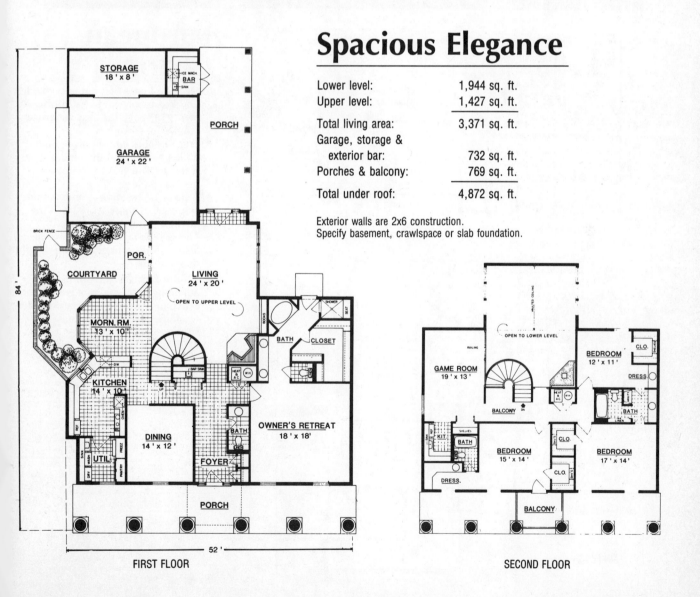

FIRST FLOOR

SECOND FLOOR

Photo by Dave Rowland Photography

European Charm

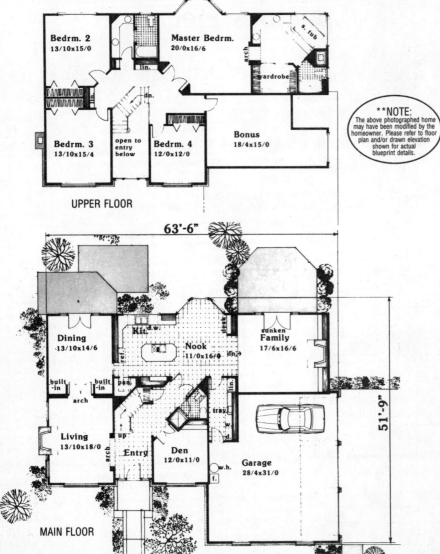

Bedrm. 2 13/10x15/0

Master Bedrm. 20/0x16/6

s. tub

arch

wardrobe

lin.

dn.

Bedrm. 3 13/10x15/4

open to entry below

Bedrm. 4 12/0x12/0

Bonus 18/4x15/0

UPPER FLOOR

**NOTE:
The above photographed home may have been modified by the homeowner. Please refer to floor plan and/or drawn elevation shown for actual blueprint details.

63'-6"

Dining 13/10x14/6

Kit.

Nook 11/0x16/0

sunken **Family** 17/6x16/6

ref.

built-in

built-in

pan.

arch

Living 13/10x18/0

up

Entry

Den 12/0x11/0

tray

w.

Garage 28/4x31/0

w.h.

f.

51'-9"

MAIN FLOOR

- Here's a home that not only exudes Old World charm, but also offers plenty of space for busy American families of today.
- French doors join the living and dining rooms, and the dining room offers easy access to an outside deck or patio.
- A huge kitchen/nook combination assures that those working in the kitchen will not feel isolated.
- The sunken family room beyond also features a fireplace and double doors to the rear.
- A front-facing den, with its adjoining bath, makes a great home office or a guest bedroom if needed.
- Upstairs, the master suite is spacious and includes an extravagant master bath and big walk-in closet.

Plan R-2093

Bedrooms: 4-5	Baths: 3

Space:	
Upper floor:	1,585 sq. ft.
Main floor:	1,792 sq. ft.
Bonus area:	351 sq. ft.

Total living area:	3,728 sq. ft.
Garage:	878 sq. ft.

Exterior Wall Framing:	2x4

Foundation options:
Crawlspace only.
(Foundation & framing conversion diagram available — see order form.)

Blueprint Price Code:	F

Plan R-2093

REAR VIEW

Spacious Western Ranch

- A three-bedroom sleeping wing is separated from the balance of the home, with the master suite featuring a raised tub below skylights and a walk-in dressing room.
- Sunken living room is enhanced by a vaulted ceiling and fireplace with raised hearth.
- Family room is entered from the central hall through double doors; a wet bar and a second fireplace grace this gathering spot.
- Kitchen has functional L-shaped arrangement, attached nook, and pantry.

Plan H-3701-1A

Bedrooms: 4	Baths: 3½
Total living area:	3,735 sq. ft.
Garage:	830 sq. ft.
Exterior Wall Framing:	2x4

Foundation options:
Crawlspace only.
(Foundation & framing conversion diagram available — see order form.)

Blueprint Price Code:	F

Floor Plan

110'-0"

DECK

BEDROOM 16'-6"×20'-0"

wdw. seat

BATH 12'-7"×12'-2" skylights

raised tub

WC

Shower

SUNKEN LIVING ROOM 30'-0"×20'-0"

DINING 15'-9"×14'-0"

steps down

vaulted ceiling

clerestory window

linen

dresser

raised hearth

WALK-IN DRESSING ROOM 11'-3"×7'-6"

folding screen

WET BAR

furnace

steps down

PANTRY

KITCHEN 15'-4"×11'-6"

ref.

dw.

CLOSET

LINEN

STOR

BATH

LAV

BEDROOM 12'-0"×14'-6"

BEDROOM 12'-0"×14'-6"

POWDER ROOM

CLOSET

CLOSET

ENTRY 15'-3"×15'-3"

NOOK 11'-6"×10'-0"

DECK

wdw. seat

wdw. seat

FAMILY ROOM 15'-0"×24'-0"

LAUNDRY skylight

D W

Shower

BATH

furnace

wh

THREE CAR GARAGE 31'-10"×23'-8"

BEDROOM 19'-0"×13'-0"

CLOSET

STORAGE

64'-0"

wdw. seat

Plan H-3701-1A

UPPER FLOOR

MAIN FLOOR

Deluxe Main-Floor Master Suite

- Traditional-style exterior with modern floor plan. Dormers and stone add curb appeal to this home.
- Formal entry with staircase leads to formal living or large family room.
- Large kitchen is conveniently located between formal dining room and secluded breakfast nook with bay window.
- Private master suite has tray ceiling and walk-in closet. Master bath has corner tub, shower, and dual vanities.
- Large screened porch off family room is perfect for outdoor living.
- Large utility room with pantry and toilet are conveniently located off the garage.
- Second floor features two large bedrooms with walk-in closets and two full baths.
- Optional bonus room (624 sq. ft.) can be finished as a large game room, bedroom, office, etc.

Plan C-8915

Bedrooms: 3	Baths: 3½
Space:	
Upper floor:	832 sq. ft.
Main floor:	1,927 sq. ft.
Bonus area:	624 sq. ft.
Total living area:	3,383 sq. ft.
Basement:	1,674 sq. ft.
Garage:	484 sq. ft.
Exterior Wall Framing:	2x4

Ceiling Heights:
First floor:	9'
Second floor:	8'

Foundation options:
Daylight basement.
Crawlspace.
(Foundation & framing conversion diagram available — see order form.)

Blueprint Price Code: E

Plan C-8915